Incarnation of the Gospel in Indian Culture

Incarnation of the Gospel in Indian Culture

A Study of the Art and Poetry of Pulidindi Solomon Raj

B. S. Moses Kumar

CWI

Christian World Imprints

First Published in 2019 by

Christian World Imprints
Christian Publishing & Books from India
H-12 Bali Nagar, **New Delhi-110015**
info@christianworldimprints.com
www.ChristianWorldImprints.com
Phone: +91 11 25465925

ISBN 13: 978-93-5148-367-0
ISBN 10: 978-93-5148-368-7

Cover : Art by P. Solomon Raj

Printed in India.

Dedicated

To the Loving Memory of My Parents!

Rev. Balla Moses & Mrs. Pulidindi Krupavathy

Contents

Acknowledgements

I am grateful to God for every rare blessing He has poured out upon my life, and now for this special privilege of doing my second Ph.D. in the field of my interest for the last four decades, and continuing! It was indeed an enriching experience on many counts.

I am in eternal gratitude to my godly parents, Rev. Balla Moses and Mrs. Pulidindi Krupavathy, ministers of the Gospel, who had reared all my siblings and me in the fear of the Lord and in His blessing - providing good education to all in spite of their meager means, and thus producing three Doctorates from among their Children and one from their Grand Children, apart from innumerable Masters.

I am deeply indebted to the Hon'ble Chancellor, Dr. Jetti A. Oliver, and the Hon'ble Vice-Chancellor, Bishop Prof. R. B. Lal for their godly leadership and encouragement. I am honored to do my Ph.D. in Theology in the historic Sam Higginbottom University of Agriculture, Technology and Sciences under their leadership!

I am grateful to my Supervisor and Dean, Faculty of Theology, Bishop Dr. Dhirendra K. Sahu, for all the guidance and encouragement extended throughout.

I appreciate the kind help of Dr. Vimal Kant Singh in the early stages of the work, and of Dr. Sam Peedikayil Mathew at the final stages of the journey.

I am grateful to Dr. P. Solomon Raj, for the inspiration he had been, and for the many times of interviews and valuable interaction with him, digging deeper and deeper, and always coming out with newer treasures!

I am indebted to Prof. David Zersen, President Emeritus of Concordia University, Austin, Texas, who has ignited my interest in the study of the works of Solomon Raj, and who collaborated with me in bringing out a Festschrift in his honor, *Planting in the Native Soil: Studies in Gospel Inculturation*.

I further express my deep admiration to Prof. Gudrun Löwner, Head of the Department of Mission and Ecumenics, United Theological College, Bangalore for her personal visit to Donald Ashram, her comprehensive orientation about Christian art and artists, and her encouragement all along in my research on P. Solomon Raj - furnishing valuable source material.

I express gratitude for all the Supporters of my Ph.D. Project from our Family and Relatives through their prayers and financial gifts enabling my continuation and now my completion of the Project.

I am grateful for the wonderful family of International Pentecostal Holiness Church, of which I am a part all my life beginning from my early childhood. I salute all the trail of leaders and missionaries, who blessed me with their godly leadership in nurture, encouragement, equipping, mentoring, restoring, and blessing me with serving opportunities, and the inexpressible joys and manifold honors! I appreciate my journey together over four decades with all the dear colleagues in IPHC Ministerium in India and across the world.

And, last but never the least, my love to Dora, the God-given woman with me in all my agonies and achievements in our 'life together' for over 40 years! She has been my Prayer Supporter, beyond all! She has been an important part of my story! I am further grateful to our dear daughters and sons and their spouses, who are our pride, and all our grand children, who are our crown!

B. S. Moses Kumar

Preface

A rural, illiterate family in Godavary delta area of the State of Andhra Pradesh in South India was visited by the light of the Gospel through the advent of Lutheran Missionaries in the late nineteenth century. Besides being transformed by this light, God in His providence had ordained that the impact of this family would touch the ends of the globe through one of the sons of this family. The present research about this saga has been a delightful exercise and a pleasant experience all along, and one cannot but wonder 'how great is our God'! The author deems it a rare honor to have studied the depths of His grace, richly manifested in the history of this family, and in the life of P. Solomon Raj who hails from this family.

The story begins with Pulidindi Abraham, who was the first generation Christian of Neggipudi village. Father Abraham had two sons – Pulidindi Lazarus and Pulidindi Prakasam. Of the two, Prakasam had higher education having graduated in Agriculture from Coimbatore. Obviously he was the first graduate from among this tiny village. He had two sons, both well educated. The eldest son lives with family in the U.S.A., and the other one in the motherland.

Pulidindi Lazarus was a schoolteacher and his wife Naomi was a Bible Woman of those days, promoting non-formal Christian education among the rural masses through story and song. Lazarus also had two sons, Solomon Raj and Aaron, but he was first blessed with a daughter by name Krupavathy. A son named Asheerwadam who was the second issue, and a daughter named Lily Elizabeth the last issue, did not survive beyond infancy and early childhood. The three who survived had become schoolteachers in the manner of their father. But Solomon Raj had ascended to greater heights gradually – not only obtaining higher education overseas, but ultimately imparting education to many in turn, overseas. Whereas his siblings had never crossed the boarders of their State, Solomon was destined to cross even the national boundaries touching all the continents, except of course, the land 'down under'. One of his grand daughters, however, now lives in Australia, and one of his grand sons now works in Illinois, the State where Solomon had his post graduate studies in graphic arts in the USA.

The ancient Wiseman had aptly expressed that 'the fear of the Lord is the beginning of wisdom'. Solomon Raj, who was named after the ancient Wiseman, had this 'fear of the Lord' and a simple faith in His Good News. The entry of the Gospel into this remote village and into his little heart had produced a thinker and a theologian out of him. And nothing could keep him from impacting the uttermost parts of the world through his pen and the paintbrush, and the writings and art that had emerged there from. The little exposure that the author had in a 'close-up' for just over a decade had given him the spur to dig deeper, and here is the fruit of his labors. I hereby express my deep appreciation to Solomon Raj for all that he had accomplished, and the woman behind facilitating, and my deep gratitude to the Triune God Who was at work with them and through them.

Krupavathy, his eldest sister had her role in the early education of Solomon Raj and in giving him in marriage to Mary Sarojini, only sister of her husband, Balla Moses. And this work is dedicated to honor their memory!

Being proud of a familial legacy with global impact,
B. S. Moses Kumar

Abbreviations

ABM	American Baptist Mission
ACAA	Asian Christian Arts Association
ACC	Andhra Christian College
ACTC	Andhra Christian Theological College
AELC	Andhra Evangelical Lutheran Church
AJPS	Asian Journal of Pentecostal Studies
AKMI	Anil Kant Ministries International
APCC	Andhra Pradesh Christian Council
B.D.	Bachelor of Divinity
B.Ed.	Bachelor of Education
B.Sc.	Bachelor of Science
CARAVS	Christian Association for Radio and Audio Visual Service
CBM	Canadian Baptist Mission
CCA	Christian Conference of Asia
CD	Compact Disc
CMS	Church Mission Society
CSI	Church of South India
CISRS	Christian Institute for the Study of Religion and Society
ELM	Evangelical Lutheran Mission
ICAA	Indian Christian Arts Association
IMS	Indian Missionary Society
ISPCK	Indian Society for Propagation of Christian Knowledge
ISSU	India Sunday School Union
JNAFAU	Jawaharlal Nehru Architecture and Fine Arts University
LCA	Lutheran Church in America
LMS	London Missionary Society

M.S. / M.Sc.	Master of Science
NBCLC	National Biblical, Catechetical, and Liturgical Centre
NCC	National Christian Council
NCLC	National Catechetical and Liturgical Centre
NMS	National Missionary Society
RAVEMCO	Audio Visual Aids Committee of the National Council of Churches
SCM	Student Christian Movement
SHUATS	Sam Higginbottom University of Agriculture, Technology and Sciences
STBC	Samavesam of Telugu Baptist Churches
TAFTEE	The Association for Theological Education by Extension
TECCA	Theological Education for Christian Commitment and Action
VEM	Wuppertal Mission in Germany
WCC	World Council of Churches
YMCA	Young Men's Christian Association

Scripture Quotations in the body of the dissertation are from the cited sources as given below:

ESV	-	English Standard Version Wheaton, Illinois: Crossway, 2007
HCSB	-	Holman Christian Standard Bible Holman Bible Publishers, 2016
NKJV	-	New King James Version Nelson's NKJV Study Bible, 1997
NRSV	-	New Revised Standard Version, Iowa: World Bible Publishers, Inc., 1989

Foreword

Presenting the Gospel to contemporary society has been a challenge to mission workers through the centuries. With the resurrection experience of Jesus, the disciples of the Lord took it upon themselves to preach the Gospel, moving in every possible direction and reaching out to the many lands and the languages. The hardships never mattered. This is one side of the scenario.

Much later, 16th and 17th centuries witnessed the advent of the missionary movement with a deep urge and a sense of urgency to take the Gospel to every habitation on the earth. The denominational churches and mission societies dared to travel to the nations of the world and planted churches and service centres, largely unmindful of the local art, culture and the dialect.

Leading people to the saving Grace was deemed to be such a sacred privilege that nothing else mattered. The Gospel was passed on with the meaning and scope of the culture it belonged to. Thus the Gospel was presented as a potted plant. In some cases it grew rooted in the local soil; and in many cases, it grew in the un-melted pot sustaining its home culture. The theologians, Gospel activists and men of God became conscious of this unintended consequence, where the potted plant churches grow with no relevance to their local culture, art and dialect.

Opening the minds and hearts to the Pentecost experience, we see how one message reached many languages, each being able to understand in his/her own setting with nothing alien whatsoever. Here was a clear paradigm shift for the Gospel to be preached culture-conscious. Several early church fathers in every denomination have become conscious of this fact and made a beginning to understand and appreciate the significance of local art, culture and dialect in the Gospel work. The notion of a Christian culture was set aside because, into every culture penetrates the Gospel of Jesus and should thus be seen, heard and experienced.

The present book *"Incarnation of the Gospel in Indian Culture"* emerges out of a study of the art and poetry of Rev. P. Solomon Raj, the Poet-Artist par excellence, not just in India but among the continents of the world. Solomon Raj had this great burden for the Gospel to be seen and experienced in Indian art and culture. It was his life-time struggle to see incarnation of the Gospel in Indian poetry, dialect, drama, art and culture. This passionate story was fittingly brought in to focus by the study and research of Bishop Moses Kumar.

Moses Kumar is a serious researcher, a passionate Gospel worker, an able administrator, voracious reader, a prolific writer, and above all, a humble servant of God, who seeks pre-eminence to others denying privileges to self. Here he made a through study of the significance of art, culture, poetry, and the dialects to understand incarnation of the Gospel.

The reader will be greatly benefited as the book is not only insightful but greatly inspirational, revealing the Gospel as vividly shown through the life, service and witness of Rev. Solomon Raj.

As the well known adage goes, *"ratnalu ralle – Mahatmulu manushyule"* (diamonds are also stones and great souls are also ordinary people). And once these are recognized, there is a whole lot of difference! This book brings out the hidden diamond, Dr. Solomon Raj, who is already a shining example in expounding incarnation of the Gospel in Indian culture. We owe it to Bishop Moses Kumar for this master piece thesis for a Ph.D. of SHUATS, which is now a regular book for the benefit of all mission workers. The reader will see and experience the Gospel in the lens of Indian art and culture. I have therefore great pleasure in commending the book.

Dr. Jetti A. Oliver, Ph.D.
Chancellor – SHUATS

Introduction

The Gospel or the Good News of God for humans was personified in the life and work of Jesus Christ. The Great Commission of Jesus Christ, as recorded by the Gospel writers[1] is to go 'Into all the world' and preach it 'To all the creation'! This mandate is for all His disciples until 'the end of the age'. Jesus includes everyone, everywhere in the great host of recipients of the Gospel, and therefore the Church in all times is given the awesome responsibility of heralding the Gospel to every generation. The 'whosoever' dimension of the Gospel envisages embracing of recipients from across the multi-ethnic globe, irrespective of creed, color, culture or nationality. As such, it is obvious that the Gospel transcends and transmits into all cultures.

The dynamics of cross-cultural communication of the Gospel brings to the fore the challenge of adapting to the host culture in order to be relevant and meaningful, rather than imposing one's culture upon the recipient culture. The modern missionary movement resulted in an inflow of missionaries from many different denominational persuasions from the West into all the nations of the world including India, and they delivered their cultural baggage along with the Gospel. The scandal of the Gospel in a 'western garb' - with western clerical robes and ritual, liturgy and hymnal with western music, and western art and architecture in relation to places of worship had been a hindrance to the natives curtailing ready acceptance. D. T. Niles, the Sri Lankan evangelist, laments: "The Gospel came to us as a potted plant. We have to break the pot and set the plant in our own soil."[2]

As Solomon Raj remarks, the problems of the Gospel in encounter to the host culture are not peculiar to India but this was something, which has been going on from the time of the New Testament. "The culture of any community

---

1 . Matthew 28:19-20, Mark 16:15, Luke 24:47, Acts 1:8.

2 C. Michael Hawn: *Praying for the World: Exploring Asian hymnody* https://www.reformedworship.org/article/june-1999/praying-world-exploring-asian- hymnody - accessed March 24, 2018.

finds its expression in its art forms, songs and stories, in its folklore, and in its way of living and the whole world view of that community."[3]

'Incarnation of the Gospel in Indian Culture' is to present the Gospel by means of relevant and meaningful communication processes in our own cultural mediums. The Gospel is pictured as 'a seed that is sown in the soil of culture', and as such the plant bears the mark both of the seed and the soil. In Asian countries, Christianity is like a potted plant, which needs to be rooted in the cultural soil of the East. Incarnation of the Gospel therefore connotes the need for the Gospel to be communicated in a given culture in such a way that it is identified with the culture in which it is presented, rather than remain alien to the culture.

Contextualization means the active work of translating the Gospel into a culture that doesn't have an indigenous expression of Christianity. As defined by Pope John Paul II, it involves the twin dynamics of 'the incarnation of the Gospel in native cultures' and also 'the introduction of these cultures into the life of the Church'. Incarnation of the Gospel means that the unchanging Gospel changes its form and format, and becomes real in a new culture, in such a way that it identifies with the culture in which it is presented. The Lausanne Movement propels the Church from "Seeing *culture as a problem* or a barrier to communicating the gospel" to "*Celebrating culture* as the God-given context of our identity and as the fertile ground for the ongoing incarnation of the gospel and the Kingdom."[4] The concept of 'incarnation of the Gospel' obviously had been espoused and expounded by the Lausanne Movement. And it conveys the ideal of the Gospel taking roots in indigenous cultures and blooming where planted. According to Joshua Russell Chandran, the goal for contextualization is not to simply dress up Western theology in Indian robes or in non-Christian terminologies, but to enable people from where they are to answer in a never ending way, Christ's invitation to a contextualized conversation: 'Who do you say that I am?'

Much discussion had gone into the problem of 'presenting the Gospel in the western garb'. This process - with all its problems and prospects - may be deemed as 'incarnation of the Gospel' and this had been the talk of ages, the need of the hour, and the focal theme of the present study. An analytical study of this issue will be made in the light of ***'the Art and Poetry of Pulidindi Solomon Raj'*** - as Solomon's manifold works of art and poetry provided a conspicuous example for this process. The Problem ultimately is - Can the Gospel be presented in Indian context through the art and culture of Solomon Raj or other similar means?

This Study is undertaken with the following Objectives :

- To analyze the western cultural baggage on the life of the Indian Church;

3 P. Solomon Raj: *'Indian Church and Response to Culture'*, Unpublished Paper.

4 *Gospel Contextualisation Revisited*, Haslev 1997 Consultation Statement, http://www.lausanne.org/haslev-1997/consultation-statement.html - accessed March 24, 2018.

- To narrate the incarnation of the Gospel in the Indian context;
- To analyze the literary and artistic creations of Solomon Raj;
- To articulate the theological themes embedded in his art and poetry;
- To evaluate the evangelistic means initiated and implemented by Solomon Raj.

Major compilations of art only are analyzed briefly here, with limited scope for evaluation of each of the individual work. All the rich symbolism of Solomon's art could not be explored in detail in the present work. Even the theological themes embedded in his art could not be fully fathomed or envisaged. However, the present study is hoped to aid inspiration for further exploration and deeper exposition.

This study is an interdisciplinary investigation into the issue, making use of insights from different disciplines like theology, hermeneutics, ecclesiology and church history.

- Library research – which entails study of all the writings by and about Solomon Raj, and other related literature;
- Personal interviews with the Artist-Poet and his relatives and colleagues - which are targeted to solicit the data on the formative influences, the inspiration behind different pieces of art, and the particular interpretations by the artist;
- Exploratory visits made to St. Luke's Lalit Kala Ashram for the last many years at periodic intervals. The Artist founded this Ashram at Vijayawada in 1994.

The First Chapter deals with **Review of Literature** related to the process of Incarnation of the Gospel, and to the art and writings of P. Solomon Raj.

A Historical Perspective of **Incarnation of the Gospel in Indian Culture** is undertaken in the Second Chapter. *'Incarnation of the Gospel'* means presentation of the Gospel in an alien culture in such a way that it is identified, and made 'at home' with the host culture, without imposing unnecessary cultural baggage, and the encumbering non-essentials.[5]

Much discussion and study have gone in the history of the Indian Church into the problem of 'presenting the Gospel in the western garb'. Many experiments have been made at different times in different places by different pioneers in the field, to offset the problem and to present a viable option. The particular pattern of Solomon Raj, in the backdrop of an historical perspective, is hoped to provide a challenge with some feasible insights.

The Third Chapter, on the **Life and Work of P. Solomon Raj** enumerates the humble origins and formative impacts of Solomon Raj, which propelled him

5 Acts 15:28 *"For it has seemed good to the Holy Spirit and to us to impose on you no further burden than these essentials".* (NRSV)

attain higher pinnacles in literary, artistic and theological realms. It shows how he could march from the ranks of his formal profession to the peaks of his creative vocation - beyond the denominational bounds, beyond the national bounds, and beyond retirement.

The Fourth Chapter deals with **'Theological and Evangelical Perspectives'** of the **Art and Poetry of P. Solomon Raj**. An analysis will be made of his methodology in presenting the timeless message of the Gospel in a timely mode by means of literary works in Telugu and English, as well as works produced or reproduced in other languages - with special emphasis on the theological themes embedded therein. A brief mention of his early works on Christian communication would not be out of place at this juncture. The Christian Publishing House (of the Lutheran denomination) at Rajahmundry published two of his works in Telugu on *Audio-Visual Aids* and *Story Telling* back in late 1950's.

A detailed study and evaluation will be made of what the researcher deems his *Magnum Opus,* namely, *Liberation in Luke's Gospel,* which was published in German, Dutch, and English, and which contains wood block prints with matching meditations on twelve themes of liberation - all taken from Luke's Gospel. These 12 colored woodcuts of *Liberation in Luke's Gospel* with matching meditations went round in many Exhibitions in Germany, Netherlands, and Switzerland before they appeared in a booklet. Of late, it is commendable that Solomon Raj could bring out his *'Liberation in Luke's Gospel'* into Telugu also (entitled *Luka Suvarthalo Vimochana Prasakthi*) - with beautiful rendering of the accompanying meditations for each of the twelve themes of liberation in fitting Telugu poetry. The rest of Solomon's works in art and poetry are presented in this Chapter with a theological commentary.

The Fifth Chapter is **'Evaluation'** which analyzes Solomon's *Evangelistic Innovations,* and endeavors to portray *'An Evangelist in the Making'*. An Evangelist in his own right, Solomon communicated the Christian message beyond the confines of the Christian community, to a wider global human community, through his innovative art and poetry! This chapter assigns due consideration for his unique 'Literary Creations', unparalleled 'Theological Proclamations' and unprecedented modes of communication - beyond the familiar, beyond the theological jargon, beyond the normal confines, and beyond his times.

In Conclusion *'A New Paradigm of Evangelistic Means'* initiated by Solomon Raj with a new hermeneutic of evangelization will be seen. This analytical study is hoped to inspire the emerging generations across the nations. It is also hoped to inspire the reader for further reflection and innovation. This work does not claim to be exhaustive, but attempts to be a reliable source-book that aids further research as Solomon Raj continues to speak for generations to come through his works - literary and artistic.

1

Review of Literature

A study of 'Review of Literature' is undertaken at this juncture, with a statement of justification and need for the present study at the end. Review of Literature may be analyzed under five divisions, as follows:

- Selective Works on Incarnation of the Gospel;
- Dissertations on the Works of Solomon Raj;
- Reviews on the Published Works of Solomon Raj;
- Articles and Essays on the Works of Solomon Raj;
- Researcher's Exploratory Studies.

Works on Incarnation of the Gospel

Since the Research Problem deals with the challenge of ***Incarnation of the Gospel in Indian Culture***, a preliminary review of literature on the issue of incarnation or inculturation of the Gospel is in order. There had been extensive research and writing on the issue. In view of limitations of space and time, two vitally important works, from Catholic and Protestant standpoints, may be selectively cited:

i) A Handbook on Inculturation[6]

This work by Peter Schineller, a Jesuit scholar, serves as a Manual for Inculturation. The author deals with the 'what' and 'why' of inculturation in the very first chapter of the book and then traces the process of inculturation that was at work in the Catholic Church chronologically. The 'how' of inculturation also was dealt with in the fifth chapter with examples from Nigeria and Latin America. "Wherever the gospel is lived, wherever it is preached, we are obliged to search for ways in

6 New York: Paulist Press, 1990.

which the good news can be more deeply lived, celebrated and shared" - Peter believes. "This process is inculturation: an attitude and method necessary for any Christian ministry"!

ii) Christianity Made in India: From Apostle Thomas to Mother Teresa[7]

This much-awaited seminal work was written by Prof. Roger E. Hedlund, the director emeritus of Mylapore Institute of Indigenous Studies, and the Chief Editor of *Oxford Encyclopaedia of South Asian Christianity.* The author takes the readers on a tour through the centuries from Apostle Thomas to Mother Teresa - "Beginning from Jerusalem" in the Introduction "To the Ends of the Earth" in the Conclusion. The author traces the process of incarnation of the Gospel that has been at work in the Protestant Church chronologically – with Thomas and the First Christians in the first century, and after a thousand years of silence, with Ziegenbalg, William Carey, and Pandita Ramabai, and eventually Mother Teresa in the twentieth century.

In other words, this work "discusses the indigenization of Christianity in the Indian context, set in the larger context of the exceptional growth of the church in the non-Western world during the twentieth century, which has been characterized by a diversity of localized cultural expressions". Hedlund affirms the reality that "wherever the gospel goes, it takes root in the local culture"!

iii) Planting in Native Soil: Studies in Gospel Inculturation

In addition to the representative works cited above is the Festschrift in honor of P. Solomon Raj, *Planting in Native Soil: Studies in Gospel Inculturation.* Intended to be a Reader, this work, edited by Prof. David Zersen and Bishop B. S. Moses Kumar, contains enlightening studies by 19 scholars from four continents on Inculturation - mostly with reference to the works of Solomon Raj.

Solomon "uses a variety of styles to communicate his message, including Indian symbolism, Ethiopian iconography, Japanese and German woodcarving and theological reflection." There is a comprehensive Curriculum Vitae of Solomon Raj, appended to this volume.

7 Minneapolis: Fortress Press, 2017.

Dissertations on the Works of Solomon Raj

Three works of research are done so far in India and overseas, in the form of dissertations at Masters level:

i) "Dr. Solomon Raj: A Christian Artist"

This earliest work on Solomon Raj was a dissertation Marie Dominic Cicilya submitted to the Faculty of Stella Maris College, Madras in 1995 for the degree of M.A. in History of Fine Arts. This work contains 37 works of Solomon Raj at random, and is primarily an introductory study. The researcher assesses the artist as

> a volatile person, exploring various creative spheres such as painting, writing poems, carving and creative crafts. All these spheres project the artist as a devout Christian … This dissertation brings to light the real artist with a vision, who liberates, sets trends and conveys a prophetic message to the society through his works. He is a pilgrim who continues his journey to see his best performance in each of his endeavor.[8]

ii) "Solomon Raj, Prophetic Artist in India"

Another significant research was done by a Dutch scholar, Jojanneke Dekker, with the above title, on Solomon's art as a medium of inculturation of the Gospel in India. It was a Master's Dissertation submitted to the Faculty of Theology, Utrecht University, Netherlands in 2006. Having spent several weeks at St. Luke's Lalit Kala Ashram, Vijayawada, and having interviewed the artist at length, Dekker presents Solomon Raj as an innovative communicator of the Gospel through the media of art. She is a Lutheran theologian working in the Protestant Church in the Netherlands (PKN). This work is rather a fruit of Participatory Observation than mere Library Research. Participatory Observation is a "research technique in anthropology and sociology characterized by the effort of an investigator to gain entrance into and social acceptance by a foreign culture or alien group so as better to attain a comprehensive understanding of the internal structure of the society."[9]

Dekker has written another analytical commentary on Solomon's reputed Batik - 'Thirst for Justice' - with rich imagery and symbolism, and proclaiming need for 'Righteousness like a Stream Ever-Flowing.'[10] Solomon made this batik in 2001 at the request of Brot für die Welt (Bread for the World) - to specifically make a meditation cloth (Hungertuch). It was first shown at the Kirchentag (the

8 Unpublished dissertation, (1995:2).

9 https://www.merriam-webster.com/dictionary/participant%20observation accessed March 24, 2018.

10 http://www.artway.eu/content.php?id=1315&lang=en&action=show - accessed April 9, 2018.

huge biennial congress of German Protestants which takes place in various cities in Germany) to focus attention on the right of every person in the world to have access to clean and sufficient drinking water. Water is desperately needed in dry and barren desert areas. This thirst is equivalent to the cry for justice of people in desperate situations - the cry of all times in all places.

With traditional confines and rigid mindsets of the Church folks, Solomon feels 'like a prophet crying out in the desert' - "It is a struggle to make Indian Christians see the necessity and the possibilities of the use of art. Their view on art has to change to let it have a positive influence on their life and faith". Dekker sums up Solomon's contribution:[11]

> Raj's art does have the potential to wake people up and touch people ... It is art that is accessible, even for people from non-Indian cultures ... does contribute to the inculturation of the gospel, as people from all over the world understand and experience the gospel in a new way when they meditate or ponder on it ... Raj, like a prophet, makes free the way for a new use of art in India; the use of art for the communication of the gospel message.

iii) "A Study of Indigenous Symbols in Selected 'Batik Paintings' of Pulidindi Solomon Raj as Means of Communicating the Gospel in India"

With the above title, K. Sam Mathew wrote his Thesis for the degree of M.Th. and submitted it to the Senate of Serampore College in 2009. This study focuses on the rich symbolism in the art of Solomon Raj, but again it has a limited scope as the study was of just some selected Batiks of Solomon Raj. The investigator has taken well three sets of test audience - Christians, non-Christians and professional artists - to pose his questions and to record his findings. He affirms "indigenous symbols can be an effective means of communicating the Gospel, and art forms can function as a common language to reach beyond the boundaries of religion, culture and language to communicate Gospel in India."[12]

Symbols by definition are 'open' and different answers for meaning of symbols is quite natural and expected. This prospect of different perceptions is useful in a sharing situation because at the end each participant will be enriched and each understanding will be enlarged. Solomon remarks, "freedom to be honest to one's own response is good and useful". Differences, even if they are serious, must be welcomed, since the participants are honest to say what they got from the picture. If some people thought in this experiment that fire symbolizes 'hell' we should not be disappointed or surprised. For example, Solomon's symbol of fire among German audiences suggested the bombs in World War II. This

11 Unpublished dissertation. (2006: 103).

12 Unpublished dissertation. (2009: 11).

negative suggestion may be strange and disappointing to the artist, but this is what happens with symbols. White color is not always a symbol of happiness in some cultures; it is symbol of sadness.[13]

It is interesting to see Solomon Raj emerge as a 'Christian artist' initially, and successively evolve as a 'Prophetic artist' with passage of time, and with ascending stages of maturity. Experimenting a multitude of art processes, he has presented a new hermeneutic of indigenous symbolism in communication of the Gospel. The present study at doctoral level continues to add to the growing interest and ongoing exploration on Solomon's works in arts and literature.

Reviews on the Published Works of Solomon Raj

Many articles and reviews were written about Solomon Raj or his works by many authors across the globe. Solomon's seminal work was his doctoral dissertation with Birmingham University under Prof. Hollenweger. In this section, it is apt to touch base with the Reviews on Solomon's seminal work and its sequel, which is a follow-up research, by some reputed critics like Stephen Fuch, an anthropologist, and a couple of missiologists, H. L. Richard, and Alle G. Hoekema.

i) Stephen Fuchs' Review

Stephen Fuchs, SVD, a famous anthropologist, came to *India* as a young missionary in 1934 from Austria and lived more than 60 years in India. He was the Founder of Institute for Indian Culture, Mumbai, a research center-cum-library. His review on Solomon's seminal work, *'A Christian Folk Religion in India: A Study of the Small Church Movement in Andhra Pradesh, with Special Reference to the Bible Mission of Devadas'* deals with the problem of how far inculturation in the local culture is permissible to a Christian Church. Fuchs wonders about faith-sustainability among converts who were "only superficially instructed in the Christian faith which they have recently accepted".

Yet the value of the 'Group Churches', as Solomon Raj calls them, cannot be undermined, if systematic discipleship among the new converts is undertaken. They are seen to be representing "valuable links between the foreign and rather distant Mother Churches and the prospective converts among the local non-Christian population", as these Group Churches are "intimately connected with the old folk religion". Finally, Fuchs had categorically portrayed the popular appeal of this indigenous faith movement in comparison to the seemingly foreign expression of Christian faith, as given below:

> Since Devadas' audience was mostly illiterate, all teaching had to be done orally. He preached and taught, using to full effect the imagery of the local people. To communicate his message he used also hymn singing accompanied by music instruments in much the same manner

13 Solomon's E-Mail dated April 22, 2010 to Prof. Gudrun Löwner.

as the ballad singers of the region. Devadas himself was a gifted poet and composed devotional songs, which were sung in genuine Indian melody and metre, while the Lutheran (Church) had few such songs. Most of their church hymns were translations from western languages and had to be sung in the western style of music. The foreign character of the Lutheran Church became most conspicuous in the form of their singing and worship, while that of Devadas' followers was fully indigenous. He had also his own style of prayer, meditation, and Divine worship, which was better adapted to the mentality of the local people than the official Lutheran liturgical style.[14]

The situation was somewhat rectified, in course of time, and it was not all Western translations of hymns the Lutheran churches ended up with. Many converts from other faiths came up with devotional lyrics in Indian classical music, and the compilation of Andhra Christian Hymnal with a combination of both came into vogue in 1893, with completely revised edition in 1966. It is a grand testimonial to this transition, and though it remained steady for long, in recent times a new dimension is added when even the many popular songs from 'Songs of Zion' used by the Brethren churches, and other lyrics mostly used by 'group churches' at last have made their way into the Hymnal and being freely used by the Lutheran and other liturgical churches.

ii) H. L. Richard's Reviews on Solomon's Seminal and Sequel Works

Solomon's seminal work was his doctoral dissertation[15] under Prof. Walter J. Hollenweger, a Swiss theologian and author, recognized as an expert on worldwide Pentecostalism. This was a study of the small church movement in Andhra Pradesh, with reference to the Bible Mission of Devadas. It was originally published by Verlag Peter Lang (Frankfurt) in 1986, and the Indian revised edition was published by Centre for Contemporary Christianity in 2004, with a reprint in 2009.

Solomon's sequel work[16] was a study of the other Indigenous Missions in Coastal Andhra Pradesh. With an unquenchable quest, Solomon had resumed the study of new Christian movements in Andhra Pradesh with the survey of some 73 indigenous missions. This work contains couple of scholarly expositions by Prof. Roger Hedlund and Bishop P. Victor Premasagar.

In the process, Solomon addressed practical issues such as the following with enlightening insights:

- ministry of the Spoken Word,

14 https://nirc.nanzan-u.ac.jp/nfile/1414 p. 147. accessed April 6, 2018.

15 *"A Christian Folk Religion in India: A Study of the Small Church Movement in Andhra Pradesh, with Special Reference to the Bible Mission of Devadas."*

16 *"The New Wine-Skins: The Story of the Indigenous Missions in Coastal Andhra Pradesh, India."*

- equipping the saints for the work of the ministry,
- ministry of the printed page,
- dreams, visions, miracles and healings, and,
- bread and butter concerns (stewardship).

H. L. Richard wrote a fitting review on both the above works.[17] At the outset, Richard points out that these two works are closely related, as indicated in the subtitles. The first is Solomon's doctoral research while the second is his 'follow-up research, looking more for breadth than depth'. Richard concludes: "Students who want to understand the meaning of Christianity need to look beyond creed-based definitions to the grass-roots realities of the movements introduced here."[18]

iii) Alle Hoekema's Reviews

Alle G. Hoekema, professor of missiology at the Vrije Universiteit, Amsterdam, has written a couple of reviews on Solomon's following works:

- *"Biblia Pauperum. The Poor Man's Bible."*[19]
- *"St. John's Gospel. A Gallery of Hieratic Art."*[20]

Hoekema, in his review on *Biblia Pauperum,* points out how Solomon's attention was drawn to the subject back in 1960's while at Indiana University, but was rekindled in Finland when Hans-Ruedi Weber commented on his work with woodcuts that they reminded one of the *Biblia Pauperum* of the Middle Ages, and eventually led to the publication of his *Biblia Pauperum* in 2008. Solomon has limited the number of pictures on each page and the total number of pages - instead of seven pictures, he only has the main three of the classic triptychs, and instead of 40 pages, he only has ten - thus reducing the idea of the *Poor Man's Bible* to its essence: "the New Testament images in the centre and the two Old Testament types on either side of the central picture."[21] Again Hoekema points out that Solomon replaces the written *tituli* and *lectiones* of the original example by 'brief and often moving meditations'. Like its famous predecessor, this work too will be a 'teacher's aid' rather than directly come into the hands of the really poor.

In his review on *St. John's Gospel: A Gallery of Hieratic Art,* Hoekema states that the aspect of 'an inward directed spirituality' added to his work. He

17 Published in *Global Missiology, Review & Preview,* October, 2004 www.globalmissiology.net - accessed April 4, 2018.

18 *Global Missiology, Review & Preview.*

19 In *Exchange,* Journal of Missiological and Ecumenical Research, Vol. 38, The Netherlands: Brill, Leiden-Boston, (2009:381-388).

20 Unpublished (Copy from the File of P. Solomon Raj).

21 P. Solomon Raj, 'The Sequence' in *Biblia Pauperum,* (2008:40).

fittingly sums up that during many decades Solomon holds a very special position among the Christian artist-theologians in Asia, and "his way of transmitting and transforming theology is exemplary to many theologians and missiologists in the West".

iv) Siga Arles' Evaluation

Prof. Siga Arles presents an analysis of Solomon's seminal work, elucidating the relevance of Solomon's insights from his doctoral dissertation for broad theological discussion.[22] Solomon identifies six themes, exploring the role of an indigenous movement within Indian Christianity. They provide a helpful analysis for the continuing developments in India, and around the world, as given below:

- *The Rise of Indigenous Churches - a Global Phenomenon:*

It was attested that the Spirit of God was moving the missional scholarship to consider these new church movements around the world in the twentieth century. Contemporaneously Solomon went to Birmingham and explored the reality of what was happening in the church. He saw three categories of "independent group churches" in Andhra Pradesh:

- so-called revival groups remaining in the denominational churches, yet developing their own structures as charismatic groups within the major church bodies;
- other groups that broke away from mainline churches becoming a kind of dissident bodies, working independently;
- a third type, small in number, remaining outside the major churches as open rivals, and highly critical of the historic churches.

Of these, Solomon selected the Bible Mission of Father Devadas for his study. What Father Devadas saw as the ethos and status of the Lutheran Church of which he was a member was not adequate to satisfy the needs and spiritual longings of his people. Hence, he went into a 'search mode' for relevance and meaningfulness, and invented new and indigenous approaches - using songs, worship style and ministry patterns - to discover 'a satisfying religion and religious experience'. Solomon saw here a reflection of the worldwide movement of the Holy Spirit bringing renewal in the church movement through new religious initiatives. He did not disown it as heretical or as rebellion against the church, but saw it in a positive light affirming it.[23]

- *The Cultural Unsuitability of the Western Church in Indian Soil:*

In numerous ways Solomon has identified how the Western form of Lutheran Christianity was unsuitable to the rural masses of Andhra Pradesh. While

---

22 *Towards a Renewed and Relevant Church*, in "Planting in Native Soil" (2014:1-9).

23 Siga Arles, *Towards a Renewed and Relevant Church*, (2014:3).

narrating the characteristics of the non-white indigenous churches, he identified certain tensions between mission churches and the indigenous churches. Perhaps the Western pattern of the church made it look irrelevant and hence, it did not attract people to keep it growing and increasing through the centuries.

- *The Absence of Dreams, Visions and Healing*

The rural people were often in need of healing - of their bodies, minds and their emotions. They needed interpretations for their dreams and visions. But this was neither accommodated nor encouraged in the kind of Lutheran theology and ministry in rural Andhra Pradesh. Jesus healed people and he calls his disciples to do greater things than what he did. The church is divided into people with either *charismania* - an over enthusiastic love for gifts - or *charisphobia* - an undue fear of spiritual gifts. Healing is a popular gift that the *charismaniacs* seek. The right use of healing is a welcome means of ministry. But there is much misuse of healing and an all too limited use of healing in a world of much brokenness and illness.

Near the end of his dissertation, Solomon deals with dreams, visions and healing. He notes the lack of any meaningful teaching or practice of these in the Lutheran church and observes their presence and use in the Bible Mission. This provides a corrective input for the church in Andhra Pradesh, which could help the church worldwide!

- *The Church was Priest-Centered and Priest-Dominated*

The intention of God is that the redeemed shall be incorporated into the body of Christ - the church around the world. The *laos* includes the laity and the clergy together. The role of the clergy is to be servant leaders to teach and train the members in their faith and practice. Instead, the clergy have often taken control of the church, laity left as mere pew sitters and spectators. It was so in the pre-reformation period, but Martin Luther shared the conviction of the Priesthood of All Believers. Every man and woman in Christ is to be trained to fulfill the calling to ministry in the world. It is unfortunate that this Protestant ideal was lost often in the post-Reformation period.

- *The Priest should Equip the Saints – The Laity*

The World Council of Churches at the second Assembly in Evanston in 1954 pursued the theme "Laity Formation", with much concern for the laity. In 1953, Lesslie Newbigin presented his classic statement in *The Ministry of the Church: Ordained and Unordained, Paid and Unpaid.* In spite of the many efforts ever since, the sad reality was that everything remained priest-centered. Solomon has attested the significance of the laity emphasis and the Latin American initiatives of TEE and commended the new church movements as pro-laity and positive.

- *The Folk Church*

Solomon is committed to the Peoples' Church – the folk church! To arouse a theology suitable and relevant for such a peoples' church is part of the concern in his thesis. Every lay member of the church in whatever job one finds himself/herself ought to be involved in society constructively, with a personal sense of mission. In the final quarter of the Twentieth century when contextualization became a strong theme and propelled the church around the world to consider the plight of the subaltern people, and theologians began to engage in contextual theologies such as the Dalit, Tribal, Feminist, Black and Minjung theologies, the church is moving closer to the people! It is turning into a peoples' church. This is a welcome sign for mission of the church in imitating the incarnational pattern of Jesus Christ whose kenosis model influences a theology for our times.

Solomon has interpreted the church in India and the movement forward into newness of renewal, revival and transformation. He brought global similarities in the marching order and provided parallel information to show how it is the Spirit of Christ, Who is at work moving the church into this new path.

Articles and Essays on the Works of Solomon Raj

There are many articles and essays on Solomon Raj and his works by different people, reputed in different fields of study. *Christian Themes in Indian Art: From the Mogul Times till Today,*[24] a seminal work on Indian Art by Anand Amaladass and Gudrun Löwner gives a detailed biographical essay on '*Solomon Raj*' portraying Solomon as an 'autodidactic' artist, and a 'bridge builder' whose message is well received. His oeuvre is 'dominated by presentations of Christ. His early black and white woodcuts depicted nearly exclusively the suffering Christ'.

Other works may be classified and listed as follows, which are duly acknowledged in the Bibliography:

i) Indian Writers in Telugu

Couple of Indian writers, familiar with the works of Solomon have written analytical essays: Prof. K. Anandan of Telugu University, Hyderabad has written a Foreword to a couple of Solomon's works - in *Daiva Gnana Siri* and in *Upamana Malika*. Prof. K. Job Sudarshan of Andhra Loyola College, Vijayawada has written an analytical essay, "*A Pleasant Bridge Between Indian Culture and Christian Faith: A Charioteer of Christian Literature and Art Expression*" published in "Swarna Deepika."[25] Here he pays a tribute to P. Solomon Raj:

> Raj is a restless cultivator in the literary fields. Along with *Shathaka, Dwipada* and *Geya* genres in Telugu literature he also accomplished creditable works in *Yaksha ganas, Udaharana Kavyas*, which even experts hesitate to attempt.

24 New Delhi: Manohar Publications, (2012:255).

25 Telugu Christian Journal, January 20, 2006.

Job Sudarshan has also written Foreword to a couple of Solomon's works in "Kim Kartavyam" and "*Gaana Kusumalu*".

ii) Indian Writers in English

Many Indian writers, familiar with the works of Solomon have written critical essays in English, as acknowledged in the Bibliography. D. Sanjiva Dev has written on *'Rhythmic Vision' - An Appreciation of the Art Work of Dr. Solomon Raj.* Dr. Balantrapu Rajanikantha Rao and R. M. Challa have written analytical essays. In his preface to this book, *Gaana Kusumaalu*, Karanam Balasubrahmanyam Pille aptly remarked that though Solomon Raj might have written countless books before, his life attained its fulfillment just with these lyrics.[26] Others include Dr. Stephen Joseph and Prof. Sumita Roy of Osmania University.

Some Indian authors wrote essays about the works of Solomon Raj, in the Festschrift in his honor: Pulidindi Augustine Jyothi Raj, Dr. Chilkuri Vasantha Rao and T. Venkata Rao.

iii) Western Writers

Many writers from the West too were familiar with and appreciative of the works of Solomon Raj. Herbert E. Hoefer has edited the work, *Christian Art in India* mentioning about Solomon's art works. Another book by Masao Takenaka and Ron O'Grady, *The Bible through Asians Eyes* mentions about the art of Solomon. Many authors like Michael Hardy, Volker Kuester, Joe Ubelmesser, Martha Frederiks and Joshida Megumi have written reviews and essays in Solomon's books. Walter J. Hollenweger and Gudrun Löwner have also written detailed essays on the works of Solomon.

The following Western authors have written essays about the works of Solomon Raj, in the Festschrift in his honor: Jojanneke Dekker and Eric J. Lott - a Dutch and an English author respectively. Prof. David J. Zersen had fallen in love with Solomon's art in 2003 when he first saw it at *Kirchentag* in Berlin, and ever since he writes consistently on the works of Solomon Raj, as acknowledged in the Bibliography.

iv) An Artist Colleague

Jyoti Sahi, another Indian artist-theologian is a younger colleague of Solomon Raj, and he has written a couple of essays on Solomon Raj, published in couple of the Festschrifts, the second one in honor of Solomon Raj himself:

- *Solomon Raj: Artist with a Cosmic Vision* [27]
- *Solomon Raj and the Prehistoric Origins of Dalit Art* [28]

---

26 *Sahabhavana*, in *Gaana Kusumaalu*, (2002: xiv).

27 *"The Yobel Spring"* Vol. 1 (2013:31-40).

28 *"Planting in Native Soil,"* (2014:145-151).

Both the above works are judicious evaluations of Solomon Raj and his works. Jyoti Sahi met him first in 1980 in London, and he worked with Solomon in the Indian Christian Art Association. In 1990, in a talk on Indian Christian Art at the Hermansburg Mission, Jyoti Sahi tried to show how the theological viewpoint of different Indian artists had influenced their art, and how their art expressed a theology through the way in which they had represented Christian themes. There is also a variety of cultural and theological underpinnings to their art.

All the Literature cited in this Chapter thus far, in addition to researcher's personal exploratory studies listed in the following folios, serves as the secondary source material for this dissertation. All the writings by Solomon Raj, published or unpublished, of course, are the primary sources, as given in Bibliography at the end.

Researcher's Exploratory Studies

Having studied available literature on Solomon Raj and his various works on art, poetry and other literature by different artists and authors, as reviewed in the preceding pages, an effort is made now to review some of the exploratory studies by the present researcher:

i) Bhaki Sahitya from the Heart of Solomon Raj

The scope of this essay confines our attention to the theological themes of Solomon's *Geetha Malika*, with an exciting exercise through his 44 steps up on his *Bhakti yaatra* (devotional pilgrimage), which may be called *Songs of Solomon.* The major theological themes in these *bhakti geetas* (devotional songs) pertain to the author's views on God the Father, Christology and Eschatology. An analytical study of these themes in the light of the songs was presented in this essay. This exercise enables the reader to appreciate the richness and ethos of some of Solomon's theological thought. His Theological Proclamations are woven mainly around his conception about the Father God, the Incarnate Son, and the hope of glory at the end of life's journey. His strong belief in the triune God was expressed in the first two themes above, and his intimate relationship with God through his life's journey seems to have produced an unwavering assurance in His unending care at the end of life as we see in these songs.[29]

Solomon has written three poetic works, which the present researcher was privileged to edit. The first two were published in 2012, when Solomon turned out to be a nonagenarian, and the last one in 2014:

- *Daiva Gnana Siri: Prayers and Proclamations*
- *Upamana Malika: Parables of Lord Jesus*

29 *Bhakti Sahitya from the Heart of Solomon Raj* in P. Solomon Raj; *Geetha Malika*, Delhi: ISPCK, (2010:93-144).

- *Paul Gerhardt Kirthana Sahityamu (The Hymns of Paul Gerhardt: A Free Translation)*

The researcher has written Foreword for these three works:

ii) Thirst for Vaividhya

Solomon's thirst for creative variety already kept him on higher pinnacles as a writer in Telugu literature, as he successfully employed different genres in each of his five published works in Telugu. The present work is a grand testimonial to his continuous thirst for *vaividhya* - creative variety in writing. *Daiva Gnana Siri* is an anthology of 157 poems on various Biblical themes. In his Introduction, the author beautifully and clearly portrays the didactic value of poetic literature, especially in relation to the Biblical narratives and proverbs. Expressing the Biblical truths in native and cultural idiom and phrase would make it relevant and revelatory. Solomon emphatically elucidates the necessity of the 'incarnation of the Gospel in Indian culture' here in this work, as well as in most of his previous writings. To read the Biblical narratives and sayings in simple verse, to enable the listeners have the benefit of lucid understanding of the said teachings, and to engage the audience in fruitful interaction for better understanding and appreciation of the Biblical truths - all this entails to the didactic purpose of this anthology.

The addition of 29 poems written as *shashtyantas* at the end makes this anthology a rare combination of his love for poetry and his love for devotional verse. The author narrates the 'what' and 'why' of *shashtyantas* in his Introduction. Of the seven prepositions in Telugu literature, the sixth one (*kin, kun, yokka,* etc.) when applied to God, the Lord, or Christ, it becomes a word of worship, praise and prayer. These words used with the sixth preposition, in poems, describe Christ's attributes and works, and these are poems of praise. As Prof. K. Anandan points out it is common to write six of such *shashtyantas* addressed to the Patron of a particular work, but the way Solomon Raj added 29 *shashtyantas*, in praise of his Lord, is unique.

A couple of *'Dandakas'* at the very end of this work further makes it a rare piece of Christian literature in Telugu. Solomon Raj maneuvers his pen, his imagination, and his capacity at *vaividhya* (creative variety) with great ease and unique skill here, as often done. This work is one of the unique writings in Telugu literature, with Christian *'Dandakas'* at the end. *Dandaka* is a prayer to different gods, and there are many *dandakas* in Telugu literature addressed to different gods of the Hindu pantheon. It is a literary style of poetry seen in Sanskrit and Telugu languages. The ever-innovative mind of Solomon Raj spurred him to pen a couple of *dandakas* in profuse praise of Jesus Christ.

iii) Didactic Literature from the Pen of Dr. P. Solomon Raj

Oral culture prevailed in every society, aiding communication through songs, proverbs and stories. Solomon tried to preach the Gospel and also celebrate in his own heart the good message through song and story. The subject matter of his writings as well as of his art had been Christian themes from the Bible, but the means of its proclamation or presentation had been diverse and distinguished. The three-fold dynamics of *pratibha* (talent), *vyutpatti* (scholarship), and *abhyasa* (practice) have had a rare mingle in the hands of Solomon Raj, and have produced what we see with our eyes – physical and spiritual!

The thrust of each of his writings had been *didactic*, and Solomon Raj now turns his eyes on the parables of Jesus Christ. The present work deals with some twenty parables – not just as narrative, but also with an interpretative treatment. The poet very skillfully introduces or summarizes each of the parable with his profound reflection. This work may rightly be styled as reflective poetry. For example, in the first Parable on 'Wheat and Tares' the poet summing up reflects in the closing lines as follows:

> We have seen You're longsuffering;
> How can we know this divine truth
> when we find fault with others?

Parables are a unique means of Jesus' instruction and teaching, and the purpose of a parable is to convey a single central truth. Solomon focuses on the message of Jesus in the parables through his reflective verse. He opines that a reading or singing of these parables in verse would bring joy and delight, and that this would be more attractive, and easier to remember. He anticipates that these would help in better appreciation of the Word, and aid in sharing the Gospel. In fact, at the very beginning, in his poetic Introduction to this work, the poet envisions that all the parables Jesus taught would become stepping-stones to heaven (*paralokamunaku sopanambulu*). Elsewhere he acknowledges that these sayings and stories are adequate signposts (*Neevichu suktikathalu chalunu maadu kannulu deruva).* Again, it is amazing to see Solomon Raj, a communicator all his life across cultures, communicate profound Scriptural truths, with an unusual ease and an unending elegance in Telugu verse. Countless truths are communicated as words of wisdom, and herein lies the didactic value of this writing.

In the process of enunciating the parables, we often come across a 'conversational mode', the poet skillfully employs, whereby, he reasons with God on what seems a puzzle from the human end, or affirms God on things that sound justifiable. This human-divine conversational mode further ensures 'I-Thou' relationship with God. This pattern of reflective verse has been interwoven throughout the text. The conversational mode is also seen at interpersonal level where the poet reasons with the readers or the audience on the ways of God. Though there are twenty different parables, this dialogical mode ensures continuity in the whole work, and makes it readable and profitable. In fact, the way the poet skillfully engages God in a dialogue is unique. It is not a straight narration as it is in the Bible, but it is a response of our heart to the everlasting instruction of the Lord.

iv) Paul Gerhardt's Hymns: A Review of Telugu Rendering by Solomon Raj

The incessant and exploratory mind of Pulidindi Solomon Raj has produced a few things of beauty in art or verse, which are 'a joy forever', and which have brought much delight to the people of God across the nations for more than six decades. Of late, the eye of Solomon was intently searching valuable resources, for example, in the area of Hymns of the early church and through the Reformation period. In the process, he was drawn to the *'Spiritual Songs'* of Paul Gerhardt, a post-Reformation hymn writer with hundreds of hymns to his credit in German language. Many of these were translated into English and sung in the churches for centuries.

Solomon was not new to Gerhardt's hymns, as he had listened to some of them in the churches during his global itineration in 1980's. The message and the structural beauty of these hymns are remarkable. Solomon never thought of rendering them into Telugu language during those bygone days. Now after some three decades, it is interesting to see him, in his nineties, do the present study on these Hymns. This first-ever Telugu rendering is a great contribution, beyond any doubt, to the Telugu Church. Though these hymns were originally translated from German into English, and now from English to Telugu, one wonders at the depth of their meaning, and the creative imagination and elaborate thought on the themes Paul Gerhardt touched. The Telugu rendering sounds almost like an original work by itself, rather than a translation. Solomon translated some six of those hymns and this gives the reader a foretaste into the rich devotional literature of Gerhardt in particular, and of the Reformation heritage in general.

Gerhardt wrote some of these hymns during The Thirty Years' War, a major military conflict of the seventeenth century in European history – a conflict, which started between the Catholics and the Protestants. It was a series of wars fought by various nations for various reasons, including religious, dynastic, territorial, and commercial rivalries. A struggle that began as a religious conflict had ended as a confrontation waged for secular political reasons. It is amazing to see a 'song' to the Lord in the midst of turmoil around, and it is unfathomable how Gerhardt was gifted to present the manifold themes of Christian Faith in such a voluminous and profound hymnody, even in such a disturbing environment of warfare around.

Solomon has several works to his credit in translation - from Telugu to English and vice versa. Now with the translation of some of the Hymns of Gerhardt from English to Telugu, Solomon has done yeomen service to the Telugu Church. The unending thread of thought given for a certain theme is evidenced in most of these hymns of Gerhardt. Solomon has done a rendering of these hymns bringing home to the reader the depth of meaning in the message envisaged. Solomon also has been doing a study of the Greek Hymns in recent times, and it is anticipated that another volume from the pen of Solomon Raj would be forthcoming on the content and theology of the ancient Greek hymns. When all is said and done, we have a rich treasure as six hymns were rendered into beautiful Telugu for the first time:

- Why Without, Then, Art Thou Staying?
- A Song of Christian Consolation and Joy
- Of the Appearance of the Angels
- Now With Joy My Heart is Bounding
- Scarce Tongue can Speak, Ne'er Human Ken
- Now Spread are Evening's Shadows

Solomon's choice of the above six hymns out of hundreds is in deed a skillful choice, and they together present a cohesive and compact message for the reader in a simple and beautiful rendering. The fifth song is the only hymn Gerhardt wrote 'Of the Holy Trinity'. The first one is from Gerhardt's collection of hymns on 'Advent', while the third and fourth songs are from his collection on 'Birth of Christ - Christmas'. The second song is from Gerhardt's collection of 'Songs of the Cross and Consolation'. The last song Solomon translated is the last hymn from Gerhardt's collection of 'Morning and Evening Songs'. Solomon must have found some solace and preparation at his own evening of life spending time in meditation with this Evening Song. Solomon has faithfully endeavored to envisage the ageless message from Gerhardt's Hymns by means of this wonderful effort. 'The wonder that is worship' is conspicuously demonstrated in Gerhardt's spontaneous lines in his voluminous work. Solomon introduces the Telugu Church in some detail to this rich heritage by this endeavor.

v) Liturgical Interests and Lyrical Innovations of Pulidindi Solomon Raj: An Experiment at Indigenization

This was a study by the researcher of the liturgical interests of Solomon Raj, and the lyrical innovations resulting there from, which together constitute an experiment at indigenization.[30] Being exposed to the contemporary trends of indigenization, and the free worship styles of modern day charismatic movement, Solomon transcended the traditional boundaries and adopted the relevant and usable modes of indigenous expression of one's faith. '*Kim Kartavyam*', an hour-long dance and song drama in the 1970's, was his brainchild. Using the *Kuchipudi* style, a famous local form of Hindu dance, he created a unique form of communicating the Christian message. In this, Solomon touched new heights in liturgical renewal and innovation. Use of some Sanskrit, and simple but pure

30 *"The Yobel Spring"* Vol. 2, (2013:431-437).

people's Telugu as means of communicating the Christian message helped him reach a much wider public, crossing religious barriers. This reward was achieved mostly through his songs on the stage and on the air through Radio Voice of the Gospel (*Suvartha Vani*), which work Solomon had headed for ten years during 1967-77. The song dance rendering of the famous prayer of St. Francis of Assisi, with well-known Indian melodies and so called footwork became a well-appreciated and favorite art form to the Hindu elite community in those days.

From early times in ministry, Solomon had manifested a profound interest in the hymn-tradition or song tradition among Telugu speaking people. On this subject he made an in-depth study and, with much understanding and insight, presented a few papers on related topics in different Academies around the world, some of which were published in various Journals. Apart from this theoretical understanding, we see several Lyrical Innovations in the writings of Solomon Raj. His major contribution, *Gaana Kusumaalu* (Song Flowers) consists of 44 original Lyrics in both classical and popular tunes - "fairly well known and much appreciated for their composition, message and the melody".

Solomon Raj is also known for his simple but beautiful verse in English. Most of his publications of art works, batik or woodcut, are adorned with accompanying short meditations and reflections in simple but profound verse. We see him at ease while translating songs and poetry from Telugu into English. He did the bulk of the translation work on the (some 34) Telugu songs of Kalagara Subba Rao, 'a radical Hindu devotee of Christ', who wrote songs of deep mystical devotion to Christ, and left behind a small community which continues to worship in the tradition (*sampradaya*) which he forged. Further, Solomon translated selected Telugu works of Boyi Bheemanna, a *Dalit* secular poet, into English for a Project of the Telugu University, Hyderabad, which is yet to be published.

In 2010, he translated his own lyrics in *Gaana Kusumaalu* into English, which was published as *Geetha Malika*. Solomon has such a track of producing original pieces of verse in English, and translating pieces of poetry and lyrics from Telugu to English. Solomon did a study in more recent times, of the Greek Hymns of the third and fourth century A.D., unfolding the content and theology of these historic hymns. His translation of these works from English into Telugu is rich with local idiom to the extent they appear to be original works, while they are just his translations.

As mentioned earlier, his essays on song tradition, and the subsequent essays published with each of his recent works are a valuable treasure with many interesting facts and enlightening insights.

vi) Songs of Solomon from Sambalikan: An Analytical Review[31]

A manuscript in English with eleven songs, which Solomon wrote with musical notations during 1989-91 at Sambalikan, the Asian Institute for Liturgy and

31 Journal of Contemporary Christian, Vol. 5 No. 4, 2014.

Music in Manila, came to light in recent times. Dr. Feliciano, the head of the Sambalikan, a Catholic and an expert in Western Music, wanted to give harmonic tunes to these hymns but it remained a task unaccomplished. This collection of songs, however, was fortunately published in the Appendices of *Geetha Malika*.

The whole luster of this collection springs forth from the profound depth of the theological themes embedded therein. The themes of God's Protection, Man's Longing for God's *Darshan*, the Call of God, the Disciple's Response, Hope for the Future and the Final Destiny were all woven well into these lyrics, with rich imagery - Biblical and indigenous. Though this was his first exercise, it was all spontaneous and filled with the cardinal themes of Christian faith. Solomon wrote three songs about the Incarnate Lord, and two songs each on the following themes:

- Irresistible Call and Disciple's Response;
- Love and Grace;
- Mother Earth, Weaver and the Potter; and,
- The Sunset of Life and Forgiveness.

It is conspicuous that Solomon has exhibited an enlightened realization about environmental stewardship. He seems to be a rare combination of classical taste and modern reflection.

vii) Essays on the Internet

Two of the researcher's essays on internet about two series of woodcut works of Solomon are given below:

- *Liberation in Luke's Gospel: An Artistic Appreciation and a Theological Analysis*[32]
- *Solomon Raj's Gallery of Hieratic Art in St. John's Gospel: A Thematic Appreciation*[33]

These are analytical works in detail, expounding the theological themes embedded therein. The first work is a collection of 12 works portraying 12 themes of liberation - all from Luke's Gospel. And the second work is a sequel, with a collection of 13 works on Johannine icons. The notes by the researcher in the above Internet articles are used in a blog on *Holy Week Art from India (Solomon Raj)* by Dr. Paul Neeley,[34] Professor of the class on 'Cross-Cultural Perspectives

---

32 http://www.artway.eu/content.php?id=1366&action=show&lang=en accessed April 6, 2018.

33 http://www.artway.eu/artway.php?id=588&action=show&lang=en accessed April 6, 2018.

34 http://globalworship.tumblr.com/post/140920564975/holy-week-art-from-india-solomon-raj accessed March 25, 2018.

in Christian Worship' at the Robert E. Webber Institute of Christian Worship, in Jacksonville, Florida. For over two decades, Solomon has worked with woodcuts, and he also produced three other series of art on the Life of our Lord Jesus Christ, Caring for God's Creation, and Jesus' Encounter with Women.[35] This is in addition to the many individual woodcut works by the artist.

viii) 'Soliloquies in Solitude'[36]

This work by the researcher is a compilation of 127 poems, which Solomon composed as an octogenarian and as a nonagenarian, with the commentary depicting cultural, natural, existential, philosophical and Christian themes embedded in Solomon's poetry. As David Zersen described in his Foreword, Solomon is revealed in this collection as "a poet who has shared many personal expressions of his faith in his observations of the world around him". The descriptive as well as the reflective poetry of Solomon in his sunset years was salvaged by the researcher, and appended in this volume, preserving these lines of wisdom and fun.

All the above studies by different authors, including the researcher, mirror well the rich potential of the artist-theologian in different dimensions. Yet none of them are exhaustive, and there are many countless realms yet to be explored from amidst the vast gallery of Solomon's handiwork. In view of limited scope of the above works, justification for undertaking the present study is obvious. Much discussion and study have gone in the history of the Indian Church into the problem of 'presenting the Gospel in the western garb' - analyzing the good, if any, and the bad of it. Though many experiments have been made, at different times in different places by different pioneers in the field to offset the problem and to present a viable option, the particular pattern of Solomon Raj, in the backdrop of the historical overview, is hoped to provide a challenge with some feasible insights.

Solomon is a 'universally known Brahmin' who needs no tags - as the Indian idiom aptly describes, and his name shines in the foreign skies in a unique way.[37] Yet, he is less known and least recognized among his own people in his own nation. Even the present researcher has been exposed to Solomon Raj, in some detail, just over the last one decade and a half. This occasions the urge to quarry the mines of the literary and artistic contributions of Solomon, with special reference to his 'Evangelistic Innovations' - culminating in '*Incarnation of the Gospel in the Indian Culture*'.

---

35 This work contains 10 of Solomon's woodcut prints, with text by Jorg Dantscher SJ in German.

36 B. S. Moses Kumar: *Soliloquies in Solitude*, New Delhi: Christian World Imprints, (2017:viii).

37 This idiom - 'universally known Brahmin' - means that no introduction is needed for a well known person, and in no way it denotes any caste nomenclature.

The need for the present study may be seen in the following considerations:

- The creative genius and the spirit of experimentation with his varied skills - literary as well as artistic - found their highest expression in this villager of South India, taking him across the oceans with global repute in an increasing manner. Though some research is being done in India and overseas on the works of Solomon Raj, the contribution of Solomon Raj to Indian Christian art is not recognized well, especially in the Indian Church. For example, as long back as 1974, a couple of Telugu Christian Lyrics penned by Solomon were for the first time released in Gramophone Recordings with the voice of a popular cine artist S. P. Bala Subrahmanyam. They were the only Christian songs heard across the length and breadth of Telugu-speaking Andhra Pradesh State in India during those earliest times for every family occasion among Christians through Public Address System. Though people were most familiar with these lyrics, the author was never known to most of them. This study is hoped to bring an awareness of the great contribution of Solomon Raj and a better appreciation of his innovations in the field.
- Unfortunately, as Gudrun Löwner points out,[38] in contrast to Catholic Christian artists like Jyoti Sahi and Sister Claire who receive a lot of orders for their art in India and abroad, Solomon entirely misses the support of his extremely conservative Lutheran Church, who are probably against his contextual art. This lack of patronage at home and overseas had kept him off from the gallery of popular reputation.
- Also, with the particular background and bent of mind of the present researcher, this study is hoped to take on an entirely different approach bringing out the ethos of such religious art and the accompanying verse, by means of a comprehensive and analytical study of the theme of '*Incarnation of the Gospel in Indian Culture*'. This work does not claim to be exhaustive, but is anticipated to be a reliable source work inspiring new generations and aiding further research.

38 Gudrun Löwner: *Theology with the Brush: Transmitting Faith through Art - Azaria Mbatha, Solomon Raj and I Nyoman Darsane*. Published in Gudrun Löwner: *Inter-Cultural Dialogue in Art and Religion*, New Delhi: Manohar, 2018.

2

Incarnation of the Gospel in Indian Culture: A Historical Perspective

'Gospel' is the word ringing in the world for over the last two millennia on an increasing scale with an ever-increasing euphoria - in accordance with the Great Commission of Jesus Christ[39] and the much-awaited jubilant consummation at the end of the age prophetically portrayed in the Book of Revelation.[40] *Gospel* is a word of Anglo-Saxon origin, meaning "God's spell", i.e., 'word of God', or rather, according to others, "good spell", i.e., 'good news'. It is the rendering of the Greek *evangelion*, i.e., "good message." It denotes primarily "the welcome intelligence of salvation to man as preached by our Lord and his followers."[41]

Gospel is the good news about Jesus Christ, the incarnate Son of God - about His person and work in Time. Eternity precedes and follows time, in a continuum, without end. Incarnation of Jesus Christ portrays His person and work in time. With due consideration for the person and work of the Pre-Incarnate and Post-Resurrection Christ, the Gospel primarily concerns about His atoning work on the cross for the remission of sins of humanity, and about the salvation bought by the blood of Jesus Christ. What a glorious salvation! - Wrought not by human works or merit, but by His work on Calvary, and freely received by faith through God's grace. The Great Commission Jesus gave His disciples, before His

39 Mark 16:15 "Go into all the world and preach the gospel to every creature."

40 Rev. 7:9-10 "… behold, a great multitude which no one could number, of all nations, tribes, peoples, and tongues, standing before the throne and before the Lamb, clothed with white robes, with palm branches in their hands, / and crying out with a loud voice, 'Salvation belongs to our God who sits on the throne, and to the Lamb!'"

41 http://www.websters-online-dictionary.org/definition/gospel
Source: Easton's 1897 Bible Dictionary - accessed March 12, 2018.

ascension, was recorded by the Gospel writers. 'Into all the world' and 'To all the creation' - this mandate holds good until 'the end of the age'.[42]

Jesus includes everyone, everywhere in the great host of recipients of the Gospel- people from 'every tongue, tribe and nation', and therefore the Church in all times is given the awesome responsibility of heralding the Gospel to every generation. The 'whosoever' dimension of the Gospel envisages enlisting of recipients from across the globe, irrespective of creed or color, culture or nationality. As such, it is obvious that the Gospel transcends and transmits into all cultures, and then and only then can it be meaningfully communicated to each people group on earth. Joshua Project, an unreached peoples research initiative, helps us in defining what a people group means: "For evangelization purposes, a people group is the largest group within which the Gospel can spread as a church planting movement without encountering barriers of understanding or acceptance."[43]

The Greek word *ethne*, translated 'nations' in Matthew 28:19, literally means 'people groups'. Though the reputed author, Prof. Vishal Mangalwadi deplores the definition of 'nation' as "people group" to be a 'destructive definition',[44] for it "led the American church away from the need to disciple America", the definition by Joshua Project is adopted in this paper for clarity of the global Task of Evangelization. And Jesus intentionally declared: "And this Gospel of the Kingdom will be proclaimed throughout the whole world as a testimony to all *nations* [*ethne*] and then the end will come."[45] This should be so not only to herald the coming of the Lord but also to hasten the 'glorious liberty of the children of God' for which 'the whole creation groans and labours with birth pangs.'[46] A recent treatment of this aspect is also seen in Howard A. Snyder's *Salvation Means Creation Healed.*[47]

Gospel is never presented in a vacuum but always within a particular culture; Gospel is said to shine in its true luster through the lens of a culture. Thus Gospel and culture co-exist together and never can thrive in isolation. In his article *'Indian Church and Response to Culture'* Solomon Raj examines some aspects of the Indian culture and shows how the church had responded to culture in its various art forms and literature in particular, and to the whole set of assumptions and worldview in general. He points out that "the problems of the Gospel in encounter to the host culture are not peculiar to India but this was something which has

42 Matthew 28:19-20, Mark 16:15, Luke 24:47, Acts 1:8.

43 www.joshuaproject.net - accessed November 16, 2017.

44 https://www.facebook.com/search/str/vishal+magalwadi+on+ethne%2C+nations/keywords_blended_posts?filters_rp - accessed November 16, 2017.

45 Matthew 24:14, English Standard Version.

46 Romans 8:21-22, New King James Version.

47 *Salvation Means Creation Healed: The Ecology of Sin and Grace: Overcoming the Divorce Between Earth and Heaven, Eugene,* Oregon: Wipf & Stock Publishers, 2011.

been going on from the time of the New Testament ... The concept of culture is very complex and hence it is difficult to precisely define what it is. The culture of any community finds its expression in its art forms, songs and stories, in its folklore, and in its way of living and the whole world view of that community."[48] The Webster's dictionary defines culture as "the integrated pattern of knowledge, belief and behavior that depends upon man's capacity for learning and transmitting knowledge to succeeding generations" and as "the customary beliefs, social forms and material traits of a racial, religious or social group." It is also described as "the integral pattern of human knowledge, belief and behavior that depends on humanity's capacity for learning and transmitting to succeeding generations."[49]

Teresa Chai[50] aptly points out, "When scrutinizing the relationship between the Gospel and culture, one discovers different words are used to explain the process of what happens when the Gospel moves from one culture to another" and Chai presents various terms that have been employed:

- Accommodation
- Adaptation
- Indigenization
- Incarnation
- Translation
- Rereading of Scripture
- Communication
- Conceptualization
- Inculturation

With all its problems and prospects *'Incarnation of the Gospel in the Indian Culture'* had been the talk of ages in the Indian Church History, and the inevitable need of all times. Solomon in his seminal work graphically points out:

> The present image of the church, however, is not quite familiar to the people of the land. The voice is familiar but the image is strange (Jacob's story). There is much in the outward structure of the church, which gives it a strange appearance, a peculiar foreign color.[51]

Presenting the Gospel by means of relevant and meaningful communication processes in one's own cultural media may be deemed as 'incarnation of the Gospel'. The Lausanne Movement propels the Church from "Seeing *culture as*

48 P. Solomon Raj: *'Indian Church and Response to Culture'*, Unpublished Paper.

49 https://www.merriam-webster.com/dictionary/culture - accessed March 22, 2018.

50 *A Look at Contextualization: Historical Background, Definition, Function, Scope and Models,* AJPS 18:1 (2015:3-19).

51 P. Solomon Raj: *A Christian Folk Religion in India: A Study of the Small Church Movement in Andhra Pradesh, with Special Reference to the Bible Mission of Devadass,* Bangalore: Centre for Contemporary Christianity, (2004:273).

a problem or a barrier to communicating the gospel" to "*Celebrating culture as* the God-given context of our identity and as the fertile ground for the ongoing incarnation of the gospel and the Kingdom."[52] The concept of 'incarnation of the Gospel' obviously had been espoused and expounded by the Lausanne Movement. As such it conveys the ideal of the Gospel taking roots in indigenous cultures and blooming where planted. Incarnation of the Gospel connotes that the Gospel is communicated in a given culture in such a way it is identified with the culture in which it is presented, rather than remain alien to the culture, allowing the Gospel seed to bloom where it is planted. An analytical study of this issue will be made in this work *'with reference to the Art and Poetry of P. Solomon Raj'* in the backdrop of a historical perspective.

The broad spectrum of denominational Christianity that entered the Indian soil, in modern times, had brought with it diverse doctrines and patterns of worship. Therefore we often see Christianity in a Western garb. Much discussion and study have gone in the history of the Indian Church into the problem of 'presenting the Gospel in a western garb' – analyzing the good and bad of it. Though taking the alien culture becomes a necessity at the initial moment, for practical convenience, due to difference in language and cultural practice, it doesn't mean it should become a perennial feature of our experience.

With passage of time and critical reflection, the journey should be characterized by an ongoing effort of adaptation and indigenous innovation. Many experiments have been made, at different times in different places by different pioneers in the field, to offset the problem and to present a viable option. A survey of the many instances from the earliest times of Indian church history and the ongoing process of indigenization of the Gospel until modern times will be analyzed in this chapter. Though manifold endeavors at inculturation were made in and through the Indian Catholic Church, a summary of a few outstanding instances spanning from early 17th Century to 20th Century, will be seen in the following pages. A handful of pioneers in the Protestant Missions who have done their best at evolving an indigenous Church are briefly presented. A brief study of Christian art in India is also made with special reference to the Bengali artist Jamini Roy and the contemporary Christian artists with global reputation from North India and South India - Frank Wesley and Jyoti Sahi. The particular pattern of Solomon Raj, in the backdrop of an historical ecumenical overview, is hoped to challenge current and future generations in this direction, and provide feasible insights for further exploration and research.

Early Church History

India cradled many religions and also extended its abode of welcome to other major religions of the world. The history of Indian Christianity, according to

52 *Gospel Contextualisation Revisited,* Haslev 1997 Consultation Statement, http://www.lausanne.org/haslev-1997/consultation-statement.html - accessed February 13, 2018.

tradition, has its genesis in the very first century, when Apostle Thomas arrived in 52 A.D., preached the Gospel and established churches in Kerala.

i) Thomas Christians

Andrew Todhunter has pointed out, "Kerala's Thomas Christians – like Christians elsewhere in Asia and in Africa and Latin America – have made the faith uniquely their own, incorporating traditional art, architecture, and natural symbolism."[53] And Roger Hedlund rightly remarks[54] that "Indian Christianity is of apostolic origin, and in its multiplied manifestations is found in historical continuity with the stream of faith flowing from New Testament times into our own." As Roger Hedlund pointed elsewhere,

> The essential point is that this earliest Christianity is one of the ancient religions of India (as the late Prime Minister Nehru pointed out). Christianity in India therefore is not a foreign import (although the Thomas-figure might have been an outsider). Christianity was firmly planted in Indian soil long before it arrived in Northern Europe.[55]

The very presence of the so-called Thomas Christians in India is a living testimonial of indigenous Christianity for the two millennia of the Christian era. Christianity came to South Asia at a very early time, and it "adapted itself the prevailing culture". As Roger Hedlund observes:

> According to tradition … the community of Thomas Christians originated in the mission of St. Thomas in India. Historically, indigenous Christianity has a two-thousand year tradition in South Asia. Cult and culture combined to preserve a Christian community, which is authentically Christian as well as thoroughly Indian. The Thomas Christians have been an integral part of the social and religious fabric of the region for nearly two thousand years.[56]

Modern Church History: Catholic Missions

Any study about the Gospel and its adaptation to Indian culture brings out the name of Robert de Nobili of the Madurai Mission to the fore. Adaptation in India, in earlier times meant western Hymns sung to western tunes duly rendered into

---

53 Andrew Todhunter: *In the Footsteps of the Apostles,* National Geographic – March, (2012:47) Quoted by Roger E. Hedlund: *Christianity Made in India: From Apostle Thomas to Mother Teresa,* Minneapolis: Fortress Press, (2017:12).

54 *Indian Christianity: Charismatic and Ecumenical,* In "Planting in Native Soil: Studies in Gospel Inculturation", Ed. David Zersen & B. S. Moses Kumar, Delhi: ISPCK & Austin: Concordia University Press, (2014:57).

55 Unpublished Paper for the IAMS assembly in Malaysia (2004:1).

56 Roger E. Hedlund: *Christianity Made in India: From Apostle Thomas to Mother Teresa,* Minneapolis: Fortress Press, (2017:81-82).

vernacular languages. The Church, of course, is universal, and when we sing in western tunes we are in fellowship with the faithful across the globe, just as when we use some set prayers and doxologies from ancient saints we have fellowship with the Lord's people across the ages. Of course, the orthodox Christians in Kerala have adopted architecture, oil lamps et cetera all from Kerala Hindu culture. Having justified thus, it is vital to recognize that we have failed to speak the language of our land, and the idiom of our forefathers in the process, and ultimately failed to appeal to the appetite of the Indian mind.

i) Robert de Nobili – A Pioneer at Indigenization

Robert de Nobili (1577-1656) ushered in the Catholic Ashram (*sanyasa*) Movement as a modern phenomenon in the late sixteenth century. It acquired a definite shape only in the later half of the twentieth century. The critical moments of the movement are intimately connected to the life and theology of some charismatic Catholic leaders. Robert de Nobili was regarded as the "father of adaptation".

An Italian Jesuit missionary of the Madurai Mission, having arrived in Madurai, Tamil Nadu in 1604, de Nobili soon realized that Christianity had failed to make deep inroads into the world of caste Hindus. Convinced that Christian missionary activity would not succeed unless the Christian message is presented to the Hindu cultural and religious elite, he identified himself culturally with the Brahmin community.

He learned Sanskrit and undertook a deep study of Hindu philosophy and Tamil culture. He adopted the lifestyle, customs, and dietary practices of a Hindu renouncer (*sanyasin*), calling himself the "Roman Brahmin". Further, by distancing himself from fellow Jesuits, and living in Brahmin *agraharam*, de Nobili sought to dispel the prevailing idea among the Tamils, about the Christian missionaries as outcasts (*parangis*) and low castes because of their meat-eating habits.

When Christianity was called as *parangi markkam* (way of the uncountable), de Nobili called Christianity as *Satya Vedam'* (true religion). His second experiment was learning Tamil and their customs and manners. With penance and chastity as vows of his religious order, he chose to be called *sanyasin*. With approval from church authorities he wore saffron cloth and wooden sandals, and decided to lead a life entirely on alms. His third experiment was adopting the Raja caste, with his royal ancestry (from Otto II). He also acknowledged valuable elements in Hindu sacred writings and compiled a book to show that Christianity was a religion, which crowned the Vedas as the Fifth Veda.[57]

57 Though the de Nobili experiment failed, his Jesuit successors continued his heritage for many decades. According to one statistic, by the end of the nineteenth century the Jesuits had gained thirty-five Brahmin converts from the two districts of Tiruchirapalli and Thanjavore in Tamil Nadu.

Through these and other measures, de Nobili sought to incarnate the Christian faith in Indian forms to make it acceptable to caste Hindus. As a missionary, de Nobili's interest in adaptation was primarily missiological, aimed at gaining high-caste Hindu converts to Christianity. However, due to ecclesiastical opposition of other Orders, the de Nobili experiment was put to rest for time being.

ii) '*Christha Purana*'[58]

Meanwhile, Fr. Thomas Stephen S.J., known as Apostle of Salcete, wrote *'Christha Purana'* (Story or Epic of Christ) in Romi Marathi in 1616 in Rachol, also known as Raitura, a village in Salcete, Goa in south-western India. Located on the left bank of the Zuari River it was home to the famous Rachol Seminary. Amonkar translated it in Devnagri Konkani. It was used for 70 years in churches of Bardez, Tiswadi and Salcete, but later withdrawn in 1684. Fr. Stephen had learnt the Konkani/Marathi from Brahmins of Salcete in order to write *Christha Purana*[59] in Romi Marathi. Amonkar informed that at that time Marathi was the written language and Konkani the spoken language in Goa. The new converts had only two prayers in Konkani. Amonkar described Fr. Stephen as the real author who understood the need of the time, producing Christian literature in people's vernaculars.

iii) Catholic *Sanyasins* and Ashram Movement

Brahmabhandav Upadhyay, a Brahmin convert acquainted with Hindu Reformers of the times, was convinced that Christianity could never reach the mainstream of India unless it appeared in Hindu garb. He urged Christian missionaries to adopt the attires and lifestyle of Hindu *sanyasins*. His zeal for adaptation led him to the lifestyle of a Hindu sanyasin. He established a Catholic ashram on the banks of River Narmada. His experiment too failed due to ecclesiastical opposition.

But his emphasis on *sanyasa* had great impact on the next generation, especially on the three monks of Shantivanam, namely, Jules Monchanin, Henri Le Saux / Abhishiktananda, and Bede Griffiths. Monchanin was convinced that Christianity in India should attain an indigenous character. Henri Le Saux joined Monchanin in this initiative - both embracing *sanyasa* and founding *Saccidananda Ashram* in 1950. It was the first Catholic Ashram in the post-independence era. Taking on Indian names these 'maverick monks' adopted Hindu ascetic lifestyle and sought to integrate Hindu spirituality with Catholic monasticism. They created a context and climate for interreligious dialogue. Bede Griffiths, known as Dayananda was the most influential and he called for an inculturated Christianity that is totally Indian and totally Christian.

---

58 http://www.ucanindia.in/news/%e2%80%98christha-purana%e2%80%99-and-%e2%80%98goenchem-savasarikikan%e2%80%99-released/34447/daily accessed March 25, 2018.

59 *The Christian Puranas,* Goa: College of Rachol, 1616.

Shantivanam and Griffiths became the inspiration for other ashrams that mushroomed since the 1970's. During his tenure as the *acharya* (spiritual leader), Griffiths initiated many natives and Westerners into *sanyas*, some of whom have established their own ashrams, as follows:

- Anjali Ashram founded by Amalorpavadoss in Mysore, which still exists today.
- Christa Prema Ashram in Poona founded by Jack Winslow in 1929, no more existing now.
- Jeevan Dhara Ashram founded by Vandana and Eshpriya at Jaiharikhal.

They all seek to live the legacy of the pioneers. And there were thirty such Christian ashrams during these times in India. While pioneers of the ashram movement and inculturation were foreign missionaries, native theologians, priests and nuns serve as leaders and defenders of the movement in current times.

The heart of Saccidananda Ashram is a simple chapel dedicated to the Christian Trinity with Hindu titles (*sat-chit-ananda*). There is no human *guru* since most Catholic ashrams regard Christ as the real or true *sad guru* of the ashram. Saccidananda Ashram adopted Hindu forms not only in terms of architecture, but also in lifestyle, dietary practices, and worship, while preserving its Catholic identity.

iv) National Biblical, Catechetical, and Liturgical Centre

D. S. Amalorpavadass (1932-1990), a Catholic theologian of South India, played a significant role in the renewal of the Catholic Church in India. He founded the National Biblical, Catechetical, and Liturgical Centre (NBCLC) on Hutchins Road, Bangalore in 1967 and was its Director from its inception till 1982. He worked vigorously to renew the Indian Church and initiated scholarly discussions and invited the learned scholars of India on to an ecumenical platform. There was much adaptation in architecture, ritual and attires.

v) Catholic Charismatic Renewal

The Catholic Charismatic Renewal is a spiritual movement incorporating aspects of Charismatic practice. It is influenced by Pentecostal teachings with emphasis on personal relationship with Jesus. The Golden Jubilee Event of the Catholic Charismatic Renewal in 2017 recounts fifty years of Charismatic Renewal in the Catholic Church. This ushered a new era and brought a new dimension in the life of the Catholic Church bringing the Gospel closer to the people through the gifts of the Holy Spirit and through many new means in the respective cultures of the world. The media has brought the experience and the fruit of the Revival into every ethnic section, with countless indigenous expressions of the Gospel. The Spiritual Renewal make things relevant, increasing response of the people to the claims of the Gospel as they seek deeper experience, intimate relationship and being effective witnesses.

The Renewal Movement brought to India by Minoo Engineer in February 1972 spread the blessings through National Conventions, Conferences and Seminars in different places through the close of the 20th century. The Potta Ashram at Potta in Thrissur district of Kerela, was founded in 1977, and in spite of many controversies, continues to reach out to all over India in current times. The Retreat and Renewal Centers connected with it are widespread geographically and catering in different vernaculars.[60] There was a new release in indigenous singing and charismatic worship, and the manifestations of the Spirit, with healing and deliverance.

Modern Church History: Protestant Missions

In major sections through the length and breadth of India, there has been an awakening near the end of the 19th Century through some great Indian thinkers, who related themselves with their times and climes and endeavored to evolve an indigenous Christian theology. A brief historical survey of this process of indigenization among Protestant Missions is given below.

i) Sadhu Sunder Singh (1889-1929)

A serious religious conflict with the death of his beloved mother and of his elder brother at the age of fourteen, eventually led to his conversion to Christianity. He was a Sikh anti-Christian and had thrown stones at missionary preachers, and even burned a copy of the Bible. He wanted to obtain the realization of God and in his utter despair he decided to take his own life unless God would reveal Himself to him. With a vision of Christ at a very strange place, on the railway track, he decided to become a Christian. Sunder Singh had a fascination for Tibet and he went to Tibet in 1928, but had to return due to a violent hemorrhage. In September 1929 he made another attempt and never returned. His desire must have been fulfilled - to die as a martyr for his faith.

He produced eight short books in Urdu, and English translation was done with the help of A.J. Appaswamy and T.E. Riddle. *At the Master's Feet* was the first one in 1922. The basis of Sunder Singh's theology is said to be similar to Paul's direct experience of Jesus Christ. His Christian life goes back to a definite experience of the risen Christ and his spiritual life based on constant communion with Christ in prayer. The aim of prayer is union with God - union of two free personalities rather than absorption in the divine. His method of teaching by

60 In Bangalore, Faridabad, Elavur in Thiruvallur, Kamba village near Kalyan, Chintamanipudur near Coimbatore, Karnad in Mangalore, Premagiri in Kurnool, Muthangi, Toopranpet, Karunapuram near Warangal, Habsiguda in Hyderabad, Pulakkattukara near Thrissur, Thavalom near Palakkad, Paravoor in Kerala, Athirampuzha near Kottayam, Meerganj near Bareilly, Khetri near Guwahati, Jalalkhali in West Bengal, Vincentian Ashram in Kolkata.

use of parables was that of his Master; he draws his experience from everyday life, nature, and the books he read including *Upanishads*. All his life he preached wherever he was invited.

His messages, writings and books were enthusiastically accepted both by theologians in the West as well as by the missionaries in India. His theology was clearly Christocentric, as he preached Christ and his own experience of Him. He openly denounced Hinduism and used Johannine terminology in his speeches. His contribution to Indian Christian theology had a profound influence on many Indian Christians. His *Gospel in an Indian Cup*, is an all time attraction to both Indian Christians and non-Christians.

ii) Pandita Ramabai (1858-1922)

Ramabai, a high caste Brahmin, lost her faith in traditional Hinduism and became a Brahma Samajist. Her husband died two years after their marriage and she moved with her baby Manorama to Poona. She joined *Prartana Samaj*, and established Arya Mahila Samaj for the education and emancipation of Hindu women. She wrote *Stree Dharma Neethi*, a book dealing with questions of morality and justice for women in Hindu society. She came to know of Jesus Christ and Christianity through some mission contacts.

Ramabai left for England. She corresponded with Nehemiah Goreh about Christianity and converted to Christianity in 1883. She went to America to enlist support for establishing a House for Brahmin child widows. On her return to Poona she started Sharada Sadan as a secular institution. Led by a famine in Maharashtra she started the Mukti Mission at Kedgaon. Ramabai's pioneering leadership in the movement for liberation of Indian women was her great contribution. She attained the Pentecostal experience of the indwelling Christ in the end and translated the Bible into Marathi her mother tongue.

Ramabai's main contribution to Indian theology lies in questioning the relevance of the dogmatic Christianity imported to India from the West, and in her honest search for a spiritual authority for an Indian experiment defining Christian faith in relation to service in society. The denominational structure within the church was confusing as Christianity adds denominational divisions to an already caste-divided Hinduism. She believed that the only answer to it for missionaries and preachers of all denominations is to establish one united Christian church - an indigenous church to Indians, for only then will they 'be worthy' to preach Christ to the Indians.

iii) Narayan Vaman Tilak (1862-1919)

Narayan Vaman Tilak, a Chitpavan Brahmin was convinced of the Christian faith through a causal encounter with a Christian stranger who gave him a New Testament. Tilak was baptized in 1895 and worked within the framework of the American Marathi Mission. He taught Hinduism and Indian languages in its theological seminary. He was ordained in 1904. He became a Christian *sanyasi* in 1917, seeking to gather round him a group called 'God's Darbar', a 'brotherhood of the baptized and unbaptized Disciples of Christ'. Christian poems written by Tilak include many lyrics, used in congregational worship and for evangelistic proclamation.

Tilak's theological ideas are embodied in his poems and lyrics. Marathi poetry with its rich tradition has provided many a saint-poet of the past. Tilak followed that tradition in his poems on Christian themes. He was a pioneer in innovative movements in Marathi poetry considering the Marathi saint-poets as a preparation for the Gospel. His greatest contribution to the nation was his poems of which he left a very large collection. He also gave the western Indian Church many devotional lyrics to express their devotion to Christ.

Tilak sings praises to God, the one Creator of heaven and earth, which reveal His glory, and he speaks of God as 'the Home of all our trust', as father-mother, source of life and love and as the foundation of all existence. For Tilak, Jesus Christ is God's *avatar*, the love incarnate, historically once-for-all event, but existentially a daily occurrence for Christians and in the life of the church. It was the cross of Jesus Christ that made the deepest impression on Tilak.

He experienced a certain ecstasy in his vision of the crucified Christ; he sang:

Hast thou seen the Lord, Christ crucified?
Hast thou seen those wounded hands? Hast thou seen His side?
Hast thou ever, ever seen love that was like this?
Hast thou given up thy life wholly so be His?

In his poems, sin and salvation by grace have an important place. He uses terms like *adhi, vyadhi*, *bhranbi* and *avidya* to characterize sin, and *bhakti salokotta, sanipatta, sarupata* and s*ayujata* for salvation in Christ. Tilak was firmly committed to the indigenization of the Indian Church's worship, pattern of life and mission, and certainly his lyrics and poems made a great contribution towards this end. He believed in a church larger than the institutional church of baptized Christians only; but the *Durbar* of God and the church of his concept was a brotherhood of the baptized and unbaptized disciples of Christ, which included adherents of other religions who acknowledged the Lord Jesus Christ, the Son of Man, as their guru and imitated his path of utmost love as manifested in the cross.

iv) Vedanayagam S. Azariah (1874-1945)

V.S. Azariah was born in a Nadar family in Tinnevelly to an Anglican pastor. His greatest urge was 'Evangelization of Indians by Indians' - Indian Men with Indian money and Indian direction! He was instrumental in organizing Indian Missionary Society (IMS) and founded National Missionary Society (NMS). He was ordained in 1907 and consecrated as the first Indian bishop of Dornakal diocese. He attended World Missionary Conference as an important speaker at Edinburgh in 1910, and later at Jerusalem (1928) and Tambaram (1938). At Tambaram Conference he pleaded the church to recognize the centrality of evangelism. As a veteran leader of the National Christian Council (NCC) of India for many years, the nationalist movement of India under Mahatma Gandhi influenced his thinking and action. He did not want the church to be a static community guarded in 'minority status' by legal safeguards. He wrote many books in English, Tamil and Telugu, on the structure of the church.

Being primarily an evangelist, Azariah's contribution has been in the theology of evangelism. His theology embodied in *India and the Christian Movement* (1936), a revision of his earlier work, *India and Missions* (1909) calls for recognition of evangelistic mission and corporate life of the church. He believed that a missionary church must move towards an organic unity, overcoming existing confessional divisions and becoming increasingly indigenous. This means foreign missions and missionaries must become friends and not masters, helpers and not directors of the indigenous church. This was his passionate call at the Edinburgh conference. His influence in calling for the unity of the church is seen in the Tranquebar Manifesto of 1919, which launched negotiations of church union in South India. The architecture of the Dornakal Cathedral is a standing testimonial to his commitment to an indigenous church. Many adopted this move to an indigenous church architecture later.

v) Bathineni Venkata Subbamma: Ashrams and Bhajans

Christian Ashrams and *Bhajans* were adopted even into some of the Protestant mission churches. Solomon mentions three better-known Christian Ashrams - *Kristukula Ashram* started at Tirupattur, *Kristhu Shishya Ashram* near Coimbatore, and Stanley Jones' Sat Tal Ashram in the foothills of the Himalayas. Solomon also mentions the Ashrams of Dr. B. V. Subbamma run in the Lutheran Church, attracting many Hindu women and new converts for a period of prayer and reflection.

B. V. Subbamma [61] was born in 1925 at Bodipalem in Guntur district. She was an Indian woman theologian and scholar, known for founding Christian ashrams. She was recognized for her analysis of introducing and planting Christianity from a cultural perspective. She was one of the first theologically trained women in India, ordained by the AELC in 1999.[62] During her high school education, she got interested in Christianity, but because of cultural divisions associated with caste system, she did not convert until 1942. In that year, she realized that she did not have to give up her caste and cultural identity to become a Christian and was baptized. With B.A. and B.Ed. degrees from India, and an M.A. in Education from New York Theological Seminary, she served as principal for Charlotte

61 https://en.wikipedia.org/wiki/B._V._Subbamma - accessed February 24, 2018.

62 https://en.wikipedia.org/wiki/B._V._Subbamma

Swenson Memorial Bible Training School for another decade. Earned a B.D. in 1968 and founded a Christian Ashram at Rajahmundry with the goal of helping women in education and training nurses, social activists and leaders.

Subbamma wrote extensively on culture, Christianity and women's opportunity. She was recognized as one of the most influential women leaders in the Third World Christian church, for her mission work and ministry. She focused on introducing Christianity to Hindu women, believing that an indigenous approach brought understanding and integration of cultures. Her seminal work "*Christ Confronts India: Indigenous Expression of Christianity in India" was published in 1973.*[63] *Her other monumental work, "Christian Ashrams: Years (1968-1993)" was published after two decades in 1993. Other masterwork, "Open Doors: New Patterns of Church Growth Among Hindus in Andhra Pradesh" was published in between.*[64]

vi) E. Stanley Jones

Another down-to-earth stalwart of indigenous methods of evangelization in India needs to be mentioned, before we move on to a new century. Though we have seen 12 of the proponents of indigenization earlier, each with their peculiar motif and orientation, the one we see in this section is most popular, and his methodology seems to be more practical, which he lived out, with lasting impact and outcome. This is a missionary extraordinary, an American by birth but an Indian by choice, E. Stanley Jones (1884-1972). Fondly and familiarly called Brother Stanley by thousands of people, he received the attention of the high castes, and the intelligentsia, being invited to speak at ancient universities and other centers of learning. Having been set apart for interpreting the Gospel especially to educated men and women, he was appointed Evangelist-at-large" to India in 1919, by the Missions Board of his Church.

Stanley Jones held mass meetings in leading Indian cities and inaugurated "round table conferences" where Christians and non-Christians sat down as equals sharing testimonies as to how their religious experiences enabled them to live better. He presented Jesus as the Universal Son of Man who had come for all people. This offer to receive Christ within their own framework marked a new approach in missions, which came to be known as "indigenization". In 1925, he wrote a report of his years of service, published in the book '*The Christ of the Indian Road*' - a best seller, sold over a million copies, influencing the course of missionary thinking.[65]

He established the Sat Tal Ashram in 1930 with the purpose of interpreting Jesus Christ in indigenous forms. It was a means of drawing men and women for a few days to study in depth their own spiritual natures and quest, and what

---

63 *Madras: Diocesan Press.*

64 *Pasadena, California: Fuller Theological Seminary.*

65 Nashville, Tennesse: Abingdon Press, 1925.

the different faiths offered individuals. The group thus gathered there attempts not to find an answer, but to be the answer, to be a miniature Kingdom of God. The Hindi word "ashram" means "away from hard work." Sat Tal Ashram is a Christian Ashram and Jesus Christ is the Guru of the Ashram. People of all faiths and of no faith are welcome to share this kingdom of God fellowship. His impact is still felt across the world through his books and through the Ashram, where he was cremated and his remains laid to rest.

Christian Art in India

Anand Amaladass and Gudrun Löwner, in their monumental work, *Christian Themes in Indian Art*, have traced their subject matter 'From the Mogul Times till Today.'[66] Prominent among Bengali Artists with room for Christian themes was Jamini Roy. Prominent among Christian artists were Frank Wesley, Solomon Raj and Jyoti Sahi. A brief treatment of these contemporary artists is undertaken below:

i) Jamini Roy

Jamini Roy was born in 1887 at Beliatore village in West Bengal. He studied painting in oils under Abanindranath Tagore. First being influenced by Western traditions, he then looked to his own culture and tribal art for inspiration. Kalighat painting, a style of art with bold sweeping brush-strokes, influenced him. He began his career as a commissioned portrait painter but later moved to discover his own, featuring a new style based on Bengali folk traditions. His quest was to make art accessible to a wider section of people, and to give an identity to Indian art. He became popular with his art exhibitions in Kolkata, London and New York City, and was honored with Padma Bhushan in 1955. The selected themes for his paintings were from joys and sorrows of everyday life, and Hindu and Christian religious themes. He evolved his own language of painting known as 'Flat Technique' and used cheap indigenous pigments and materials like lampblack, chalk-powder, leaves and creepers.to bring art within the reach of all. He passed away in 1972. He is a senior colleague of Solomon who had considerably impacted some of his art. Solomon has in common with him a lot of style features like the large fish eyes of the people.

ii) Frank Wesley

Frank Wesley was born to a Christian family in 1923 at Azamgarh, Uttar Pradesh. He was a younger artist colleague of Solomon and he belongs to Lucknow School of Painting. His paintings were a unique blend of Japanese and Indian influences. With initial studies in Lucknow, he later studied at the Kyoto University in Japan and at the Art Institute of Chicago. He was present at the first Christian art

66 New Delhi: Manohar Publishers, 2012.

consultation in Bali and is among the founding members of ACAA. Naomi Wray compiled his works in *Frank Wesley: Exploring Faith with a Brush*.[67]

iii) Jyoti Sahi

Dr. Jyoti Sahi is a contemporary artist-theologian, born in 1944 to a Christian British mother and a Punjabi Hindu father. His early studies in art were with Sudhir Khastigir, one of the early students at the Kala Bhavan at *Santiniketan*, and later went for further studies at Camberwell School of Art and Craft in London. Hailing from a multi-religious background, he uses his art to generate a dialogue between Hinduism and Christianity.

He was one of the founding members of the Asian Christian Arts Association and was a frequent contributor to its publication, IMAGE. The role of art and culture in Indian context has been one of his concerns. Jyoti Sahi started the INSCAPE (Indian School of Art for Pearce) at the Art Ashram in Silvepura, Bengaluru in 1983. His seminal work, *Stepping Stones: Reflections on the Theology of Indian Christian Culture* was published in 1986. It includes his reflections accompanying his art works, and it was a pilgrimage, a search for homeland, not just in the past but in something beyond.

Jyoti Sahi, a younger colleague of Solomon, worked in close association with him in the Indian Christian Art Association. He has written couple of essays on Solomon Raj: *Solomon Raj: Artist with a Cosmic Vision* and *Solomon Raj and the Prehistoric Origins of Dalit Art*. Both these works are judicious evaluations of Solomon Raj and his works. Jyoti Sahi met him first in 1980 in London. As with Solomon, the theme of Resurrection had been significant for Jyoti Sahi and he had taken three different approaches to depict the theme and did three different works in oil on canvas. Of all the painters of biblical themes active today, Jyoti Sahi is obviously one of the most inventive. He had been instrumental in developing a 'visual gospel language' -contextualized to Indian culture, furthering Hindu-Christian dialogue.

In 1990, in a talk on Indian Christian Art at the Hermansburg Mission, Jyoti Sahi tried to show how the theological viewpoint of different Indian artists had influenced their art, and how their art expressed a theology through the way in which they had represented Christian themes. People tend just to think of "Indian Christian Art" as a unified approach, with differences only to be found in the personal styles of artists, and their social backgrounds. But, as Jyoti Sahi has pointed out, there is a "diversity in Indian Christian art, which has also represented a diversity in the denominations from which different Indian Christian artists have come. These influences on the art expressions of artists is of course important, but there is also a variety of cultural and theological underpinnings to their art."[68]

---

67 Oakland: Pace Publishing, 1993.

68 Jyoti Sahi <jyoti.inscape@gmail.com> E-Mail Response to the Researcher Dated: Fri, Mar 2, 2018.

21st Century Missions

Though most of the so called 'mission churches' continue with their alien paraphernalia, with no significant change with times, there emerges a changing scenario in an increasing measure, that appeals to the masses, and proves to be effective in the task of evangelization and discipling. Singing in local languages, and use of local instruments has become a characteristic of such worship services. C. H. Dicran, in his study on "Hindi Christian *Bhajans*", a study in ethnomusicology, seeks to understand the meanings of *bhajan*, *kirtan*, *namjap*, and mantra from a Roman Catholic, Protestant, and Hindu perspective.[69] In this study, *Bhakti* and *bhajan* are studied in the mission of the Church, both evangelical and ecumenical. Also, the Catholic charismatic movement is observed as to how it mixes with the indigenization and contextualization of Roman Catholic worship since Vatican II. It also studies the use of many kinds of devotional songs in *satsangs* in homes and in Christian ashrams in North India.

For want of space, the study of 21st Century Missions had to be very selective and only a few examples representing Catholic, Protestant and Charismatic expressions are cited. The whole phenomenon nevertheless seems to be vitally indigenous and culturally relevant.

i) Satsang

Satsang comes from Sanskrit, meaning "to associate with true people", to be in the company of true people - sitting with a sat guru, or in a group meeting seeking that association. The word *Satsang* literally means 'gathering together (sang) for the truth (sat)'. The origins of *Satsang* may be seen in the Bhakti Movement of 15th century and the notion is well known to the followers of Hinduism, Buddhism, Jainism and Sikhism as a spiritual or devotional activity. Generally speaking, *Satsang* is a congregation of religious or spiritual people who assemble together to listen to a guru or a religious discourse or participate in some religious or spiritual activity such as devotional singing, dancing, meditation or concentration. *Satsangs* are popular among Hindus and people of South Asian origin, Rosey Johnson remarks, but "they can also be an expression of Christian spirituality".

The beginnings of adopting *Satsang* into Christianity as an indigenous form of worship can be seen in modern times. Johnson narrates how a group of creative arts specialists, gathered at London school of Theology, love Jesus and people of other cultures, and how they enjoy expressing God's love through various art forms. Leaving the shoes at the door and sitting on cushions and blankets on the floor, with leaders seated on a slightly higher platform, one is struck at the different attitude with an air of humility, reverence and service. The *Diya* (lamp)

69 "Hindi Christian Bhajans: A Survey of Their Use by Christians and a Critique by Hindu Professionals in the Music World", Unpublished MA dissertation, Briercrest Biblical Seminary, (2000:2).

was lit when some words of scripture were read. Light symbolizes knowledge in Hindu culture and it is worshipped, but here at the Christian *Satsang*, they do not worship the light but Jesus who is the light of the world. There was beautiful singing in vernacular languages with instruments like flute, *manjira* (small hand cymbals) *tabla* and *dholak* (drums) with interspersing scripture exposition, prayers and silence. Prostration is a way of humbly acknowledging the greatness of another and symbolizes selfless love and sacrifice. It is a new experience but certainly there is so much that one can learn from expressions of spirituality, which are different from our own.

At the turn of the 21st century, Anil Kant, a Hindu from a Punjabi family came to the Lord with his entire family. He dedicated himself completely to use his talents for the Lord and recorded his first Gospel album in 2002. Since then he has released 18 Gospel Albums. His songs are word based (Bible scriptures) because it is the word that breaks the yoke bringing the anointing and presence of God into our lives. Pastor Anil Kant, as he loves to be called, and his wife, Reena, have two children, Shreya and Rishabh. They too gave their lives to the Lord and together they serve the Lord as a family. Anil Kant was ordained as a Pastor in the year 2007.

The Lord put in his heart to begin a *Satsang*, a contextualized church model, which is a Fellowship relevant to our Indian Culture, reaching out to the unreached. From the year 2007, Pastor Anil Kant is holding weekly *Satsang* fellowship called 'Ashram of Life' in Andheri (West), Mumbai. Pastor Anil Kant travels extensively all over the world proclaiming the Word of God and singing the gospel. Anil Kant Ministries International (AKMI) aims to bring the Good News in a relevant manner to every Indian home, and to the nations in a manner that is popular and easily understood and accepted by them, through *Satsangs* and Media. *Satsang*[70] means fellowship with the truth. *Sat* means "Truth" and *Sang* means "With" - together it means 'Along with the Truth' and their message is: 'Jesus' is the Truth.

ii) Yeshu Darbar

The American Presbyterian missionaries, Sam Higginbottom and his wife Ethel Higginbottom came to India in the early 20th Century. Inspired by the words of Jesus Christ - 'you feed them' - Sam Higginbottom received the vision of 'Gospel & Plough' - the two eyes of his mission in India. He soon realized that the teaching of the spiritual values envisaged by Lord Jesus Christ is vital on par with teaching and transfer of agricultural technology. This ultimately led him to establish the Allahabad Agricultural Institute in 1910 with a vision to train Indian peasants in modern agricultural technology and empower them to produce more food. This was the first and foremost Institute of Agricultural Science and Technology in India. The vision to 'Feed the Hungry' was a practical vision implemented

70 http://southasianconcern.org/christian-satsang/ - accessed February 24, 2018.

by Sam Higginbottom. This has given pioneering agricultural engineers, farm implements and tools for appropriate technology for the first time in India. This Green Revolution in Allahabad was long before Norman Borlaug, the American agronomist and humanitarian, launched global initiatives that contributed to extensive increases in agricultural production, styled as Green Revolution.

Sam Higginbottom emphasized that most of Jesus' miracles on earth, while preaching the Gospel were of healing the sick, cleansing the lepers, giving sight to the blind, hearing to the deaf, speech to the dumb, making the lame to walk, raising the dead, and feeding the hungry. Thus the primary mission of the Church and of the evangelists should be to emulate the same. With this twin focus, the Institute has grown from strength to strength, from an Institute to a Deemed University and finally to what it is today - Sam Higginbottom University of Agriculture, Technology and Sciences under State Legislation - after 110 years of service to the nation! Another indigenous phenomenon in sharing the Gospel emerged on the banks of river Yamuna, within the premises of SHUATS in Allahabad, at the turn of the 21st century. Called *Yeshu Darbar*, it simply means the 'Royal Court of Jesus'[71] - probably the largest Christian Outreach program in the world. The term is used in Indian tradition when Kings would have public meetings called a *Darbar* or court. The common folks would be able to approach and appraise the Ruler of their problems. So also at The *Yeshu Darbar* - the Court of Jesus - people can come with their problems and be blessed in response to His ever extended Invitation: "Come to Me, all you who labor and are heavy laden, and I will give you rest.[72]

This ministry was birthed under the vision of Gospel & Plough, with the charismatic initiative of the Hon'ble Vice Chancellor, Prof. Dr. Rajendra B. Lal, Founder Bishop of the *Yeshu Darbar* movement. Having served the Allahabad Agricultural Institute in 1990 as a Lecturer in Agronomy department, he went to U.S.A. after his Ph.D. in Agriculture Botany. There he completed another Ph.D. in Soil Science and had a lucrative career as an Agricultural Scientist. Having received God's Call he came back to rejoin Allahabad Agricultural Institute. He was appointed as its Director at a time when the Institute was at low ebb under financial crisis. A Prayer Meeting at his house in 1994 with a handful of like-minded believers triggered the tipping point, and by the end of 1996 the Institute with a break through was out of crisis. The attendance at the Prayer Meeting rose to 50. The venue was relocated to Chapel of Brotherly Love, when the strength increased from 50 to 500.

Bishop Lal received the baptism of the Holy Spirit on February 25, 2000, with the evidence of speaking in tongues, and other manifestations of healing and deliverance. The same year on March 15th the Institute was elevated to the status of a Deemed University, the first Christian University in the country with

---

71 http://www.aaidu.org/yeshuDarbar.htm - accessed February 27, 2018.

72 Matthew 11:28 (NKJV).

Bishop Lal becoming the first Vice-Chancellor. In 2001 the number of people attending *Yeshu Darbar* rose from 500 to around 5000, and the congregation was moved out side of the Chapel, and into old Engineering Hall during rains. On October 14, 2001, Dr. Mani Jacob, Chairman, Board of Directors, Allahabad Agricultural Institute-Deemed University attended the Sunday service, saw the work of God among the people, and inspired by the Holy Spirit declared that this small group of believers will become a great and mighty Church of Indian origin. He expressed his appreciation for this indigenous Church, which preserves our heritage, values and culture.

Followed by the anointing, by 2002 around 15,000 people used to hear the Word of God in open-air setting, with miracles, healings and wonders in a greater scale. Ultimately the venue of *Yeshu Darbar* Service was moved to the Football Field known as Higginbottom Stadium. In 2003 greater crowds started attending from neighbor villages and towns - around 15,000-35,000 - as for a *mela* where people thronged for healing and deliverance. With increased outpouring of the Spirit, a heterogeneous group of believers comprising of people from all communities (all castes, creeds and religions), assembled in large numbers, i.e. 50,000 to 60,000, every Sunday to receive healing and deliverance. *Yeshu Darbar* is open to all without any discrimination, with the belief that God is not imprisoned in a specific religion but available to all people when they travel beyond their religious boundaries. The Gospel is preached with power as God confirms His word through deliverance, healing and miracles. Of late, multiplication of the Movement is seen in multiple services held in various branches.[73] Amit Thomas sees *Yeshu Darbar* as a Movement of current times, and points out:

> Yeshu Darbar (Royal Court of Jesus) Movement is playing a significant role in demonstrating the person and work of Jesus Christ in its preaching and practice. Interestingly, this movement has close affinity with the early Church. The movement, which is developed in Indian Context, is now taking its direction in the formation towards proper Indigenous ecclesiology, which would always be a point of reference for many emerging movements ...[74]

Theologians and thinkers rethink and reformulate Indian Christian Theology, in current cultural context. As traditional understanding of the Church is challenged, ancient paradigms become obsolete and new vistas and horizons open up for the 'Church beyond the Walls'. In the backdrop of this historic legacy, spanning from the early church history through 21st century Missions duly sandwiched by Catholic and Protestant Missions, and a study of Christian art in India, the present study proceeds to examine the life and work of Pulidindi

73 Such as *Yeshu Darbar* City North, *Yeshu Darbar* Presbyterian Church Fatehpur, Pratapgarh, Mirzapur, *Yeshu Darbar* Gauara Mohanlalgunj, *Yeshu Darbar* Lodhwari, Raibarelli.

74 Unpublished Ph.D. dissertation. Allahabad: SHUATS, (2017:200).

Solomon Raj in the next chapter, with detail of his early life and teaching career, and his vocation beyond the denominational bounds, beyond the national bounds and beyond his retirement, followed by successive Chapters on his Contribution in Art and Poetry, and his Evangelistic Innovations.

3

Life and Work of P. Solomon Raj

This Chapter on **Life and Work of P. Solomon Raj**[75] is an endeavor to enumerate the humble origins and formative impacts of Solomon Raj, which propelled him to attain higher pinnacles in literary, artistic and theological realms. It shows how he marched from the ranks of his formal profession to the peaks of his creative vocation. His father was a schoolteacher, and his mother was a Bible teacher skilled in informal education among women folk, popularly known in those days as a Bible Woman in the Lutheran Mission. The Gospel reached this family through the missionaries of the Lutheran Church in America (LCA). And, their home served as a parsonage for the local pastor for years, and their front yard as venue for Harvest Festival Celebrations - with grounds full of many Stalls!

Early Life and Teaching Career

Solomon Raj was born on February 21, 1921, in a Dalit family as a third generation Christian at Neggipudi, a tiny village in West Godavari district of Andhra Pradesh in South India. In many places, Solomon fondly called his *janmasthala* (place of birth) by means of a poetic epithet, *Nigrahapuri* (abode of self-restraint). As per his reminiscence this was a "beautiful piece of land with rice fields, irrigation canals, coconut and mango groves". Solomon comes from an agricultural family, and his grandfather had some lands for rice cultivation. His father was the first one in the family who went to school and qualified to be a teacher in a Lutheran Mission School.

As the third child in the family, Solomon learnt to read and write in his father's school, and while doing that he also learnt all the basic skills in the rice fields with his grandfather. He had to tend their domestic cattle in the vacation

75 Source for much of the detail in this Chapter is from Interviews with Dr. Solomon Raj.

time and he liked the out door life immensely. Swimming in the waterways was a great relief from the heat of the tropical sun. He describes his birthplace as "a picturesque part of South East coast of India where the rivers join the mighty sea". He was brought up in that 'dreamland' as the son of a schoolteacher. In the midst of "the simple rural life with sail boats on the water ways, sand beaches, coconut palms and cows and calves grazing around", he says, "I started thinking in 'pictures' before I learnt to speak in words". There were no roads and motor vehicles in those days, and the only means of travel and transportation were sailboats on the waterways.

Solomon was born into a Church movement, which existed over sixty years in Andhra Pradesh. There were a couple of mission stations at Guntur since 1842 started by American missionaries like John Christian Frederick Heyer, and at Rajahmundry since 1845 started by German missionaries. The two bodies merged as a registered indigenous body with the nomenclature of Andhra Evangelical Lutheran Church in 1927 when Solomon was six years old. There were also Lutheran Missionaries from the Scandinavian countries like Norway, Sweden and Denmark, of whom not much was written. This was the only faith expression or denomination he was exposed to in his early childhood. As a teenager, he witnessed a schism within this established church with the emergence of a charismatic segment in 1938, which later had phenomenal growth as a parallel body. In view of the policy of 'comity' only Lutheran missionaries worked in that part of the State where Solomon lived and studied. The principle of comity demarcated territorial boundaries between missionaries of various societies in order to use personnel efficiently, reduce the duplication of activities, and avert competition. When all one sees is the Lutheran expression of Christianity, the emergence of a new element naturally generates suspicion, curiosity and animosity. The initial reaction of Solomon as a young adult is not mentioned anywhere. But as he grew in faith and maturity, this must have fascinated the inquisitive mind of Solomon to study the distinctives of this other 'group' church for his Doctoral studies.

i) Parental Legacy

Solomon had great respect for his parents, and is proud of them for their rich legacy. In tune with the Biblical injunction of honoring one's father and mother, apart from other things, Solomon appropriately dedicates his *Gaana Kusumalu*[76] (Song Flowers) and its English rendering *Geetha Malika*[77] (Garland of Song Flowers) to his beloved parents. This is a fitting token of his *honor your father and mother* - expressed in verse. He was immensely proud of his father, Pulidindi Lazarus, who lived as an ideal schoolteacher, a versatile genius with a multifaceted personality:

76 Vijayawada: St. Luke's Lalit Kala Ashram, (2002:xxv).

77 Delhi: ISPCK, (2010:14-15).

A friend of the young and old,
A voice to the voiceless,
A valiant leader who declared
There should be no neglected soul in the society.

As a grateful tribute, he writes,

To his memory I offer these humble lines,
As a garland from a grateful son.

Recalling the Biblical character after whom his mother was named, he extols his mother who had a great impact not only on him but also upon countless rural folks of the times:

Naome is also the name
Of the woman who gave birth to me.
She was named after the blessed woman in the Bible.
She in her turn became the teacher and guide to
Countless poor women in our land,
Wherein is flowing the river Godavari;
She became a widow herself,
I remember her with a thankful heart.

His mother lived longer as a widow for nearly 37 years, and had been a blessing to her children and grand children, and to the many womenfolk in the villages around. The above lines are an acknowledgement to the fact that he owes his greatness to the godly upbringing by his parents.

ii) High School Experiences

When it was time for him to go to high school, he was admitted into the local High School in their small town. He liked the extra curricular activities like games, dramatics, drawing, scouting and other camps more than his studies. He became popular for making pictures in the notebooks for his classmates. As he paid more attention to this at school, he made many friends. When he could go around in the locality he went to spend his free times with a village screen painter and song writer; he was asked to mix colors with squirrel-hair brushes. Taking all sorts of humorous rolls in the school performances and anniversary celebrations became his hobby. Consequently his studies suffered and he did not get good grades in class work. At the age of eleven, his father died and his mother went to a Bible training school far away for three years. He was left with his grandparents to live along with his siblings. His older sister, Krupavathy married Balla Moses, and they lived in the same village as schoolteachers. Her impact on Solomon and his younger brother motivated them later to become schoolteachers, in the fashion of their sister and their deceased father.

Because of his poor performance in the village school, Solomon was sent away to study in a good Mission High School in a town called Bhimavaram. He lived in the dormitory with new colleagues and unknown friends for the first time in his life. But the idea worked well. Strict discipline in the school dormitory life, early rising habits, stipulated study hours, Sunday School and church attendance with friendly groups helped him very much. In addition, there was a great opportunity for activities such as elocution and essay writing competitions, and special drawing classes as a hobby. Such things filled his spare time and gave him great satisfaction, and he did well in them all. It was a great joy for Solomon to go to the Mission High school. He remembers well that on the front wall of the High School building the School motto was written in large letters, *Ora et Labora* which means "Pray and Work". He was told that it was the motto of the Benedictine monks in the monasteries in the Middle Ages, and it was a great inspiration to him.

iii) College Education

At the end of that period, six of the boys and girls passed the High School examination and they were ready to go to College. Having primary and secondary education in his native place, Solomon enrolled at Andhra Christian College, Guntur in 1940 and was graduated there in 1945 - obviously the first graduate hailing from his tiny village. It was a Lutheran College, the only college of those days in their vicinity. It was not far away, but just a few hours ride by train. And the Lutheran students were eligible for scholarships, and it was not a big burden to parents to send them to the college. The Andhra Christian College was a great institution in those days more than now. They had beautiful new facilities, new stone buildings, single room accommodation, excellent hostel meals and well known faculty - all this was a great blessing to him. It was the Second World War time and the University had moved down from a coastal city to Guntur where the Andhra Christian College was located, because of the fear of Japanese bombing. With the larger University community, it was stimulating with many cultural activities and academic atmosphere.

It was the beginning of the country's serious freedom struggle, and the 'Quit India' movement. Further, it was also a period of a renaissance of Telugu literature and culture. The so-called 'one act play' was new to the Telugu people. The days of the long three acts and four scenes and poetic narration have gone. The Registrar of the University, Mr. K. V. Gopala Swamy Naidu was a Bar-at-Law from London and he was a great enthusiast of modern drama. Solomon enjoyed the four years of study but he got an ordinary B.Sc. with Mathematics and Physics in 1945. He never relished Newton's rings in the Physics lab as much as he enjoyed Tagore's stories in the library. One act play was his favorite subject and so was the poetry of

Tagorean style.[78] He studied all the one-act plays of Victor Hugo on his own, such as *Bishop's Candle Sticks*, et cetera. He tried this genre himself with Indian themes and won first prize for a one-act play published in the College magazine, already defeating senior students. He was in the top place for art contests, story writing and acting in dramatics. The lecturers and classmates remembered some of the humorous skits in which he acted, for a long time after the event. But none of this made him qualified for higher education in science and mathematics.

iv) Formal Teacher Training

So, Solomon chose to be a graduate teacher and went into the Government Training College, Rajahmundry, where he obtained a B.Ed. degree. Thus, teaching became his vocation and he enjoyed it immensely. To be with youngsters, and to become their model gave him great satisfaction. He got married with Mary Sarojini in 1946 and started life as a schoolteacher. Mary comes from his close relations' family; she is none other than the only sister of his brother-in-law, Balla Moses. They knew each other from childhood, and as he says, "it was a marriage by mutual choice and not one of the usual 'made in India' arranged marriages".

v) Formative Influences in Art

His academic work proportionately spanned over all his vocation. As a double graduate he started his career, not as a drawing master but as a science teacher. While he was working as a teacher in the Teacher Training School at Rajahmundry in 1950, he participated in the first batch of Agriculture Extension Methods Training conducted in the then Allahabad Agricultural Institute. Thus he was an alumnus of the 1950's at Sam Higginbottom University of Agriculture, Technology and Sciences (SHUATS). In early 1970's he enrolled his eldest son, Pulidindi Abraham Jaya Raj also into M.Sc. (Agriculture) at SHUATS.

As already seen, Solomon had an inborn aptitude for arts, which was amply manifested in his making pictures in notebooks of classmates at a very young age. This aptitude for art flourished further at the College, which kept him on higher pedestal as topper in art contests. He got acquainted at an early age with other artists in the area, especially men related to an Academy, named after Damerla Rama Rao, an accomplished watercolors artist, and a native artist-instructor. With the encouragement of those artists he passed some examinations, which entitled him to certificates in drawing and painting. At the end of the day, the name of Damerla Rama Rao had shone wherever Solomon Raj is known with all his increasing repute, as he faithfully acknowledged his early mentor in art.

Alle G. Hoekema scans and evaluates Solomon's aptitude and accomplishment in a fitting manner:

---

78 Rabindranath Tagore is considered the greatest writer in modern Indian literature. He was a Bengali poet, novelist, educator, Nobel Laureate for Literature. *Gitanjali* was his classic.

> In the 1950s he discovered his gift as an artist, first specializing in linocuts and wood block printing (black and white, later coloured ones as well) and then also in designing batiks, and - though to a lesser extent - acryl paintings. Serving in the field of modern mass communication as a means of propagating the Gospel, he discovered the possibilities of using visual art in explaining the biblical narratives. Most of the art works which he published in separate booklets and books are accompanied by brief, often surprising, poetical meditations, which remind one of the work of Rabindranath Tagore and others.[79]

After a decade of teaching career, however, he was to launch his preaching career as an ordained minister of the AELC, which had spanned for over five decades - being actively involved, even after retirement.-

vi) On to Theological Studies

As he started life as a schoolteacher, a call came from the Church asking him to go to training for a fulltime pastoral ministry. The missionary Principal at the Lutheran Theological College in Rajahmundry asked him strongly to start his theological studies there - extending to a period of three years' residential study and leading to a B.D. degree. He declined to accept the call for several imagined reasons. He thought the vocation of a teacher - '*guru*' like his father - was more enjoyable. A fixed salary with annual increments, two months summer holidays to enjoy, and other similar considerations seemed alluringly good enough for him. Seven years passed by but the Lord was still chasing him 'like the hound of heaven', urging him for full time pastoral ministry. The Federation of Lutheran Churches in India has restarted the higher education program in Theology in the city of Chennai at Gurukul Theological Seminary and Research Institute. There were students from many parts of the country other than Andhra Pradesh. He decided to go to this College to study. By then he had three children, the youngest only a few months old, but he went to Chennai (called Madras in those days). There again he enjoyed life attending lectures after several years, spending long hours in the library, writing examination papers, waiting for the grades from Serampore Senate, and so on.

He was active in the Student Christian Movement (SCM), and the National Missionary Society (NMS). As the final graduation approached, the National Committee of the SCM of India sent their executive secretary to ask him if he was interested in a job with them as the Regional Secretary of the movement. He was called for a short training in Bangalore, and they offered the job. But he was more in anticipation of a Students' Chaplaincy job in his own Church, which was vacant. In that context, he came to know some important Church officials

79 Alle G. Hoekema: *P. Solomon Raj: Biblia Pauperum. The Poor Man's Bible: A Book Review, "Exchange"* 38, (2009:381-388).

like Harry Daniel, the General Secretary of the SCM, and Dr. D. G. Moses, the Chairman of the National Committee of the SCM.

Beyond the Denominational Bounds

Ultimately, he came to his own Church, the Andhra Evangelical Lutheran Church, which ordained him as a Minister in 1956, and posted him as Students' Chaplain at the Andhra Christian College. The work involved spiritual care of the Lutheran students living in four residential hostels for boys and girls, two Sunday morning services in two places, preparing every year about 20 students for confirmation, teaching Small Catechism of Martin Luther in Lent season leading to Palm Sunday when young people are confirmed in a big festival. It was a full time job with teaching Church History in the College two days a week to the students of the fourth year class. The Sunday morning services were colorful, always with some special festive occasion, and well attended. The resident teachers in the Girls' Halls gave full cooperation and the faculty of the College generally attended the services. And occasionally Solomon was preaching in the main St. Mathew's Church at English service, attended by most of the College community.

For four years he served the student community most joyfully. Miss Hazel Nagul was Principal of Stalls Girls High School, and also Dean of Women at AC College. She was a great inspiration to Solomon in his vocation. She gave him orientation about story telling and encouraged him to teach and write on audio-visual teaching methods and story telling.

i) Initiation into Christian Education Ministries

Every summer vacation, for two full months, Solomon was free to go to places like India Sunday School Union (ISSU) in Coonoor, a hill station in South India and a nice summer resort - first as a trainee, and then regularly as an instructor. It was there that he came to know some ecumenical Church leaders like the Secretary of the ISSU, the Head of Christian Home Movement (CHM), the officers of the Christian Education Movement in various denominations, and others. While moving with others in various denominations he was all the time known as a Lutheran pastor. He was given due recognition in his own denomination, and he was happy that he had never stood for election for any 'offices' in his Church. Standing for elections and occupying honorary posts was not his cup of tea.

While he was in the students' parish in Guntur, a post fell vacant in the Lutheran Seminary at Rajahmundry, that of Assistant Director of Christian Education. The work in this place involved some teaching in the Seminary, seminars and workshops for laymen and women, and production of some simple reading materials for Christians. He was called to this position and most sadly he had to leave the much-cherished ministry among young people in the College. As an ordained minister he held several jobs in the Church, mostly such as Students Chaplaincy, Communications education, and directing a Christian Radio Production Center.

His work with Christian Education of his Church lasted for a couple of years, and then came, like a bolt from the blue, another offer for a new job. Those were the days when the use of audio-visual aids was becoming very popular in the churches. Individual workers, who were mostly missionaries in their own denominations, handled most of the work, till then. In 1947, the Church of South India union was formed, the first experiment anywhere for an organizational union of Christian Churches.

About this time the audio-visual education and its promotion was being felt as the responsibility of the National Christian Council (NCC), just like Christian Home Movement which already had a desk at NCC, Nagpur. But with audio-visual aids and radio work the Churches wanted to form an autonomous body with participation of various denominations. Thus a Centre in Jabalpur was developed with all the small and scattered communications units under one head and one board to manage, namely, Christian Association for Radio and Audio Visual Service (CARAVS).

A theologically trained man was appointed as Executive Director, and Solomon's name was suggested for the post of Field Director for South India. By that time, although he was working with his own Church, he was fairly known outside his own denomination - providentially through his contacts with ISSU, the CHM and the Adult Education work. He was initially not happy to go. Since it was interdenominational church work, he reasoned whether he could fill it adequately. Also, he felt it better to stay with his own Church and do something that could be recognized easily. The decision was hard to make. As far as salary was concerned, he would get thrice what he was getting in his Church, with perks like full house rent, first class train travel, and better provident fund. At last he considered that as God's unsolicited call, as he recollected the words of a chorus, which he learnt as a Sunday School boy:

When he calls me I will answer,
On the mountains or in the valleys …
I will be somewhere working for my Lord.

ii) Multiplied Capabilities at CARAVS

Accepting CARAVS job meant moving with family to a city, travel of twenty days in a month, and training adult people from several denominations, who were unknown to him. He accepted the job on a three-year contract, but was in it nearly for a decade. The job gave him an opportunity to contact, at one time or the other, all denominations and the dioceses of the Church of South India, or later, the Church of North India, in Church Centers like Jabalpur, Rajpur, and Dehra Dun in the North, and Medak, Dornakal, Machilipatnam, Chennai, Coimbatore, and Bangalore in the South. The training camp at Bangalore used to be a central camp lasting for 15 days in residence involving theory and practice in the use of aids, including still projectors and 16 mm movie projectors. Accommodation and excellent catering arrangements were facilitated in places like Baldwin Boys' School in Bangalore. He combined Bangalore training course with Coonoor ISSU, so he could take the opportunity to teach for two weeks in Coonoor. Over nine years of interesting work, teaching people in the use of tools and methods of communication and an enjoyable ministry, was soon to change as Solomon accepted another challenge.

iii) Further Education in Arts

Earlier Solomon had very advanced practice working with the famous Rama Rao School of Artists in Rajahmundry and freelance study on Indian arts and sculpture. Then he worked for ten years as the communications trainer with the NCC of India. In those days it was called only audiovisual arts in which his basic arts skills became very useful in his teaching and preaching from the pulpit.

During the period he worked with Audio Visual education, Solomon was awarded a scholarship by the Lutheran Mission in America to go for a graduate study in Communications in 1964. He was given leave by his employing organization and he chose the Indiana State University in Bloomington, Indiana. This he did because he was told that it was a great school for communications, chosen by the Government of India scholars going for such a study under Ford Foundation Scholarships. This gave him another interesting opportunity with the Indiana-Kentucky Synod office of the Lutheran Church in Indiana. He was invited occasionally to fill the vacant parishes on Sundays and was also chosen for women's annual meetings of the Synod as guest speaker. He was taken to several places in the Synod to speak at a series of meetings for that year.

During that time he was privileged to take two higher-level courses in graphics, and Magazine production without the pre-requisite courses and he was fortunate to get A grades in those optional courses along with Philosophy of Education, Non-projected Aids, Photography (full course in educational film production starting from the story board ending with full tape with magnetic sound track voicing, etc.) It was a full course of study with 36 courses in three semesters, which was not even possible for American students, for whom it took several semesters.

Solomon thoroughly enjoyed the work as part of the requirement. This was the only academic work he had done in fine arts and he was wedded to that interest and experience in graphics, as can be seen in his later work with wood block prints and linocuts. This in fact was the fitting opportunity that brought out the best in art in his life. He vividly recounts in his *Memories*:

> I was born as a child artist and the son of a schoolteacher. I continued with freelance art, and the landscapes I made at the age of 16 have been around for some time. I never had a formal training in art till I

> went to graduate study in Indiana University much later where I did some work in graphics and magazine production.[80]

At the end of the year he passed the examinations with high grades, and obtained M.S. Degree in Communications, with graphic arts as a major. He also had a three-week working experience with a senior Lutheran pastor in a parish in Wisconsin area, and to top it all, he was given an opportunity of a one-week visit to the Holy Land on his return journey, as a paid guest of the Lutheran Mission.

iv) Beginnings of Christian Radio in Telugu

Rev. Roger C. Cann, a missionary from Canada worked in the Northern parts of Andhra Pradesh with the Canadian Baptist Mission (CBM). In 1960 when Solomon was starting his work with All India Communications Society as Field Director, Roger became his honorary colleague and helped him in several training programs in Andhra - at places like Medak, Dornakal, Machilipatnam, Kakinada and Vijayawada - serving the interdenominational church groups and institutions. In 1960 they co-sponsored a Conference of Church Leaders in Hyderabad to talk about the possibility of Christian broadcasting in Andhra, in anticipation of the forthcoming Communicators Conference in New Delhi along with the WCC Conference.

Roger Cann and Solomon attended these Conferences in Delhi and they came to know the announcement that the Lutheran World Federation was going to put up a 100 Kilowatt Broadcasting Station in Ethiopia to send Christian programs in Telugu to all East Asian countries by short wave. In the consultations, Roger and Solomon accepted responsibility on behalf of the Andhra Churches to start a production studio in Andhra Pradesh to make programs for the Radio Voice of the Gospel, which was to come up in Ethiopia soon.

At the meeting in New Delhi, they made friends with eminent Christian broadcasters like Dr. Sigurd Aske of Norway, Bishop Berkeley and others. They came back and reported the matter to Andhra Pradesh Christian Council (APCC) meeting in Vikarabad, and asked the Council to constitute a board. Then Solomon wrote a draft constitution and it was approved. Several Telugu Dioceses of the CSI, AELC, CBM, and American Baptist Mission (Samavesam of Telugu Baptist Churches) - these bodies have joined and a piece of land was leased from Krishna Godavari Diocese of the CSI, and the work of production of Christian Radio programs started in 1964 with Roger Cann as the Studio Director and Solomon as member of the Board with other elected persons.

The work under Dr. Cann's leadership went on successfully for four years. The station Radio Voice of the Gospel at Vijayawada offered free broadcasting time of half an hour a day, and organizations like Radio and Audio Visual Aids Committee of the National Council of Churches (RAVEMCO) in USA has

80 P. Solomon Raj: *Memories of an Artist,* Unpublished article, p.1.

become main donor for production costs. After four years, Roger Cann wanted to be relieved of the Radio work to go into other responsibilities of his Mission, and Solomon succeeded him to direct the work at the Telugu Studio, named Suvartha Vani (Gospel Voice).

v) Suvartha Vani and Solomon *Bani*

With his coming to Suvartha Vani, the broadcasts became more 'indigenized' and the whole enterprise had a different *bani* (pattern) - greatly oriented to Indian culture in general, and to Telugu culture in particular. New features appeared like Bible Quiz which the listeners loved to participate, listeners' groups with guided listening, and dialogue in small groups, and most of all, specially written and composed songs with Indian orchestra, Indian melodies and structure, and trained singers. With all this, Suvartha Vani broadcasts became a new attraction. Annual festivals - once on the Anniversary of the Studio, and the other during Christmas season - became open to Christians and non-Christians. Friendship with local All India Radio Station and the Government College of Music - all these brought Suvartha Vani close to the public.[81]

When Solomon worked as the Director of the Christian Radio Studio, he became more involved in fine arts as member of a secular art academy, and regularly participated in one-person shows and group shows, and more recognition came to his work. At one time the District Collector asked him to do a one-day arts seminar for the children of all schools in the city and he gave him the help of several revenue officials. Later he held an exhibition in city hall on the invitation of the Mayor, and again the District Collector cut the ribbon and paid rich tributes to his work. He specially advocated the concern for the poor and the oppressed, which came out very clearly and specifically in some of his art works.

In his broadcasting ministry with the Radio Voice of the Gospel in the 1960's, as director of a Program Production Centre in India, he had attended the biennial Studio Directors' Conferences in Addis Ababa - four times, once in every two years - and got some influence of the Ethiopian art which was in many ways similar to Indian art, if seen carefully. Once at the decennial celebration of the STATION RVOG, Solomon shook hands with the emperor Hailesalase also. During those trips he had an occasion to learn some history of Ethiopian Christianity and also to make a study of Ethiopian art, which had its influence on his Biblical art expression all along.

But his last trip in 1977 was part of his Sabbatical, and he went to stay in Addis Ababa for one year to work there. But that year the Communists under the leadership of an Ethiopian have taken away the RVOG from the Lutheran World Federation. The station was nationalized and all the missionaries were sent out.

81 A booklet was later published by the author, with some 44 of those songs under the title, *Gana Kusumalu*. An English rendering of these songs by the author himself, along with other scholarly essays was recently published by ISPCK, with the title, *Geetha Malika*.

So he could not spend the whole year of his Sabbatical but returned already after only a month there.

In all these trips and in the longer trip at the end, he studied Ethiopian art in the University and could make a deeper non-academic investigation into the arts of the country. Solomon had a big volume of Ethiopian art and art history in his library. And traces of the Ethiopian impact are obviously seen on the art of Solomon. He was very fascinated because the Ethiopian art was similar to Indian iconography.

vi) Creative Innovations in Christian Communications

During this time, he had written and produced some Bible Dance Dramas (*Yakshhaganas*) in a typical classical dance form of the area. Now some of the better known of these plays are on video cassettes fortunately, whereas in 1973, when these dramas were played to packed audiences on the stage, it was new for a Christian story to be told in dance and song art forms typically native to our culture. This was the most novel and interesting attempt of 'musical dance dramas' on Biblical themes, after the pattern of the famous Kuchipudi dances.

One of the earliest dance dramas, *'Kim Karthavyam'* - a paraphrase of the greatest Commandments of Christ - Love God and Love Your Fellowman - was most successful. This drama was heard on the National Radio, played on stage in several cities, and was talked about by Christians and non-Christians for several years, even to date. For the first time, Solomon also managed to bring Hindu play back cine singers to give voice to some of his songs, composed specially for the broadcast. Much commitment and hard work fetched ample appreciation from all over, beyond religious boarders.

Beyond the National Bounds

After he worked with Radio Production Studio for ten years, Solomon was required to move again this time overseas. He got an unexpected invitation in 1976 from the Missionary Training Colleges of Selly Oak, Birmingham for a three-year contract, which lasted for a decade. His work in the Colleges was to teach Cross-Cultural Communications to missionary trainees, along with his English colleague, Mr. Denys Saunders. By then he already had put in two decades of work in India as a communicator of one sort or the other. At the same time in England he was involved with icon painting with authentic Greek painters and then he studied the Byzantine art and made papers on the Iconography as means of worship and renewal.

i) Teaching Ministry in the Selly Oak Colleges

Relation of this work with faith and culture came mainly in Selly Oak where he worked in the cross-cultural communication or intercultural communications. The work involved with adults and already academically trained missionary candidates going to foreign countries. It was most inspiring to deal with interpersonal communications when one enters a new culture. The assumptions and the expectations, and the follies - all these were not difficult to find out, analyze and talk about in a College. There he taught the missionary candidates many things about crossing cultures, the whole matter of assumptions, stereotypes, cultural aspects, misunderstandings including problems of body language and its effects. He clearly emphasized the fact that there are no higher cultures and lower cultures, but only different cultures, which should enrich each other through sharing and understanding and enlightening interaction. In his work with the cross cultural department of the Selly Oak Colleges, Solomon was better known for visual arts and story-telling.

With one group of the Namibian students whom he was teaching, they produced together a booklet with stories and artwork from the students themselves, which was published by the central house of the Colleges. At that time he was able to study deeper in the university libraries since he was also admitted to the Ph.D. study in the Birmingham University to defend a thesis on Indigenous Church Movement in India, which included the whole idea of Non Christian culture and world view, religions, assumptions, folklore and iconography. This period of study and investigation and sharing perceptions with people coming at any time from nearly 20 different cultures was very useful, and mutually enriching.

ii) Doctoral Research under Hollenweger

With preliminary theological studies at Gurukul Lutheran Theological Seminary, Madras, his theological persuasion culminated in his doctoral studies at Birmingham University. Nobody ever imagined he would reach such heights in his academic pursuit - hailing from a rural pedigree marked by meager means. Discarding the traditional mode, he chose an innovative mode in his ministerial vocation! An ordained minister of the AELC, he never confined himself to an appointed parish of limited horizons, but soared like an eagle with renewed strength and vigor, the whole world becoming his parish – for ten years on loan from AELC to work as Communications Trainer for South India under the National Christian Council (NCC), and another ten years in Radio ministry as Director of Suvartha Vani - with creative innovations to his credit.

During the period of ten years Solomon was in Selly Oak teaching, he registered for Ph.D. at the University of Birmingham under the guidance of the Swiss professor, Walter J. Hollenweger (b. 1927 – d. 2016), a great authority on Pentecostal and Charismatic churches. He was the author of the magisterial classic, *The Pentecostals* (1972), and its sequel, *Pentecostalism: Origins and Developments Worldwide* (2005), making a deep study of the non-mission and charismatic churches in India and around the world. As Solomon's research guide at Birmingham University, Hollenweger gave him much encouragement in his work.

It was a great joy for Solomon to work with Hollenweger, who was an artist himself in song, poetry and dance. Solomon taught some courses with him in the area of art and faith. Later he had drawn from this experience for the papers he had presented here and there. He feels very grateful to Hollenweger and visited him and his wife in Switzerland later, and also met him in German Kirchentag (a biannual five-day church convention) celebrations later.

iii) Bloom of Art at Birmingham

While in Birmingham on the faculty during 1976-83, Solomon had his share of showing his art first, which had drawn many in the colleges, and later in a major exhibition at the University, which had drawn several visitors from the community. At one of the one-man shows at the Selly Oak Colleges, the Indian High Commissioner came as the chief guest and the President of the Colleges sent invitation card attractively printed in gold, which was a great honor. Some of the Colleges acquired his artwork and the one in Crowther Hall today was ceremonially installed in a prayer meeting with the President of the colleges in the chair. Similarly the arts faculty of Birmingham University acquired a batik and it has been hanging in the seminar room.

In 1980 as a part of the 1000-Year Jubilee of Advent of Christianity to Russia, and also the commemoration of the 'Triumph of Orthodoxy' (as it is called in the Eastern Orthodox Church history), Solomon was happy to be initiated into icon painting and gilding. He continued the study of icons and Eastern Orthodox spirituality, and later presented some papers at various consultations, some of which were published elsewhere, on topics such as:

- Icons for Renewal and Worship
- Icon and Eastern Orthodox Liturgy, et cetera
- The Place of Images in Communication with Special Reference to Theological Education
- Images in the Bible

The last essay was published in *The Bible and the Technologies of the Word.*[82] Birmingham gave him an opportunity for a deeper involvement and study of the cultural aspects of art, specially the history and meaning of Christian art.

iv) Further Accomplishments at Selly Oak

Four years after he left Selly Oak in 1983, Solomon had been invited again as a William Patton Fellow. This period he worked on some meditations and an essay with some of his better-known batik works, which appeared as a book in German language, *"Lebendige Flamme"* (The Living Flame). Incidentally the English version of this book with the same pictures was published later in India.[83]

---

82 Ed. by Joseph Palakeel, Bangalore: Asian Trading Corporation, (2007:210-220).

83 *Living Flame and the Springing Fountain,* Delhi: ISPCK.

Liberation Theology was developing in Latin America in the 1950's and 1960's. Solomon was impressed by the 'liberation motif' found in the most familiar texts of Luke's narrative, and he was inspired to produce 12 wood block pictures on a single theme, namely, the hand of God at liberation. He chronicles the origins of this work in a simple, yet significant manner:

> I was reading the gospel according to St. Luke in the Bible searching for passages related to freedom, liberation or what may be called redemption. Humanity, nay the whole creation needs liberation, a liberation from many kinds of bondage. So I made these pictures to bring out the idea of liberation or freedom. With each picture I have written short meditations ... the outcome of my quick reflection on each text.[84]

According to Fr. Ubelmesser, the Mission Office in Nuremberg (Nuernberg) dedicated Christmas issues of their magazine each year to a special subject on inculturation, presenting the work of a particular artist each time. Their magazine for Christmas 1984 contained eight works of Solomon Raj. "They are embedded in photos of dalits and tribals, as well as in texts of dalit literature; and this at a time, when the struggle for dalit liberation was still fresh and new, even in India."[85] When Dalit Liberation Theology was taking shape in Bangalore, South India with the reflective views of A. P. Nirmal, and was emerging as a movement to reckon with in early 1980's, Solomon has taken this message, almost simultaneously, beyond the boarders of India through his art and reflective verse. The Christmas issue of Nuremberg Mission's magazine in 1991 was entirely dedicated to the works of Solomon Raj, this time on *Liberation in Luke's Gospel.*

Again, after nearly two decades, the art in this book has been used in Chicago in 2008 and this accounts for its continued impact on the successive generations. The Lutheran Church of St. Luke of Itasca, Illinois has thoughtfully used these twelve woodcuts as basis for their 'Meditations for the 12 Days of Christmas', commemorating their centennial. Solomon was very appreciative of this work and the commentary involved in the project:

> This is the kind of response I always welcome. My artwork is not prescriptive or restrictive in any sense, but it aims at being evocative. That means that the viewers are welcome to bring their own experience and perception into play when they see the works and express their own ideas.[86]

---

84 Solomon Raj, *Liberation in Luke's Gospel,* Vijayawada: St. Luke's Dalitkala [sic] Ashram, (1996:8).

85 Fr. J. Ubelmesser, S.J. "A Word about the Artist" in *Liberation in Luke's Gospel,* (1996:6).

86 *Now We Are Free,* The Lutheran Church of St. Luke, Itasca, Illinois, 2008.

In March 1986 Solomon completed his teaching term in Selly Oak Colleges, and also completed his four years of research. It was a fulfilling moment when he was awarded an earned Ph.D. from the Birmingham University, U.K. It was a remarkable homecoming, when Solomon could be with the family, and when a new season of extended ministry would usher. In 1987, his friend Roger Cann invited him to Canada. He held a successful exhibition of his art in St. Andrew's Church in Toronto, which lasted for four weeks. All these seasons were like 'spring' for him emerging as a global artist-theologian, and evolving multifarious modes and models in art and literature.

v) Artist-in-Residence in the U.S.A.

Solomon was involved with his research in Art, Faith and Culture while teaching some mission classes on topics related to his study. Following his dissertation on Indigenous Churches and Intercultural Christian Communication, he had presented some papers to the Mission department classes. The Japanese theologian Kosuke Koyama came to give a series of lectures during that time at Selly Oak. He had the good fortune of having heard him speak with great conviction and humor, and had never forgotten the message Koyama gave through his books '*Water Buffalo Theology*' and '*Three Miles an Hour God*'. They provoked strong discussions in Intercultural theology.

While he was working in the Asian Institute for Liturgy and Music in Manila, he received a message from the President of Selly Oak Colleges that he was selected to receive the title of Fellow of Selly Oak Colleges, which is a great honor for those who worked in a meritorious way for the College in the past.

After ten years of his teaching work in Selly Oak Missionary Colleges and his obtaining a Ph.D. from the Birmingham University, the Lutheran Mission Board in New York asked him to go to USA with his wife as artist-in-residence in 1986. It was for over a year working a semester in each of the following colleges in succession - Lenoir Rhyme College at Hickory in North Carolina, Luther College at Freemont in Nebraska, and Bethany College at Lindsborg in Kansas. In all those places while doing some teaching, Solomon was deeply involved in art exhibitions, study of art and visits to various galleries and private art studios. His wife Sarojini was with him in all those travels, including the teaching stint of 8 years in Selly Oak. And she kept herself busy making beautiful tapestries, which she exhibited at Wuppertal Mission in Germany (VEM) at the time of the Düsseldorf Kirchentag.

The most important of these American colleges in a way was Bethany College in Lindsborg, Kansas. This used to belong to the old Augustana Synod of the Lutheran Mission in America from which missionaries, especially some well-known lady missionaries like Ms. Agnes Christenson, came to India and worked in Bhimavaram, near his birthplace. She established a girls' school with the same Bethany name, which is now a first grade Women's College in India. Ms.

Christenson was a student and also a lecturer in this College in Lindsborg, and it was a privilege for Solomon to go to the same College with full academic teaching qualifications. His mother worked with the missionary, Ms. Christenson, in her lady preachers group.

vi) Asian Christian Arts Association

As early as 1978, Solomon's name appeared among the artists' group in India. In those days he used to call himself a "Sunday Afternoon Artist" - since it was only a hobby to him in those days, although he had earned two certificates in art from the Government of India Technical Education department. Then he was working as freelance artist, in fellowship with well-known private and professional artists and art teachers in India.

But when the Asian Christian Arts Association was formed at an initial meeting in Chennai in 1978, his friends like Jyoti Sahi of Bangalore, Fr. Matthew Lederle of Pune and others became members, and Masao Takenaka of Kyoto City, Japan was made the President. Solomon could not be present at this meeting, but subsequently while he was in Birmingham he became a member and subscribed to their periodical, *IMAGE*. It is still in circulation and many of his art works appeared in this periodical over the years.

One of the big conferences of the Asian Christian Organization, which Solomon attended in Bali, was important in decision-making and the planning of Arts Work in Asia. Subsequently he was in the executive committee meeting of the Association on two occasions in Thailand.

More lately he went to another important conference in Bali with 'Dance and Drama in Asia' as the theme. In that conference, the TV version of his major dance drama, *Kim Karthavyam* was projected on a giant open-air screen in Bali. Two important publications appeared - one by Masao Takenaka himself under the title *Christian Arts in Asia*, and more recently another publication, *Bible Through Asian Eyes*, jointly authored by Masao Takenaka and Ron O'Grady.[87]

In his ministry with various responsibilities in India, he had relationship at different levels with different organizations, and traveled occasionally in the Asian countries like Manila, Japan, and Indonesia. From those days, Dr. Masao Takenaka, Ron O'Grady, and Solomon Saprid of Manila became his friends. In fact, Solomon Saprid, the then Audio Visual Aids Director of the Philippines Christian Council had already worked with him in India, in a couple of communication training sessions way back in 1962.

Since those times, Fr. Mathew Lederle, the President of the Indian Christian Arts Association (ICAA), also knew Solomon. And he introduced some of Solomon's early print works to his friends in Germany. Then Solomon attended two consecutive council meetings of the Asian Christian Arts Association (ACAA)

87 Hong Kong: Pace Publishing Auckland-New Zealand in association with Asian Christian Art Association, Kyoto-Japan, 1991.

convened in Thailand. About that time he was also elected as President of the ICAA with Fr. Lederle's resignation in order to facilitate the developing of Indian leadership. In that responsibility, Solomon worked with other artists and art promoters like Jyotj Sahi of Bangalore, and the Jesuit Prof. Dr. Anand Amaldass, the Rector of Satya Nilayam, Chennai.

Fr. Amaldass became the founder of an excellent arts magazine in those days which exist no more.. Two major articles from Solomon's pen have appeared in that periodical called *Sahrdaya*. Solomon had the privilege of working with Amaldass in a major seminar in communications in Chennai, conducted for the Jesuit communicators. Later, Amaldass encouraged a lady student from Maris Stella College in Chennai to do research on Solomon's work for an M.A. in Fine Arts, which was later published.

Beyond the Retirement

In 1986, his work as a church employee came to an end, when he was 'officially made retired'. But he had continued his artistic activities more intensively. When he had returned from the U.S.A. in 1986, he was elected President of the ICAA, and served for five years in this special capacity. While doing art productions in his home town, he had traveled to several countries as 'artist-in-residence' - in 1991 to St. Andrews College, Manila, for example - and doing seminars, special lectures and exhibitions.

Since his retirement, he traveled every year to Germany, Netherlands, Switzerland, England, and Japan. In Japan, incidentally he was guest of the ACAA, and learnt the technique he was waiting to learn for many years. He was a life member of ACAA and his works appeared in several issues of their prestigious periodical, IMAGE, and in other major works like '*Bible through Asian eyes*'.

i) ICAA Under Solomon's Presidency

Solomon was instrumental in hosting two of the All India Art Conferences - one in Bombay, and another in Bangalore. He was invited to the ACAA a few times and he made friends with artists from different countries of Asia. The more recent meeting was in Bali in 1998, where he had presented a demonstrated lecture on Indian Dance and Christian Faith.

During the five-year period of his presidency of ICAA, Solomon invited Ms. Gudrun Löwner for the first meeting in Bangalore. She was a research scholar of Heidelberg University and presented a paper on the work of a Sri Lankan artist. And, Ms. Timur Indya, an accomplished artist from Japan, was made an honorary fellow of ICAA. In that same meeting a new constitution was written and approved for ICAA.

The second meeting was convened in Chennai a year after that, where Dr. Singh, the Principal of Jabalpur Theological College presented the keynote address. In both these meetings great interest was evinced by artists and art patrons like Fr.

Anand Amaldass, Fr. Thambu Raj of Chennai, Mr. Jyoti Sahi, Ms. Naomi Wray the then secretary of the Association, and others. Some new members officially joined and the Association became active with local exhibitions in places like Bombay, Coimbatore et cetera, with the cooperation of the members. During that time a manuscript arts magazine was initiated with the name of *Pratima* (literally, Image).

ii) Period of Extended Ministry

In this period, which Solomon calls "the period of extended ministry", he had presented papers on art and culture, and other related topics in places such as Evangelical Academy in Hofgeismar, Heidelberg University, Martin Luther University in Halle, Evangelical Alliance at Birmingham in UK, and several other places. He presented a great paper in the Heidelberg University in those days on the subject of "*Artistic Creativity and Prophetic Inspiration*", which appeared in the important *Verbum Dei* periodical from St. Augustin in Germany. With that, the *Verbum Dei* people in Pune became his friends. Solomon became a member of Indian Missiologists while he was in Birmingham and he attended several of their annual conferences and presented some papers in Ahmedabad and so on. He was a guest of the Catholic Seminary in Pune where he gave some talks. Solomon met Professor Kosuke Koyama the famous Japanese professor while at Selly Oak. Solomon presented a posthumous paper on the work of Kosuke Koyama to a Bangalore paper "Contemporary Christian". In the Netherlands, Solomon had contributed a few articles for the EXCHANGE periodical of the Dutch Missionary Society. Three of his books in English have been reviewed in this periodical. One was on the Song Tradition in Andhra and the whole idea of Oral Communications people, which he had learnt and researched with the help of Hans-Ruedi Weber.

In India he was asked to do seminars on Art, Faith and Culture in three main theological colleges - the Serampore College in West Bengal, The Gurukul Lutheran Theological College in Chennai, and the United Theological College in Bangalore. In all these places the lectures and discourses were always accompanied by an exhibition of some of his art works, which had always provided an opportunity to relate to what was talked about straight away. In the longer seminars, time was provided to the participants to work and interact with each other. For example, in a seminar at Serampore, participants were asked to select any one picture on display and express their response to it in a short poem, song or meditation written up in a few minutes. The faculty members present were happy to see that all the 50 student participants have responded by reading out their works for others to listen. In a place called Wuppertal in Germany, Solomon did the same kind of exercise with about 20, and the spontaneous outcome, as they testified, was of a high standard.

In a couple of similar exercises at different times in Germany, Solomon engaged participants to sit in small groups and work in several stages to evolve a simple visual on topics like ecumenism. The ideas were gathered the next day, and a combined visual was made from their group exercises, and the same was printed as a linocut. On the final day copies of this visual were presented at a communion service as an offering of their work to God. Such exercises in England also helped his art expression to be closely related to faith, liturgy and pedagogy. In those active sessions, he invited each one of the participants to reflect on a piece of art work, meditate and bring his or her own perception, and share their experiences in a plenary. Some symbols in his art work became more useful for this kind of meditative exercises, and there were hardly any fixed interpretations or meanings to start with, although as the interacting develops, each person's awareness gets enlarged. He did this kind of exercise with simple pictures like 'Christ with the Refugees' wood block print, and also with groups of pictures like the 'Liberation in Luke's Gospel' prints.

There were also 'doing together' type exercises some times, like the poster production exercise on ecumenism, which was mentioned above. Some times when seminarians and students are involved he gave them an opportunity to produce their own pictures on topics of their own interest and they were displayed the next day for people to see. In those exercises, it was not the professional skill that was important, but generally the expression of an idea or the visual message. Solomon had a seminar with Professor Margull of Hamburg University, before he died, and Professor Hoerschelmann was his external examiner and guide. Solomon gave a few lectures in the Open University in Amsterdam on the influence of Pentecostalism on the main line churches in India. He led a one-week seminar in St. Colm's College in Edinburgh on faith and culture. It was he who introduced the concept of *Incarnation of the Gospel in Indian Culture.*

This expression he used often in Selly Oak in the context of Inter-cultural communication of the gospel. At one time there was difference of opinion with scholars about the difference between 'inculturation' and 'enculturation'. The word 'enculturation' is used when some culture comes where there is no culture, which is almost impossible. But inculturation is the influence, or even replacement of an existing culture with a new culture, partly of course. He still exercises his thinking along such expressions for precision in the context of culture and faith, and he is ever willing to change his ideas where necessary.

iii) Artist-in-Residence at Samba-Likhaan

The real opportunity to work and live as *artist-in-residence* in one of the East Asian countries came to Solomon in 1989 after he had lived in U.S.A. in that kind of work. The invitation came from Dr. Feliciano, the Director of the Asian Institute for Liturgy and Music (later the name was changed to Samba-Likhaan) - an artists' community within an amphitheater-garden complex, a home to more than a hundred artists-in-residence from all over the world. Notable among these are painters like Solomon Raj (India) and Ng Buan Cher (Malaysia). Solomon's designation was Artist-in-Residence and the scholarship came from the World Association for Promoting Christian Higher Education in Asia with an office in New York. He had done some art works (batiks) for the institute and organized some "friendly' evening demonstration sessions for those who were interested. Between the Asian Institute for Liturgy and Music and the St. Andrews Theological College on the same campus he did not know where he belonged, as he gave some lectures in the Theological College on invitation.

iv) At the Tercentenary of the Finnish Bible

The second interruption was an invitation from the National Council of Churches in Finland to do a commemoration seminar for two weeks with Dr. Hans-Ruedi Weber who was just retiring from the World Council of Churches. In fact it was Weber who suggested Solomon's name, and the occasion was the celebration of the Tercentenary of the translation of the Bible into Finnish language. Solomon had an encouraging period of time with Weber, again after he retired from Selly Oak, since he knew him before and Weber had some of Solomon's artwork in his publications. Solomon had seen Finland for the first time. In the Helsinki Conference they shared the podium and taught several things in the seminar. Solomon had the opportunity of meeting some icon painters of Finland, which was a special privilege in addition to the interesting sauna bath experience.

v) Japan Visit and Impact on Wood Block Printing

In 1992 Solomon completed his assignment in Asian Institute for Liturgy and Music. Then Dr. Masao Takenaka, the President of ACAA has invited him for a short period of study and observation of the Japanese Wood Block printing. Solomon read about the special Japanese printing in books but he only practiced the Albrecht Durer type of raised block printing. He never tried the very fine Japanese style with rice paste and fine paper, and also never tried the so called intaglio printing in which ink is filled in the dug away narrow parts of the block and sucked by the wet paper. In this method water mixed inks are directly applied to the block, a little bit of rice paste is then applied on it, slowly rubbed around by special brushes, wet paper is spread on it, and pressed over with what is called a barren. Solomon went with his wife to Kyoto City and was accommodated in the excellent Kansai House. He was introduced to some Japanese artists, and observed the whole process and the materials used directly from them. He also learnt how to use the special carving tools of Japan. It was a fascinating experience with Japanese block printing technique, and he also met some well-known senior Japanese art producers (although they only make the design and leave the details of the work to juniors under their guidance).

vi) Far-East Experiences

While Solomon was in Kyoto, Dr. Takenaka had arranged for him to give a lecture in 1991 at Doshisha University where the latter was a Professor Emeritus. Solomon heard long ago that the great Indian artist colleague, Frank Wesley had worked there as artist for some time. Solomon was also invited to give an exhibition and lecture in the Kyoto City High School and other places. He found out that after about twenty years since he was there, they still had in that high school one of the batiks they bought from him. At the time they had the experience of joining in the famous Japanese tea ceremonies, which he never forget. Tasting the tea with cherry flowers floating in the cup, while looking at the distant low Skyline of the hills is a typical Japanese feast. Dr. Takenaka himself was a great cook and he with his wife invited Solomon and his wife to their interesting table. He personally made a very typical meal on a rotating hot plate right in the middle of the table.

This happy and enjoyable three weeks in the Far East did not come to an end, as thought. In a place called Yogyakarta in Indonesia there was a Catholic communications school. Solomon was invited by the Director of that institute to do a seminar in communications. He went there and showed his art in an exhibition in the school and gave a couple of talks in communications in general and Asian music and drama in particular - with the example of the musical Bible plays he was then composing in India. On that occasion, he had the opportunity to meet some experts in communications. He was also introduced to a great Indonesian artist, who had a big ashram in Yogyakarta with many facilities for visual art and dance. His sons were also strongly involved in his work and they themselves (two of them) were very talented in their fields. For the first time he had realized that many names of places and persons are derivatives or adaptations of the Indian names.

He had the opportunity to see Ramayana and Mahabharata performance in folk drama style in Indonesian language. It was quiet similar to the ancient Indian song story used in leather puppets and other forms of rural communications in India. Those folk art forms have now almost disappeared with the coming of cinema and television. He was always grateful to that kind of cultural exchange between India and Indonesia, not to speak of the passage of religious teachings and practices between the two countries. In Bali Island, for example, he had seen a full-length performance with elaborate dress materials, mainly dramas showing the basic idea of the strife between justice and injustice or good and evil. Visits of this sort have helped him to get a better idea of inter-cultural exchange already happening from many centuries ago.

Solomon attained many laurels – and his global fame had been multi-dimensional. It is significant that some of his works - both literary and artistic - first appeared in German. As Fr. Joe Ubelmesser, pointed out, Solomon has lived his life - at least part of it - as a citizen of the world. Having done 'service for the Gospel' in Africa and studied art in the United States, he lectured in

England often visiting his numerous friends in Germany. He was certainly 'Out of Place' geographically, and vocationally. Though Solomon Raj seems to have been 'displaced', with service in the Lutheran Church for only 5 years, he was 'not misplaced'; in fact, he was 'well placed' in an international, inter-cultural and inter-denominational arena where he served for 45 years, enriching the wider body of Christ and enhancing the use of indigenous medium in his evangelistic mission.

Of late, Solomon made a couple of visits to Hyderabad, giving Seminars on Art, Faith and Culture at Andhra Christian Theological College (ACTC). During the first visit, he was felicitated at the College with distinguished guests, and then held an exhibition of his art at the State Art Gallery. During the second visit also he gave a three-day seminar at ACTC and donated many of his works. Solomon also visited Maria Clara's Biblical Art Gallery. While here he also received an award by Aradhana TV in Ravindra Bharathi, where Solomon first gave the performance of his famous dance-drama, *Kim Kartavyam* in 1975. Soon after, on his visit to the College, his artist-theologian colleague, Jyoti Sahi inaugurated Solomon Raj Art Gallery at ACTC. The much-delayed honor of a Festschrift for Solomon Raj was accomplished when Prof. David Zersen collaborated with the researcher. *Planting in Native Soil: Studies in Gospel Inculturation,* with 19 contributions by friends of Solomon Raj, was published in 2014. Dr. J. A. Oliver, the Hon'ble Chancellor of Sam Higginbottom University of Agriculture, Technology and Sciences released the book at Zion Bible College Auditorium, Vijayawada on January 30, 2015.

For the last 15 years, with a halt for their global travels, Solomon and his wife were living at Vijayawada marching through the natural challenges of ageing and the accompanying ailments. Solomon however was involved locally in Vijayawada Bible Seminary when Stephen Joseph was the Principal, giving seminars to the Faculty and students. Though Solomon was steadily making his finishing touches and coloring on some of the incomplete icons during these years, his paintbrush seems to be steadily snoozing. But his pen seems to grow sharper, as he produced voluminous works in English and Telugu during the later years in his nineties. Prof. David Zersen remarked:

> To some degree, poetry is a friendlier form of creative expression for him because in his 90s he can no longer dip the batiks in the vats of hot wax. Nevertheless, there is aggressive and anxious power in the words that he pens while he and Mary quietly await their calling.[88]

Solomon lost his life companion, Mary Sarojini, on 13th October 2017, after seven decades of togetherness. She was with him together - in all his global travels and destinations, in all his challenges and accomplishments, in all his valleys as well as his peaks and pinnacles. As long as she was before his eyes, he was like a

88 Foreword, *Soliloquies in Solitude* by B.S. Moses Kumar, New Delhi: Christian World Imprints, (2017:viii).

tiger, but now he feels loneliness and disorientation. They were really 'made for each other', and she was in deed the woman behind him! As per the wise remark of B. W. Berry Sr., Solomon Raj was "skillful in using his hands, his head and his heart" and so, "he is an artist", as will be seen in the following Chapter. And, he seems to fulfill Berry's injunction: "*Whatever you do, make art.*'[89]

89 "A man who works with his hands is a laborer.
One who uses his hands and head is a craftsman;
but the one who is skillful in using his hands, his head and his heart...he is an artist.
Whatever you do, make art." - B. W. Berry Sr.

4

Art and Poetry of Solomon Raj: Theological and Evangelical Perspectives

Introducing the artistic and poetic yearnings of Solomon Raj and presenting a critique of his evocative art and reflective verse is the task at hand. Solomon Raj of the Pulidindi clan, hailing from an obscure but picturesque village in South India, became a popular personality on account of his art in its manifold forms, and his writings in their multiple genres!

He composed poems in Telugu from his early childhood, and continued ever since in spite of structural complexity. The subject matter of his writings and his art had been Christian themes, but the means of its presentation had been diverse and distinguished. The thrust of his writings had been *didactic*. His innovations found no bar on any known or unexplored modes in presenting the Gospel. A study of the multiple methodology of his work through his 'pen and paintbrush' is taken up in this chapter by evaluating Solomon as an Artist, as a Poet, as a Lyricist and Hymn Writer, and as a Multifaceted Genius.

Solomon Raj – As An Artist

Christian art has three primary purposes: "depicting the actual events of the Bible, depicting the events of the Christian life, and communicating the message of the Holy Scripture in a visual form." Solomon with all his efforts has gone to achieve one more purpose: "to make the Gospel relevant in the given culture through his pen and paint brush."[90] Thus he emerges as an advocate of 'Incarnation of the Gospel in Indian culture'.

---

90 Dr. Stephen Joseph: "Introduction" to *Etched Icons: Art Faith and Culture* by P. Solomon Raj, Vijayawada: St. Luke's Lalit Kala Ashram, (2009:8).

Solomon, as an artist had earned global recognition for nearly half a century, and his works continue to inspire future generations. The Jesuits of Nuremberg had undertaken publication of his batik works through their Calendars in 1987 and 1992. Calendar was also done by Missio Aachen, Germany. His art was also used in some historic posters as follows:

- Basil Mission 75 Years Jubilee (1815-1990) Poster had his batik picture and his poem in German translation.
- Christian Conference of Asia (CCA) Poster, with a very interesting new design on **Freedom and Unity of the Church.**
- Two Posters on Christus hat viele Gesichter - Christ has Many Faces or Images. - appeared in German and Dutch.
- Finally, the Bread for the World Poster - batik on **Thirst for Justice**, with several symbols, illustrating his idea of inculturation.

His major works, preserved for posterity in 6 published works, are introduced here, with special emphasis on two - *Liberation from Luke's Gospel* and *St. John's Gospel: A Gallery of Hieratic Art.*

i) Living Flame and Springing Fountain

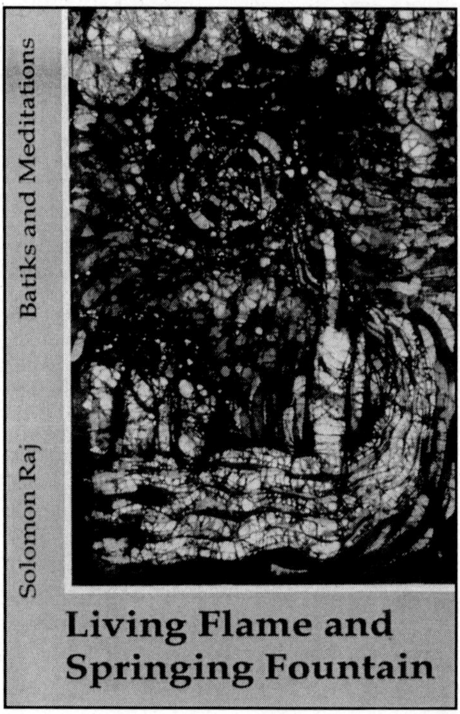

Published in his 70's, this work majored on his selected 'batiks' - a collection of 34 with matching meditations. The Nuremberg Mission Office originally published this in German in 1988. The Indian Society for Promotion of Christian Knowledge (ISPCK) published an English edition in 1993 introducing the Artist, while Christian Literature Society (CLS) had introduced the Poet (through publication of *Puja Mandiram* in early 1970's).

James Massey commends that this collection uncovers 'the prophetic aspect of Dr. Solomon's personality', and presents him as 'an Indian artist theologian'. Solomon "besides being a most successful artist, is also a Prophet and a Contextual Theologian in a real sense."[91] Solomon's profound treatise,

91 *Living Flame and Springing Fountain* (1993:6).

'Experiments with Art Expression' adorns this work. D. Sanjiva Dev judiciously comments: "each of his works, either poetic or pictorial is a living rhythm vibrant with light and delight", and "his art reflects and reveals his spirituality."[92]

ii) Fiery Wheels: Art Works and Meditations

Published in his 80's,[93] this work contains 29 batiks, 5 woodcuts and 3 acrylics all in color, plus 12 woodcuts in black and white. Volker Kuester portrays Solomon as a 'communicator of the gospel in word, image and dance.'[94] A wheel is a strong religious symbol in Hinduism, and Solomon related this symbol to the Scripture text proclaiming 'the Kingdom Manifesto' in Luke 4:18-19.

Solomon learnt batiks from Hindu artists in Hyderabad but the intercultural elements, religious symbolism and its interpretation followed. His batik on the Christian interpretation of the wheel first appeared in Hans Ruedi Weber's '*Immanuel*.'[95] Wood block printing is an ancient Japanese art form, popular in Germany before the invention of printing press. Solomon worked in Philippines for a couple of years, and went to Japan to study special wood block printing while he was already involved deeply with Durer and German graphic artists.

iii) Etched Icons: Art Faith and Culture

Published in his late 80's, this work presents 59 coloured and 7 black and white 'etchings' - all together 66 works. Solomon's Prologue enlightens the reader about

92 *Rhythmic Vision,* "Living Flame and Springing Fountain" (1993:103-104).

93 *Fiery Wheels: Art Works and Meditations,* Vijayawada: St. Luke's Lalit Kala Ashram, 2003.

94 Dr. Volker Kuester: Renunciation of *Inculturation as Aesthetic Resistance,* 'Fiery Wheels', Vijayawada, (2003:100-122).

95 *Immanuel: The Coming of Jesus in Art and the Bible,* Grand Rapids: Wm. B. Eerdmans, (1984: 19-21).

icons and different types of etchings such as dry points, aquatints, and the interesting grainy effect, special to aquatints. Though he was into making 'icons' all along, they were not reproduced in print, but remained in their original state and elegance.

Except for icons, all the published works of his art invariably appear with a matching meditation. Solomon's works had been enjoying acclamation from many around the globe, ever since the start of his 'journey as an artist'. The Jesuit Mission Office in Nuremburg had the distinction of producing several works of Solomon in their publications, and having several of his original works on permanent display. The pictures with verse have been reproduced in magazines and periodicals, being meaningful to Christians in many countries - more so with his multi-ethnic, multi-linguistic and multi-cultural audience from other faiths. Several of his works have appeared as title page illustrations, posters and cards.

Couple of his other published works, obviously the first and the last - significant for their serial form are: *Liberation in Luke's Gospel*[96] and *St. John's Gospel: A Gallery of Hieratic Art.*[97] The researcher's analytical evaluation on these works, with art reproductions, is available on the Internet.[98] During 1970's, Solomon made a deeper investigation into the issue of Liberation in the backdrop of Latin American Liberation movement. Finding ample source for Liberation in Luke's Gospel, he addresses this challenge, bringing out beautifully the good news of the Lord's Liberation from diverse situations.

iv) Liberation in Luke's Gospel

This may be considered the *magnum opus* of Solomon Raj, on par with his seminal work, '*A Christian Folk Religion in India*'. Though not voluminous, this work of color woodcuts (12"x18") with meditations was widely known, being

96 *Liberation in Luke's Gospel,* Vijayawada: St. Luke's Lalit Kala Ashram, 1996.

97 *St. John's Gospel: A Gallery of Hieratic Art,* Vijayawada: St. Luke's Lalit Kala Ashram, 2010.

98 http://www.artway.eu/content.php?id=1365&action=show&lang=en
http://www.artway.eu/artway.php?id=588&action=show&lang=en

published in German (1991), Dutch, English (1996), and Telugu (2010). A combination of 'Image and Word', these 12 works are like 12 Gates of Heaven ushering one into the riches of God's great liberation. Solomon did these prints during 1987-88, as part of his research at Selly Oak Colleges, England, where he was professor of cross-cultural communications. The color wood block prints in this dissertation are reproduced from the Originals made afresh by the artist in 2006.

The purpose of this publication was "for meditation, Bible study and prayer in groups". Solomon's treatise on 'Art and the Gospel' enlightens the reader about the process of wood block prints and use of images in church life. This critique presents the artistic significance, and theological analysis of the themes embedded. Bishop Sam Amirtham extols the liberation motif in the Bible, which was artistically portrayed by Solomon:

> Solomon Raj, resting in St. Luke's tradition, uses pictures, poetry and prose to articulate this liberating messages [sic] of Jesus Christ in this gospel according to Solomon Raj. It is an original contribution of the Indian church to the whole *Oikoumene*.[99]

Fr. Ubelmesser extols Solomon's work and the ethos of such religious art, from a firsthand experience: "His paintings, batiks, woodcuts and his verses are in all their Indian garb a beautiful expression of our common faith in Jesus Christ and his gospel. ... he has spent most of his life just doing this: integrating our faith with brush and word.[100]

The wood block printing technique had its superb expression in the hands of Solomon in the cut and the color of each work - with beautiful imagery and rich indigenous symbolism. In Telugu edition, Solomon presents a brief description of

99 Sam Amirtham, *Liberation in Luke's Gospel,* (1996:5).

100 Ubelmesser, *Liberation in Luke's Gospel,* (1996:7).

Signs and Symbols used in these works. They are like 'mini parables' with a voice of their own and a meaning.[101] The symbolism in each of these works is identified with its particular meaning and message. The 'descriptive titles' of the 12 works, and the distinct types of liberation are noteworthy. Since the primary focus of all these works is *liberation*, the order of the sub-titles is used in the following analysis.

Liberation from Social Prejudices

'The Handmaid of God' is from the *Magnificat*[102] - 'blessed' Mary's Song of Praise. It extols the theme of 'the bonded becoming the blessed' - reminding us of 'gender liberation'.[103] The prejudice for women in the Jewish society needs no mention. Prejudice for a place is also obvious in the way Mary's town of Nazareth was belittled.[104] Whether women are spoken high or treated low, Solomon could see the divine perspective that leaves no room for 'social prejudice':

101 *Luka Suvarthalo Vimochana Prasakti,* Vijayawada, (2008: 6-7).

102 *"For he has looked on the humble estate of his servant.*
For behold, from now on all generations will call me blessed". (Luke 1:48).

103 The prejudice for women in the Jewish society needs no mention for anyone who knows the Jewish Prayer: "Blessed art Thou, O Lord our G.D. King of the universe, Who hast not made me a woman". And also the prayer to be said by a Jewish man every day: "Thank God for not making me a Gentile, a woman or a slave" (from Jewish Talmud).

104 "Can anything good come out of Nazareth?" (John 1:46).

For all that we know
when God decided to become incarnate
He chose to enter
the womb of a woman.

Solomon emerges as a Champion of Women Liberation. Concluding each reflection with some profound saying - expressed in couplets and stanzas - the end of this first work in Telugu reads likes this:

He has gone down and seen the depths of divine will
Who desires the progress of womankind.
(*stree jaati pragatini aasinchuvaadu*
daiva sankalpaambudhini digi chuchinaadu).

The symbol of star in gold color at the upper right corner signifies heaven and divine revelation. Viewing it as sun which "brings the light that frees all humanity from darkness", "Humankind, represented here by the four women, waits for the coming of the Light of the World in a spiritual sense."[105] Solomon has produced similar series of 12 woodcuts, 'Jesus with the Women'[106] - upholding the place of women!

Liberation from Darkness

'Darkness and Sin' is based on Simeon's song.[107] Jesus is portrayed here as 'a light for revelation' granting 'liberation from darkness'. Solomon reminds us how Indian sages prayed from times immemorial: *'Tamas'oma Jyothirgamaya,'*[108] and hastens to declare:

Light is knowledge
Light is wisdom
Light is a sign of immeasurable holiness.
When God made the dance of creation
Light was born first.

The adjective that qualifies 'holiness' is very profound: 'immeasurable' since it is infinite. 'Holiness' is not something relative but is an absolute; it is one of the essential and eternal characteristics of God. Holiness of God, is infinite and immutable!

---

105 *Now We are Free,* (2008:7).

106 *Jesus begegnet Frauen,* München, 2000.
The book with these woodcut prints and matching devotions by Jorg Dantscher, S.J., was published in German about two decades ago.

107 *"For my eyes have seen your salvation that you have prepared in the presence of all peoples, a light for revelation to the Gentiles, and for glory to your people Israel."* (Luke 2:30-32)

108 The meaning of this Sanskrit *sloka* is - 'Lead me from Darkness into Light'!

Here is an allusion to the image of 'dance of creation'[109] as Solomon talks about creation by God. He adapts this imagery here and a genuine prayer is penned for personal enlightenment and for universal awakening:

> *So give me the gift of Light*
> *let darkness be cast behind*
> *and let the universe be awakened*
> *into that glorious morning*
> *which shall not be darkened*
> *by another night.*

Light is acknowledged as a 'gift' from God, and it cannot be attained but only received. The recipient experiences liberation from darkness, as darkness is 'cast behind' by a power higher than oneself, God Himself. People are shown in the picture to be drawn from all over to the light for revelation.

109 Wikipedia: *Tandava*, http://en.wikipedia.org/wiki/Tandava, p. 1.
According to Hindu mythology, Shiva '*tandava*' is "a vigorous dance that is the source of the cycle of creation, preservation and dissolution".

Here is a reference to the fatal fall of man when Satan tempted, and consequently the universe, as well as the heart of man, was darkened. The concluding reflection in Telugu conveys the following meaning:

> The mind of the wicked that loves darkness
> cannot see there is such thing as Light;
> Those who desire the state of darkness
> cannot smell the Heavenly Light.[110]

Solomon anticipates with prophetic hope for 'that glorious morning which shall not be darkened by another night.'

Liberation from Oppression

'Oppressors and the Oppressed' - again from the *Magnificat* declares "*He has brought down the mighty from their thrones and exalted those of humble estate; he has filled the hungry with good things, and the rich he has sent away empty.*"[111] The curse of sin upon mankind necessitated the Incarnation! Here is a beautiful imagery of a tree - 'the tree of sin' bearing fruits of 'classes and castes', and 'unjust structures' heaping oppression and injustice upon mankind. Consequently, "*Some get rich at the cost of the poor / some get fat / from the perspiration of the week.* Classes and castes not only perpetuate the existence of the oppressed and the oppressors, but they serve their contradicting destinies as 'rungs for the high' and 'crushing berths for the poor'.

110 *Luka Suvarthalo Vimochana Prasakti*, (2008:11).

111 Luke 1:52-53.

There is rich symbolism in this work. The wheel in the center is a sign of divine fullness and perfection and His eternal blessing. The Lord's wounded hand is within the circle - the hand is the means through which His blessing flows; and the wounds are the mode of the flow.[112]

As the scriptural foundation spells above, God the Equalizer ensures 'Justice for All' by His two-fold intervention: bringing down the mighty from their thrones and exalting the humble; and filling the hungry with good things and sending away the rich empty. Solomon longs for the advent of such a redeemer and His redemption:

The redeemer will bring
justice to the poor one day
taking his place
with those who are oppressed.

The Redeemer identifies with the oppressed, as "He was oppressed and afflicted" (Isaiah 53:7), and ultimately takes his place with them when he took their sorrow and suffering, and died on the cross. Here we also see the thumb and the pointing finger joined, symbolizing the unity of Christ's divine and human natures.[113] Danzer with intent reflection comments on the Byzantine symbolism embedded in this woodcut.[114]

Liberation from Hunger

'The Lord Remembers the Hungry'[115] - Using this passage related to the 'Last Supper', Solomon communicates the truth that the Lord remembers the hungry and ensures liberation from hunger. The Lord's body given for others not only satisfies the spiritual hunger of people, but also challenges and enables them to feed the hungry. Solomon encourages the reader to participate in this ministry of sharing, which ensures the prospect of a great reward:

---

112 "...with his wounds we are healed" - Isaiah 53:5 (ESV).

113 *Now We are Free,* (2008:11).

114 The hand of Jesus, bearing the scar of the crucifixion, is raised in blessing. The artist explains: 'The thumb and the first finger is the Byzantine symbol of Christ blessing and teaching. This is a well-known symbol from Eastern Orthodox iconography connecting the two natures of Christ, the human and the divine ... I have used this symbol many times to indicate the two natures of Christ.' The six followers that Solomon Raj places around the circle of blessing have looked and have seen. They seem to come away from the blessing in a variety of moods. One lifts up his arms in a sign of victory, others look like they have resolved to follow a certain course of action. And still others are singing hymns or reciting psalms. All show individual expressions on their faces, but their arms and hands seem to converge in fellowship. The circle of the believers is where the hungry are filled with good things, where the celebration is held.

115 *"And he took bread, and when he had given thanks, he broke it and gave it to them, saying, 'This is my body, which is given for you. Do this in remembrance of me.'"* (Luke 1:52-53).

Break the bread, break the bread
share your bowl of rice
there are many hungry souls around.
... and your reward will be great.

Break your bread, break your bread.
Whenever you share your bread
and part with your cup
there is always communion.

As Danzer remarks, Solomon combines here two familiar incidents in the life of Jesus.[116]

Liberation from Barriers

'*We and They*'[117] - The Divide between the human community resulting from man-made barriers and the predicament of such discrimination is well brought out in the following lines:

---

116 *Now We are Free*, (2008:13). The feeding of the five thousand near the start of his ministry and the institution of the Lord's Supper towards its end - In between these two events Jesus directs every disciple to work for freedom from hunger in every sense of the word ... Note that one follower shoulders a large basket at the end, one of the twelve containers in Luke's story ... These symbols of God's superabundant grace announce a time for thanksgiving.

117 *"And people will come from east and west, and from north and south, and recline at table in the kingdom of God". (Luke 13:29).*

Who is in, who is out
in these man-made boundaries?
Trenches that people cannot cross
Walls that nations cannot scale
... Castes do not mix
colours do not blend.

Solomon laments about these man-made barriers, which keep the humankind apart, and he graphically portrays this *Divide* through the symbol of *Yin Yong*. On one side are the depressed and the downhearted while on the other side those who rejoice. The line that divides these two must go away and all must share the joy of the Lord. Solomon anticipates that day when east shall meet with the west (across the continents) and north with the south (within the nations), and ultimately 'saints and sinners shall share the kingdom of God'.

Liberation from Guilt

'More Love and More Forgiveness'[118] - In a dramatic incident at a prominent Pharisee's house, a sinful woman had done something that is forever memorable. Solomon reflects on the ensuing theme of forgiveness in simple but beautiful verse by means of an immutable equation:

The more my sins
The more is my love.
The more my love
The more is the forgiveness
I receive.

The title in Telugu is loaded with strong adjectives meaning 'Infinite Love - Incomparable Forgiveness' (*Amitamagu Prema – Atulitamagu Mannimpu).* Mary here adores the feet of Jesus, portrayed through the sign of His wounded foot. The ascending perfume is a symbol of prayer that rose up from her heart. This woman of 'ill repute' entered the room 'uninvited', and her tears of remorse and repentance knew no bounds as they wet Jesus' feet. She endeavors to dry them

118 *"Therefore I tell you, her sins, which are many, are forgiven - for she loved much",* (Luke 7:47).

with her hair and in the process kissed and anointed them with a precious perfume.

Solomon uses rich imagery as he explains the grand outcome of the event. Just as snow melts when the sun shines on the icy peaks, 'the dirt and the dust get washed away down the hill' when the tears of repentance flow from one's heart. The sinful woman became a sanctified woman, when God's gracious forgiveness was granted in response to her genuine act of penitence. His joy and His peace filled her heart as the 'perfume's captivating aroma' filled the room. Gone was the guilt, which had heavy toll on her for long. The compassionate Lord proved that no sinner who comes to Him will ever be cast away.

Liberation from Bondages

'The Fourfold Bondage' - This picture shows Jesus reading the scroll from prophet Isaiah when he first visited the Nazareth synagogue. This *Nazareth Manifesto* of Jesus envisages the four-fold liberation, which symbolizes 'coming of the kingdom of God'. Solomon reflects on this as he heralds the Good News of hope:

> *The poor and the hungry*
> *the oppressed*
> *and the downtrodden;*
> *the casteless and the cast out*
> *shall hear the good news*
> *of hope.*[119]

---

119 *The Spirit of the Lord is upon me,*
because he has anointed me
to proclaim good news to the poor.
He has sent me to proclaim liberty to the captives
and recovering of sight to the blind,
to set at liberty those who are oppressed,
to proclaim the year of the Lord's favor. (Luke 4:18).

The Kingdom of God is the embodiment of the 'good news of hope' - nothing less and nothing else! The four-fold liberation here is portrayed through rich symbolism. We see an eye on the right hand of the Lord, a sign that the blind will see! In the upper right hand corner are the wounded feet of Jesus, a sign that the lame will walk! A broken chain around the head of the Lord is a sign of 'liberty to the captives' and the oppressed! Finally we see a scroll around the shoulder of the Lord, a sign of the 'good news to the poor'! Danzer points out another significant symbolism: "Our Lord has one hand raised in proclamation, the other set in blessing".

Liberation from Demonic Powers

'Demons and Devils' [sic][120] - In this dramatic scene, Jesus 'ordered a whole band of evil spirits to come out of an unfortunate man' and delivered him. Presenting the theme of 'liberation from demonic powers' from the story of the 'Legion', Solomon laments - 'people in many lands still live in the fear of demons' and therefore he longs for liberation for all:

> *We all need to be freed*
> *from demonic powers*
> *from demons that bother us today –*
> *demons, may be,*
> *of a different kind.*

In the Telugu version, the different kinds of demons are hinted: the demon

120 *"Then the demons came out of the man and entered the pigs, and the herd rushed down the steep bank into the lake and were drowned",* (Luke 8:33).

of drunkenness, of discord and strife, of lust for money, and the demon of corruption. We can still think about other demons of our times such as racism, terrorism, gender discrimination, molest, domestic violence and so on, which plague our society today.

Liberation from Too Many Cares

'Needle in the Haystack'[121] - Title is not a biblical phrase, but it describes 'the many cares that seem to pile up in our lives, reaching haystack proportions'. The search for only one thing needed, as Jesus tells, suggests 'looking for a needle in our haystack'. Solomon remarks that in the good olden days, things like family, children and wealth to enjoy were considered ideals. But as things change, the world became more complex.

As a result,
Goals and values shift
desires and ambitions keep expanding
and in the haystack of too many cares
humanity lost the needle
of life's compass.

---

121 *"But the Lord answered her,*
'Martha, Martha, you are anxious and troubled about many things,
but one thing is necessary.
Mary has chosen the good portion, which will not be taken away from her." (Luke 10:41-42).

Mary with folded hands is a sign of devotion and Martha tightly clutching her jar is a sign of anxiety and worry. The bird above on the branch is a reminder of God's Word.

Liberation from Bodily Concerns

'Body and Soul' - The 'flowers of the field' and the 'birds of the air' Jesus uses as a means of his didactic exercise, and through these He nails down the challenge of trusting God for all needs.[122] These three objects are beautifully pictured in this work - the birds above and the flowers below (*Indianized* and pictured as lotuses). The man who delights in the Law of the Lord is shown worry-free putting his hand in the hand of God.[123]

Liberation from Burdens

'Burdens of this World' - Solomon uses this text to depict the loads and burdens humans carry all their lives,[124] and beautifully portrays the 'Suffering Servant'

---

122 *"Therefore I tell you, do not be anxious about your life, what you will eat,*
nor about your body, what you will put on.
For life is more than food, and the body more than clothing." (Luke 12:22-23).

123 Danzer remarks that "The artist's audience in India would immediately respond to the lotus blossoms, symbols of spiritual life and objects encouraging meditation. Freedom from worry about bodily cares emancipates the mind to tend to the soul." - *Now We are Free,* (2008:23).

124 *"And he said, 'Woe to you lawyers also! For you load people with burdens hard to bear, and you yourselves do not touch the burdens with one of your fingers'."* (Luke 11:46).

alongside humans, Who carried the load of Sin upon Himself on the cross. With much enlightenment on the philosophy of life, he simply conveys a fact:

> *There are some things*
> *which we know*
> *and others*
> *which we do not know.*
> *We know there is suffering*
> *in this world.*

Many things, this side of heaven, we may not know; but we all invariably know that 'there is suffering in this world'. We often do not know the 'why' of it, in our own lives, and also in the lives of others.

This 'mysterious' element of suffering is like a puzzle and every puzzle has its answer; it is only a matter of time when we find it. With inner assurance Solomon encourages: "We wait for God's liberation from suffering, we wait for God's answer". The common tendency of the fallen human race is to shift loads instead of sharing burden. As a result, some carry more of the burden and heavier loads than the fortunate few.[125]

125 Danzer points this out as he comments:
"The warning about not to load people with burdens they can hardly carry is one of six woes listed by Luke when summarizing one of our Lord's table talks. A positive command is implied

Liberation from Fear of Death

The last work depicts the resurrection of Jesus Christ.[126] The 'imaginative title' Solomon gives to this portrait is 'Gentle Brother Death'. This is obviously the description he borrowed from St. Francis of Assisi, who called Death as 'Gentle Brother'. Solomon in the accompanying verse addresses many philosophical questions and perplexities about what happens after death:

At the time of death
where does the soul make its journey?
To the land of the fathers,
or the land of Gods?
Into the night or into the day?
Into the cloud or into the lightening?
Into the full moon or the new moon?
Into the dark fortnight
or the bright fortnight?

in his follow-up observation about helping those who are struggling. The Apostle Paul later summarized Jesus' message: 'Carry one another's burdens'."

From perception of the portrait, Danzer makes further enlightening comments:

"But the compelling image in the picture is the cross, slashing across the scene, putting everything in perspective. Jesus carried our burdens, even to death on the cross. Our proper response to God's mercy is to help free others from their burdens."

126 Luke 24:1-2.

In the midst of these perplexities, Solomon comes up with a certainty that has ample scriptural foundation:

But we surely believe
that death is the doorway
to a new life
more glorious and more wonderful.

As Danzer comments, this last image "pictures Christ the Liberator lifting people out of their coffins and giving them new life".

When Christ had conquered Death, the doors of death were broken, and Death was bound captive with chains at the feet of Christ. We see couple of angels above - one blowing a trumpet, a sign of resurrection; and the other carrying a child, a sign for the angels taking spirits to heaven.[127]

Ever since '*Liberation in Luke's Gospel*' appeared, Solomon's paintbrush has mounted many pinnacles in producing other series at different times on different themes as listed by himself.[128] Whether in Color, or Black and White, all these works are on different Biblical themes from different texts and contexts. The first two series were out of supply, probably since they were not printed as a book. The third series on Women was published in German. The fourth series are of course published as a book.

127 Danzer rightly sums up the message:
The Christ figure assumes the shape of a dynamic cross, energy bursting forth from the center. Jesus elevates a young person with his right hand and another - it looks like a woman - with his left, giving them new life. In response, the skies are filled with jubilation and the redeemed seem ready to burst into a song: 'Our souls are waking. Our bonds are breaking ... Now and forever. Alleluia'. *Now We are Free,* (2008:29).

128 1. Life of Our Lord Jesus Christ – 12 Woodcut pictures in color
2. Caring for God's Creation - 12 Woodcut pictures in color
3. Jesus' Encounter with Women – 12 B/W Woodcuts
with Text by Jörg Dantscher, a Jesuit Provincial (München: 2000)
4. Biblia Pauperum: The Poor Man's Bible – 10 B/W Triptychs

See Solomon Raj, P.: *St. John's Gospel: A Gallery of Hieratic Art* (2010:56)

However, a different kind of serial work was his 'Life of Jesus Christ' in color in a zigzag fashion on a wood panel, an available copy of which is given above. Starting from the Angelic Annunciation to Mary (on the top left), the portrait presents 17 events of the Life of Jesus culminating with Ascension of the Risen Christ (on the bottom left). It is a unique and interesting masterpiece by Solomon in multi-color.

v) St. John's Gospel: A Gallery of Hieratic Art

A genuine sequel to 'Liberation in Luke's Gospel' didn't appear until after four decades. At last, '*St. John's Gospel: A Gallery of Hieratic Art*' was published in 2010, as a fitting sequel and a grand culmination of Solomon's published works on art. While Liberation series are 12 different accounts on a single theme - all from Luke's Gospel, the present series are 13 images on different themes - all from John's Gospel.

John's Gospel is rich with imagery and symbols, and Solomon fondly calls it 'the Gospel with images and symbols.'[129] Whereas the Synoptics used parables,

129 Solomon Raj, P.: *St. John's Gospel,* (2010:7).

John used symbols. This must have inspired Solomon to come up with his creative and colorful icons in John's Gospel and he "takes us beyond the verbal imagery to see what eyes of faith can see through his art."[130] Solomon has done these woodcuts in color in 2009. Five of the 'I AM' sayings of Jesus are used in these woodcuts. The remaining eight are symbols and scenes from John's Gospel related to Jesus, His words and works. An analytical review of each of these works is presented, with reproductions facilitating ready access.

The Door

The first image is *The Door*. As Solomon did this, he wrote his instant reflection, as a matching meditation - not a philosophical jargon but an intimate and personal application, with fresh realization of the purpose of a door:

> The door is open for me
> To go in and hide my head from danger.

This image was not a closed door, but an open door - with new avenues and treasures opening up for those who enter in. There is also the picture of a shepherd at the entrance, signifying the great Good Shepherd, Who feeds and guards. There

130 David Zersen: "Solomon Raj and his Johannine Icons", *St. John's Gospel* (2010:15).

is a fountain springing from the threshold of the door, signifying the 'still waters' where the Shepherd leads the sheep.[131] Solomon mentions the deep symbolic meaning of bread, water, and light: "Water is a very old and widespread symbol, a symbol for cleansing, cooling, and quenching the thirst."[132] The symbolic use of 'water' is found not only in Solomon's art but also in his poetry and lyrics.[133]

Solomon identifies himself with a 'wandering wayfarer' who finds the 'door' 'after a long journey'. What a safety and what a solace he finds as the door is sighted:

> My limbs are tired and sore
> I come through the open door
> There is no fear to me any more.

Though the door is there all the time, it is the moment when it is found that brings in the joy in the journey to those who desperately needed it! It is a personally fulfilling search, which ushers in the realization: "My Lord, You are the door"!

Yes, He is in deed 'the door of the sheep', and "If anyone enters by Me, he will be saved, and will go in and out and find pasture."[134] A door always opens up opportunities, and Jesus, as the door, ensures opportunity, even a second chance for one and all - including the frustrated. We see a staff also on the Shepherd's shoulder -'the rod and the staff', they sure do comfort the 'wandering wayfarer'!

The Bread from Heaven

Solomon conveys a three-fold message through the second image, *The Bread from Heaven*. The bread and the cup are pictured here, but more significantly portrayed is the 'Giver' of the Bread. It should be rightly so - for He "gives food to all flesh."[135] In the lower part of the picture, the hungry folks flock to the Giver for bread - for their sustenance. They rejoice as they receive from His bounty. The kind of food peoples eat may differ - "rice, gruel, or bamboo roots" - but the Source remains the same. The clouds at the top are symbolic of the source of the

---

131 The prophetic vision of Ezekiel also comes to mind with 'water flowing from under the threshold of the temple toward the east'.

132 Solomon Raj, P., *St. John's Gospel, (*2010:8).

133 Sumita Roy in her Foreword to *Geetha Malika* rightly remarks: "'Water' is used as a recurrent symbol. In a poem reminiscent of the *dohas* of Kabir, Solomon writes:
Can we keep any water
In broken cisterns, my soul?
Consider it right to seek the feel of the Lord
And get the fullest joy."

134 John 10:9 (NKJV). Nashville: Thomas Nelson, Inc., (1997:1782).

135 Psalm 136:25 (NKJV), (1997:1018).

bread pointing to the heavens; for, "Every good gift and every perfect gift is from above, and comes down from the Father..."[136]

Secondly, Solomon interprets the Sacrament by means of this image. In addition to physical sustenance, Solomon takes us beyond and talks about restoring of souls through the sacrament. The meal that heals and restores is aptly portrayed:

> Lord You are the bread of life
> We partake in your broken body
> The life-giving bread
> In the sacramental meal
> To get our souls restored.

Finally, the message: "Man must not live on bread alone but on every word that comes from the mouth of God."[137] Solomon points out that this life-giving Word, the 'rhema' from the mouth of the Lord is the guide and the standard for our lives 'as we sojourn on this planet'.

---

136 James 1:17 (NKJV), (1997:2105).

137 Matthew 4:4, *HCSB,* (2016:672).

The Vine and the Branches

In one of His 'I AM' sayings, Jesus said, "I am the true vine"[138] and He hastens to tell about the vineyard keeper, who is none other than His Father. He doesn't stop there, but proceeds to talk about His disciples: "I am the vine; you are the branches". Jesus not only relates the Father to Himself and to the vine, enunciating the Father's role as the 'vineyard keeper'. He relates Himself to the disciples as they are connected to Him as 'branches'. Solomon beautifully portrays this word-picture here:

The vine and its branches
Together and not apart from each other
Lord You are the vine
And we are the branches
Unless we abide in you, we cannot bear fruit
Let us abide in You and bear fruit in plenty
And live abundantly for eternity.

There is a proclamation and a prayer in this verse: proclamation of the togetherness of the vine and its branches, of our identity as connected to the vine, and of our fruit-bearing status as we abide in Him; and, prayer seeking His enabling help to abide in Him, to 'bear fruit in plenty' and to 'live abundantly for eternity'.

138 John 15:1, *HCSB,* (2016:752).

Often we hear about word-pictures such as these from the Bible,[139] but very rarely do we come across picturization of these before our eyes. The creative genius of Solomon is uniquely employed here to present the message graphically and visually.

The Shepherd

This image portrays the incessant search of the Lukan shepherd for the lost sheep. This portrait of the caring shepherd reaching down to the lost sheep takes us to another 'I AM' saying of Jesus: "I am the good shepherd."[140] Solomon's reflection on this woodcut is well expressed:

> The Shepherd who keeps me
> Shall never fall asleep -
> Still waters, green pastures,
> Oil for my wounded and bleeding head
> A rod and a staff to protect me -
> His call I have heard
> My good shepherd, I belong to his herd.

This reflection embeds couple of Psalms in describing shepherd's care. As shepherd, He keeps us, and shall never fall asleep; and this role He fulfills vigilantly and watchfully:

> Your Protector will not slumber.
> Indeed, the Protector of Israel
> Does not slumber or sleep.[141]

Again Psalm 23, the 'Shepherd Psalm', describes the manner the Shepherd leads, and this too is expressed in Solomon's reflection. While we see in the Shepherd Psalm 'You anoint my head with oil', Solomon probably alludes to wars and bloodshed in the reign of King David as well. Thus oil symbolizes not only the joys of coronation, but also the consolation from a soothing balm.

139 As we see this image, another wood-block print by Solomon Raj comes to mind. It is on the 'Jesse's Rod' where the image of infant Jesus is seen as part of the tree at the top of the stump – Jesus Christ as the Son of David, Jesse's Rod.

140 John 10:11, *HCSB,* (2016:748).

141 Psalm 121:3-4, *HCSB,* (2016:428).

This is already one of the Psalms with most personal application and an intimate 'I-Thou' relationship. As such this description adds depth to one's personal experience as the Shepherd administers 'Oil for my wounded and bleeding head' - in addition to the still waters, green pastures and a rod of protection.

Finally, Solomon makes a personal confession on his relationship with the Shepherd: "His call I have heard / My good shepherd, I belong to His herd." That the Shepherd calls and that Solomon has heard His Call is declared above. His proven goodness and Solomon's assured commitment are indicated in the last line: "Let me learn to walk before I run and let me sit with you and learn before I talk about you with others". Solomon's Batik 'He Said 'Go' which presents His Call, is one of his globally known masterpieces of art.

The Blowing Wind and Sprouting Seed

This woodcut presents the twin images of *The Blowing Wind and Sprouting Seed*, with rich symbolism. The three-fold image of wind, egg and the seed - symbolizes life, growth and progress. The wind, by its primary nature, blows - sometimes gently and other times wildly. When gentle it brings delight; when wild it brings dread. Solomon picturizes another dimension of wind's function, which makes it an agent of progress:

The wind blows and
fills the boat sails
The boats go forward
I hear its roaring sound

As the blowing wind fills the sails, the boat goes forward; how hard the progress when the wind is static and unfavorable!

The Poetic Muse of Solomon, with all certainty, hears its roaring sound - though its origin and destination are never seen. Solomon beautifully communicates this propelling role of the wind in the upper part of the portrait. He talks about the seed, pictured in the lower part of the portrait, and portrayed in a couplet:

The seed sprouts gently,
breaking the earth
And it grows to become a tree some day.

What a life-giving potential in a tiny seed and what a potential for growth! These two images are sandwiched by another image: 'The egg hatches and a living chic emerge'.

Solomon's imaginational faculties soar, as he amplifies the teaching of Jesus Christ on New Birth. There is the simple proclamation about the course of wind that none can tell for sure. Finally there is the ultimate proclamation that 'new life' is nothing else but 'the gift of the Great One alone'.

The Word

In this image, Solomon portrays the nature and purpose of the Incarnation. As '*the Word primordial*', the Word was co-eternal with God the Father, and was equally active in creation.[142] Therefore, the Word who was with God was rightly called '*Co-creator with God*'.

142 Primordial comes from two Latin words *primus*, meaning "first" and *ordiri*, "to begin." So this means "first of all, original. When something is primordial, it has existed since the earliest time...".
www.vocabulary.com/dictionary/primordial - accessed on March 23, 2018.

Vachah, the Word primordial
That Word who was with God and
Co-creator with God
He who once became incarnate
So we may live in fellowship with Him
He who died once and rose again
He lives from eternity to eternity
The Alfa and the Omega.

The Word '*once became incarnate*', with the purpose - '*So we may live in fellowship with Him*'. The estranged relationships, as sin marred them, are resolved and restored - All made possible because the Incarnate Word '*died once and rose again*'. The Scroll in blue rolling down from above is symbolic of The Word Who took flesh and dwelt among us.

The crown of thorns on the head symbolically indicates the suffering and death the Incarnate Word had to undergo to accomplish '*fellowship with Him*' for the fallen humans. The cross was not an after thought, but part of God's eternal plan: 'The Lamb slain from the foundation of the world.'[143] But crucifixion is followed by resurrection; He rose again and lives forever. As '*He lives from eternity to eternity*', He is '*the Alfa and the Omega*'.

Though this woodcut is named '*The Word*', Solomon references to the Creator God and the Comforter God - the other two persons of the Godhead. The dove, pictured close to the ear, is symbolic of the Holy Spirit - speaking into the ears of the Son of Man. The last couplet adores the Triune God in worship:

I worship thee
O, God the One in Three.

Water of Life

This image touches base with the universal predicament of thirst:

Thirst unquenched
Dryness and draught
People die of incessant thirst.

In the midst of dryness and draught, '*People die of incessant thirst.*'[144] We see Jesus, the Son of Man at the well, as he felt thirsty. Jesus uttered on the cross, 'I thirst'! His thirst is physical as well as spiritual, in both the instances. Solomon hastens to talk about the '*Water of Life*':

143 Revelation 13:8, NKJV, (1997:2185).

144 'Safe Drinking Water for All' is a universal concern of all times. People of all faiths do all they can to quench people's thirst, especially in summer and other seasons of draught.

Lord Jesus, you once got thirsty too
For a cup of water
But you indeed are the deep fountain
Of Living Water

Jesus and the woman at the well is a frequent theme with Solomon and there are innumerable pieces of his art on this theme. His main concern in poetry or pictures is to depict the purpose of the incarnation - concern for the fallen and the downtrodden. In his own social context Solomon was aware of the plight of Dalits and the Protestant Christians of Andhra Pradesh.

This portrait is a vivid specimen for contextualization as the Samaritan woman is seen in the garbs of an Indian woman. Jesus introduced Himself to her as the giver of living water, and revealed that the water He gives will become 'a fountain of water springing up into everlasting life.'[145] Solomon alludes to this and extols Jesus as 'the deep fountain of living water ever springing, ever flowing'. The waters above in the portrait are symbolic of the living water Jesus gives. This eternal source makes this water satiable. In the last couplet, as with the Samaritan woman, Solomon implores the 'fountain of Living Water':

145 John 4:14, NKJV, (1997:1766).

Lord, give me that water
So that I never thirst again.

The King

This image of *The King* portrays the jubilant scene of the triumphal entry of Jesus. The King however appears 'meek and lowly', riding on an ass. The image of a crown of thorns, looming in the background, foreshadows the King's impending suffering. The symbols in John's Gospel are "not used narratively but symbolically". We do not see the crowd here but just a single individual - probably to indicate how the crowd would desert this King shortly. Solomon purposely opts for a symbolic presentation, rather than literal or historical interpretation:

> "I tried to express this symbolic aspect of the image in pictures like 'The Coming King' where the crown of thorns is not a historic part of the 'Triumphant entry into Jerusalem' story. But I added the crown of thorns also as a symbol in the background in the sky. Those who know the story see the crown of thorns in this context as a symbol and not what is happening here."[146]

Solomon ruminates the annals of human history, marked by rise and fall of kings and kingdoms. While "Kings have come and kings have gone [and] Kingdoms have risen and set", he looks to the King of kings and extols that His kingdom never ends. Yet, it's revealing and remarkable that this King never called

146 Solomon Raj, P.: *St. John's Gospel,* (2010:8).

Himself a king. He is, however, characterized by His victory in the spiritual realm: "You who conquered Sin, Death and the World"! Such a King has a claim on our souls and our all. Solomon rightly acknowledges Him and invites Him:

> Come, O King of kings
> Make your throne in my heart
> And never from there depart.

The Seeker and Savior

This image portrays the woman caught in sin brought to the presence of Jesus, the Savior. Three men are standing tall in finding fault, pointing their fingers. Pictured with phylacteries[147] on their foreheads, they obviously symbolize the three classes of critics of the day - Pharisees, Sadducees and Scribes. Solomon graphically narrated the situation in the accompanying verse:

> A woman was caught in sin
> And the men who considered themselves righteous were outraged.
> Punishment -To be stoned to death.

The men, though equally culprits in the act of adultery, try to put it all on women, amounting to gender injustice. The way of the world is well expressed:

147 The phylacteries were cube shaped small leather cases wherein were the Scriptures from Exodus 13:1-10, 11-16 and Deuteronomy 6:4-9, 11:13-21.
See more at: www.scripturessay.com/what-were-the-phylacteries-that-the-pharisees-wore/#sthash.6DochUQS.dpuf – accessed March 23, 2018.

"They brought her to Jesus - They quoted the law books". At this juncture, the urge for justice and justification surges forth through the pen of Solomon: "Who is he who never sinned?"

Further, the cry for a better solution whereby a 'cure' is sought after:
Is there no solution?
Is there no cure
For sin, other than damnation?[148]

The Sacrament

This image depicts Jesus' baptism by John the Baptist seen in the Synoptic Gospels. Solomon includes it here in order to present the significance of this sacrament. This made its place into Johannine woodcuts because of Jesus' reference to being born of water in His discourse with Nicodemus. In addition to Jesus and John the Baptist in the waters, we see the symbol of dove, signifying the descending Holy Spirit. The symbol of the sun probably indicates the time of the day Jesus was baptized, and also the dawn of a new day when Jesus would enter public earthly ministry. It may further symbolize the sun of righteousness, personified in Jesus. Anyway, Solomon nails it down categorically: "Baptism is a sacrament, / An outward sign for an inward faith."

148 These lines bring to mind "Rock of Ages" - the famous hymn by Augustus Toplady, a follower of John Wesley. This hymn speaks of a "double cure," saving us from our two-fold problem before God - sin's guilt and sin's power:

Be of sin the double cure
Save from wrath and make me pure.

Beyond Luther's *Justification by Faith*, we come to Wesley's *Sanctification by Faith* in one's spiritual journey. When all is said and done, the sinner becomes the seeker in the forgiving and enlightening presence of the Savior. And, yes, there is a solution and there is a cure other than damnation, through forgiveness of sins wrought by the shed blood of Jesus Christ.

Solomon touches base with many issues that often divide people, driving them to diverse denominations:

> Water, still water, flowing water -
> Full immersion, symbolic immersion -
> Child baptism, adult baptism -
> A new birth through baptism -
> What was John the Baptist's baptism?
> Believers' baptism, how much belief
> Is adequate?
> How much water is sufficient?

Sounds funny, but what a wide arena in the realm of interpretation, bringing the body of believers to such crossroads? Sifting the non-essentials and clinging on to the essentials is the barometer of spirituality. An ecumenical orientation fosters unity in the midst of diversity! Solomon wisely remarks that we have never clearly seen what is right among all the questions that have been asked. The final essence, on the whole, is divine-human combine: "that man submits and God accepts".

The Healing Pond

This image is related to the man with infirmity for thirty-eight years. We see the pool and sick people on the bank, and an angel in the waters. But we do not see the paralytic man. The viewer has to assume he was there too along with the sick. The pool was known as "a pond, which gave people healing" - all conditional - "if some one steps in at the right time"! 'Right time' - is the key!

Solomon reflects about the man who remained there most of the time: "Was it paralysis? Or was he getting used to the luxury of the bed?" Bishop Peddi Victor Premasagar remarked about slavish mentality among the people of Israel. Though they were out of Egypt, it took forty years for Egypt to come out of them. Complacence is sharply pointed out here by Solomon as a sin, and there is a personal prayer for healing:

> Lord heal me from the sin
> Of complacence
> A nagging hopelessness
> An acceptance of 'fate' as they call it.

There is a sound reason for making such a prayer:

> "I ask because with you
> There is a promise and assurance
> Of a wholeness and new life in abundance."

Trinity

This image is a unique attempt to portray the three persons of the Godhead. Here we see only the form of the Son - as He "became flesh and dwelt among us", and as specifically portrayed by a crown of thorns. But the rest we find are symbols such as hand, fish and dove. The Dove of course represents the Holy Spirit. The Father is represented by the symbol of hand, which signifies His omnipotence.

There is a sign on the palm of the hand, like an eye - the all-seeing eye. He is called יאר לא (El-Roi) - The God Who Sees.[149] The researcher feels that it must be an eye rather than wound, because eye is the only image in this woodcut on Trinity that represents the Father God. We also have another symbol - a fish with five Greek letters, pronounced as *ichthus*. The five letters, ΙΧΘΥΣ stand for five words, **Ἰ**ησοῦς **Χ**ριστός, **Θ**εοῦ **Υ**ἱός, **Σ**ωτήρ - meaning Jesus Christ Son of God Savior. *Ichthus* in Greek means fish, which had become a symbol of faith of the Early Church believers.

The mystery of the Trinity, or Tri-Unity is seen as "Three in One and One in Three while unending ages run". It is beautifully expressed as a "heavenly arithmetic". Though the Trinitarian formula is a mystery, it is never a myth.

The dynamics of knowing, believing, understanding and experiencing this mystery saves it from becoming a myth:

By knowing only we know this
We know only because we believe
We understand because we experience.

Resurrection and Life

The last work is a fitting finale of Christian faith and existence. We see the tomb and the stone that covers, and also the lifeless body within. There are also the images of hand - symbolic of the mighty hand of God, and lotus - symbolic of life.[150] In one of Solomon's well known woodcuts we see the tall lotus flower as the sure symbol of resurrection.

There is a long discourse in Solomon's reflection for this with three sections:

1) Philosophical questions about death and after;

149 The sign on the palm also looks like a wound - the nail-pierced mark. If so, it must be symbolizing the crucified Son of God.

150 It has been a powerful image and a spiritual symbol in many cultures through the ages. It is also considered a sacred flower in Hinduism, Buddhism and Egyptian religions. "Among its many meanings and significance, the lotus is a symbol of "spontaneous" generation, and so it also represents divine birth, spiritual development and creation itself". http://www.harekrsna.de/Lotus-FLower.htm - accessed March 23, 2018.

2) Biblical accounts of those raised from the dead; and,
3) Christ's Resurrection and His abiding presence.

In the first section, what happens after death is explored, by many questions:

Does the 'soul' leave the body at the time one dies?
Like one leaves the garment once in a while?
And does the soul join the body again
after floating around for a long time?

Or does it come back from the *pitruloka*
the land of the fathers
through the cloud and the rain and seed of soil
Or stay away in the *Devaloka,* the land of gods?
Or does it take a new body of glory
And lives for ever?

None of these questions have a solid answer, as there are many postulations leading to unending speculations. In his earlier series too,[151] Solomon dealt with the subject of death in the last work, and probes into similar questions:

In the second section, Biblical accounts of those raised from the dead are given to explore possible answers, if any, from this particular group - Lazarus of Nazareth, the widow's son, And the daughter of Jairus. But "None of them has told us what it was like / after death and what they saw / in the 'other world'."

In the third section, Solomon reflects about Christ's Resurrection and His abiding presence, and envisages an assuring answer:

But Christ rose from the dead
He appeared to his disciples
Showed his new body
And told them
Behold I shall be with you
for ever and where I am
there you shall also be.

---

151 Solomon Raj, P.: *Liberation in Luke's Gospel,* (1996:33).
At the time of death
where does the soul make its journey?
to the land of the fathers,
or the land of Gods?
Into the night or into the day?
Into the cloud or into the lightning?
Into the full moon or the new moon?
Into the dark fortnight
of [sic] the bright fortnight?

In this last section, Solomon establishes some eternal truths concerning life after death: there will be a new body; and, an eternal destination in His abiding presence. In the concluding lines of *Gentle Brother Death*, Solomon responds with an assuring answer.[152]

This journey through the Gallery of Hieratic Art has come to a happy ending. Hieratic means "extremely formal or stylized, as in a work of art" and Solomon elucidates why he called these images hieratic.[153] Solomon was confident:

> "some of these symbols, which I am using in my art work, will speak to those in my culture who are not Christians. Our culture is full of imagery and stories".

The color and the content, often mingled with rich symbolism, takes the viewers beyond "the verbal imagery to see what eyes of faith can see through his art."[154] As Megumi Yoshida judiciously remarked,

> Solomon Raj has been seeking to do theology in his Indian pluralistic contexts standing up for the weaker in society with his deep Christian faith in God. … (His) art works have a very warm atmosphere, comforting people, especially those who are struggling and suffering.[155]

Is there a new hermeneutic of the Johannine message? The 'Word become flesh' still incarnates through diverse media in the midst of different cultures and creeds - among all nations and generations!

vi) Biblia Pauperum

'Biblia Pauperum', means *'Paupers' Bible'* - the Bible of the Poor. It was a genre of Bible instruction in the early church. Priests of the medieval times used it to explain the relationship between New Testament and Old Testament, to common people. The most important thing is the typological Bible teaching - taking a

---

152 *Liberation in Luke's Gospel,* (1996:33).
We do not know all the answers
But we surely believe
That death is the doorway
To a new life
More glorious and more wonderful.

153 Solomon Raj, P.: *St. John's Gospel: A Gallery of Hieratic Art,* (2010:9).
First of all, these are very special word pictures not quickly to be interpreted like parables for example … These images may be called cryptic and highly stylized. I also tried to put these word images of St. John in somewhat stylized woodcut images, not narrative but symbolic.

154 David Zersen: "Solomon Raj and his Johannine Icons", *St. John's Gospel,* (2010:11-18).

155 Joshida, Megumi: "Abundant Grace of God in Dr. P. Solomon Raj's Art Images", *St. John's Gospel,* (2010:56).

person or event from New Testament and relating the same to a corresponding type from Old Testament.

The global itineration of Solomon Raj came to a halt probably after his Bali visit in 1998 due to advancing years. Hans Ruedi Weber causally remarked in 1991 that Solomon's work with woodcuts reminds one of *Biblia Pauperum.* This commendation proved to be prophetic as it "started a new fire in my heart", Solomon recounts, and the ultimate outcome was his *Biblia Pauperum.* The 'Solomon Predicament' never leaves any known media of communication untouched, and so he took up the task and produced this significant work.

His *Biblia Pauperum* was published in 2008, and the impact of his work has been felt across the nations soon. With ten triptychs, the Biblical message was amply portrayed and communicated through visual arts. As Prof. David Zersen rightly remarked,[156] this was "the culmination of a lifetime of creative attempts to communicate the Gospel."[157]

Solomon Raj - As A Poet

Scholars have acknowledged the contribution of Solomon to theology and art. Prof. Ravela Joseph and Prof. Busi Suneel Bhanu in their *Bibliography of Original Christian Writings in India in Telugu* acknowledged Solomon Raj to be one of the original Christian writers in Telugu. They have listed out a handful[158] of his earliest works from 1957-1978. The most significant writings of Solomon in Telugu are his varied attempts to bring out his reflections on different religious themes through different literary forms. All these works are unique literary exercises (*prakriyas*), each requiring special skill and hard work.

i) Puja Mandiram

Meaning 'House of Worship', this was a *dwipada kaavya* - verse in couplets - a poetic expression of I-Thou relationship between a devotee and his God.[159] Need for personal devotional life is emphasized without neglecting congregational worship. Solomon metaphorically names his heart as a 'temple of worship' with the refrain:

> Lord, I make my heart a temple
> To offer my worship to You!

Extoling Tagore's *Gitanjali* and Thomas à Kempis' *The Imitation of Christ*, Solomon expresses his longing for more such devotional literature as he pens *Puja Mandiram*.

ii) Veda Vinodini

Meaning 'Scriptural Amusement', this is a *Samasyapurana Kavyam*, answering a riddle. A unique creation with last line of each stanza posing a riddle, the answer is to be filled in the preceding three lines.[160] This is a *Sataka* (a composition of

---

156 P. Solomon Raj: *Biblia Pauperum:* The Poor Man's Bible, Bangalore: Asian Trading Corporation, (2008:11).

157 P. Solomon Raj: *Biblia Pauperum:* The Poor Man's Bible, (2008:11).

158 *"How to Study the Bible", "Story Telling" (Katha Paddati), "Wild Flowers" (Adavi Poolu), "A Theological Dictionary", "Christ, the King of Kings" (Raraju Kristhu),* and *"Puja Mandiramu".* "Wild Flowers", a Christian devotional with 22 meditations, was published with an Introduction by the then Moderator of Church of South India, N.D. Ananda Rao Samuel.

159 Originally published in 1978 by CLS, it was later reprinted in 1999 with three additional poems at the end, and a critical foreword by Fr. Jayabalan.

160 One example goes like this:
Problem - The light that a wise man could not see, an ass had seen! Solution - Humans sometimes cannot see the ways of God like Prophet Bilam could not see the light ahead, but his ass could see.

hundred poems) with a difference - a rare literary exercise in Christian literature. First of its kind, it presents good humor and amusement in acquisition of Biblical knowledge.

iii) Eeshodaharanamu

Meaning 'Illustration of Jesus', this is *Udaaharana Kaavyam* - an illustrative poetic exercise in portraying Jesus with a metrical poem and two songs, each addressed to Christ. It is a captivating call to Jesus in each of the seven case endings (*Sashtyanthas*) of Christ's name in Telugu. This is a very rare and high-class literary feat, following the tradition of great Hindu poetic works like *Basavodaharanam.* There was only one other Christian poet, Balli Purushotham, who wrote in this genre, *Treikodaharanam.*[161] Two other works by Solomon were published later: *Kim Kartavyam* and *Gana Kusumalu.*[162]

iv) Kim Kartavyam: Yakshagana Samputi

Meaning 'What Task?'[163] - This is a collection of five *yakshaganas,* (classical dance dramas).[164] *Kim Karthavyam* was staged in many cities of India. It was really "a break-through of all times in Indian Christian circles. Using the *kuchipudi* style, a famous local form of Hindu dance, Solomon created a unique form of communicating the Christian message."[165]

In his early nineties Solomon set himself to vigorous writing again in Telugu poetry and published three works: *Daiva Gnana Siri, Upamana Malika, and Paul Gerhardt Kirthana Sahityamu.* The researcher had the opportunity of editing them all, with a review for each. Since the last work above is a collection of Gerhardt's hymns rendered into Telugu, it is treated in the later section. Now an analysis of the first two:

---

161 Dass Babu: *Andhra Christian Hymnal (Telugu) Biographies of the 29 Poets and Their Messages,* Vijayawada: Global Telugu Christian Ministries, (2014:298).

162 Since *Gana Kusumalu* is a collection of Solomon's lyrics and hymns, they will be treated later in another section.

163 Amrutha Vani originally published it, though St. Luke's Lalit Kala Ashram later released it in 2001.

164 Other Yakshaganas in this collection include:
- i) *Chemanthi Chenu* (Jasmine Field based on Judgment scene of goats and sheep)
- ii) *Shanti Pathamu* (Dance drama on the prayer of St. Francis of Assisi)
- iii) *Charukesa Vilasamu* (Dance drama on the story of Samson and Delilah)
- iv) *Kreesthu Janana Vilasamu* (Dance drama on Nativity)

165 B. S. Moses Kumar: 'Liturgical Interests and Lyrical Innovations of Pulidindi Solomon Raj: An Experiment at Indigenization' in Praveen et al, ed: *The Yobel Spring,* Vol. 2, Delhi: ISPCK/ ACTC, (2014:434).

v) Daiva Gnana Siri

Meaning 'Treasure of Divine Wisdom', this is an anthology of 157 poems on 'Prayers and Proclamations' published on Solomon's 91st birthday. The shrewdness of his imagination, and his simplicity in expressing profound truths from the Word of God are richly manifested. Solomon portrays the didactic value of poetic literature, in relation to Biblical narratives and proverbs. Expressing Biblical truths in native phrase and cultural idiom makes it relevant and revelatory. Solomon elucidates the necessity of the 'incarnation of the Gospel in Indian culture' here. To read Biblical narratives in simple verse, to enable listeners have the benefit of lucid understanding, and to engage the audience in fruitful interaction for better appreciation - all this entails the didactic purpose of this anthology.

The addition of 29 *shashtyantas* at the end makes this a rare volume. Prof. K. Anandan remarks that it is common to write six *shashtyantas* addressed to the Patron of a *kaavya,* but the way Solomon added 29 *shashtyantas*, in profuse praise of his Lord is unique.[166] A couple of *'Dandakas'* at the end makes it conspicuous. Solomon maneuvers his pen, imagination, and capacity at *vaividhya* with great ease. These two *Dandakas* are gems in the gallery of Telugu Christian literature. A *dandaka*[167] is primarily a devotional expression.

Innovating new means of expressing his devotion to God and proclaiming his faith became Solomon's life-style. It was not exactly known when he initiated writing *Shashtyantas* and *Dandakas*. But it had been with him for more than a decade. Six of the *Shashtyantas* herein were written long ago, and appended to *Kim Kartavyam.*[168] Solomon also wrote and included a *Dandaka* in the above book, at the end of '*Kreesthu Janana Vilasam*'. He is the only Christian poet to have penned *Dandakas.*

vi) Upamana Malika

'*Upamana Malika: Parables of Lord Jesus*' is a collection of Solomon's Poetry on parables. He explains how oral culture prevailed in every society, aiding communication through songs, proverbs and stories. This work deals with twenty

166 Solomon narrates the 'what' and 'why' of *shashtyantas* in his Introduction. Of the seven prepositions in Telugu literature, the sixth one (*kin, kun, yokka,* etc.) when applied to God, the Lord, or Christ, becomes a word of worship, praise and prayer. These words used with the sixth preposition, in poems, describe Christ's attributes and works, and these are poems of praise.

167 Solomon explains the meaning and purpose of '*dandaka*':
Dandaka is a prayer to different gods, and is a literary style of poetry seen in Sanskrit and Telugu languages. There are many famous *dandakas* in Telugu literature written by well-known authors at different times, addressed to different gods of the Hindu pantheon. The ever-innovative mind of Solomon Raj spurred him to pen a couple of *dandakas* in profuse praise of Jesus Christ.

168 Solomon Raj, P.: *Kim Kartavyam,* (2001:80-82).

parables in reflective poetry! Each parable is skillfully introduced or summarized with profound reflection.

Parables are a unique means of Jesus' instruction, and "without a parable He did not speak to them."[169] The purpose of a parable is to convey a single truth, and Solomon focuses on Jesus' message in the parables through his reflective verse. He opines that reading or singing these parables in poetry would bring joy and delight. More attractive, and easier to remember, they help in better appreciation of the Word, and aid in sharing the Gospel. Solomon envisions that the parables Jesus taught would become stepping-stones to heaven (*paralokamunaku sopanambulu*). Elsewhere he acknowledges them as adequate signposts good enough to open our eyes (*Neevichu suktikathalu chalunu maadu kannulu deruva).*

Solomon communicated profound Scriptural truths, with an unusual ease in Telugu verse. Countless truths are communicated as words of wisdom, adding didactic value to this writing. In the process of enunciating parables, we often come across a 'conversational mode' Solomon employs, whereby he reasons with God on what seems a puzzle, or affirms God on things justifiable. The way the poet engages God in a dialogue is unique. This human-divine conversational mode ensures an intimate 'I-Thou' relationship with God. This pattern of reflective verse has been interwoven throughout the text. The conversational mode is also seen at interpersonal level where the poet reasons with readers on the ways of God. This dialogical mode ensures continuity in the whole work, making it readable.

Solomon Raj - As A Lyricist and A Hymn Writer

Apart from poetry, Solomon is known for his lyrics and hymns in Telugu, later rendered into English. He composed some songs in English while at Sambalikan, and translated Gerhardt's hymns and Greek hymns from English into Telugu. With considerable knowledge in theory, he wrote many essays on Song traditions, presented in academies and journals. This section will explore his works with lyrics and hymns.

i) Gaana Kusumaalu

Gana Kusumalu (Song Flowers) was a lyrical composition in Telugu with 50 songs, published in 2002. Set to music, and produced with professional artistes for radio broadcast through *Suvartha Vaani* (Voice of the Gospel) - Some of them had become popular household lyrics. Almost every cross section of the Telugu Christian populace around the world used to sing some of them, though they never knew who wrote these famous and familiar songs. "And this work is a culmination of Bhakti flowing through the twin stream of *sahitya* and *sangeetha* - beautiful verse put in melodious tune - refreshing many a wearied soul as they sing or listen to these songs".

169 Mark 4:34 (NKJV).

Most of them were written over four decades ago, and have stood the test of time! These songs in the book and the new ones are as fresh in depth and meaning today, as when written.

The devotion or feeling of oneness of humans, which recognizes the greatness of God and endeavors to express it in terms of praise and adoration, is what we call *Bhakti*. It is used in combination of another word, *prapathi*, which means utter dependence on God. *Gaana Kusumaalu* is one of the outstanding examples of *Bhakti Sahitya*[170] in Telugu. The major theological themes dealt are the Father God, the Incarnate Son, and the hope of glory. The very first song of the book "*The Destiny*" beautifully encompasses these three themes with rich Indian imagery.

The Father God

Solomon begins his song with the words, "O, our Father, God in heaven" confessing simultaneously His immanence as found in 'our Father' and at the same time His transcendence expressed in the words, 'God in heaven'. Such a transcendental God, at the same time, is approachable as experienced and expressed by Solomon in a We-Thy relationship: *We* chant *thy* sacred name.

The Incarnate Son

The Incarnation of Jesus Christ was possible not merely due to the will of the Father God but also because of the willingness of the Incarnate Son, who chose to empty Himself. Solomon extols the Incarnate Son as He rejected His glorious state (*mahimaasthali*) in order to be born into this world and show the way for humans to find a deathless destiny:

... You cleared the way
For us to reach the realms of
The deathless worlds.

We find beautiful Indian imagery when Solomon seeks the Lord's help:

In the blessed vicinity of Your lotus feet. Help us to live there ...

170 Moses Kumar: 'Bhakti Sahitya from the Heart of Solomon Raj' in *Geetha Malika*, (2010:94). *Pasidikanthulu* (The Golden Rays) cassette was produced in 1970's with 8 songs and another cassette of 8 songs, *Premajyothi Yesu Gaana Kusumaalu* (Song Flowers of Jesus, the Light of Love) was released about the same time. Prabhudeva Ministries in Vijayawada released an MP3 CD, *Golden Hits of Rev. Dr. P. Solomon Raj* with forty-five songs on Solomon's 60th Wedding Anniversary in 2006. There are 11 new compositions.

A word derived from Sanskrit root *bhaj, bhakti* means to revere. It connotes respectful devotion marked by intense personal attachment to God, which springs for a Christian from an unshakable trust in an awesome and adorable God. There is the dynamics of *Saameepya* (nearness or intimacy) between God and the devotee building bridges and ensuing I-Thou relationship.

The 'lotus feet' is a beautiful picture describing the feet of God, with refuge-worthiness for a devotee.

This imagery of lotus[171] is used several times as it meant much to Solomon. In "*The Love Song*" (No. 8), Solomon wants to touch His blessed lotus feet. In "*The Three Kings of the East*" (No. 23), Solomon identifies himself with the Wise Men and bring his 'body and mind: "To offer them to You at Your holy lotus feet ..." Elsewhere, in another song, Solomon calls the Lord:

> "And the Lord of the lotus feet
> Will all my needs then meet."

The Hope of Glory

Solomon beautifully expresses his strong faith and hope in *the realms of the deathless worlds*:

> Do Thou shed upon us
> Your shalom Till at the end we stand with
> You In the regions where there are no tears.

He invokes God, describing Him as the Ocean of Love, to come and receive him with His outstretched arms into heaven's haven of life on the last leg of life's journey. With an unshakable trust in the Lord, Who prepares mansions for His beloved, Solomon expresses anticipation seeking His help at the end of our *walk on the earth.*[172]

These three themes above are skillfully interwoven throughout the *Gaana Kusumaalu*. "*Praise the Lord*" (No. 4) is another classical song in which all these major themes are embedded. God is portrayed as holy and adorable Creator, Who, in the beginning through the work of his Son,

> Made the earth and all the creatures therein
> Also the sun the moon and the stars in heaven
> And the various seasons for our good.

---

171 Lotus in Sanskrit is *padma* and is a symbol of purity in the midst of filth, primarily representing beauty and non-attachment. Having its roots in the mud it floats on the water without ever becoming wet or muddy. Above all other religious symbolism, Solomon obtains a new revelation from the lotus as it was suggestive of the resurrection of Christ and of the believer. The Loyola Press, a Jesuit Ministry, in an article on their web page, *Examples of How Jesus Has Been Pictured Throughout History,* clearly presents the depth of the meaning of the imagery of lotus in the art of Dr. P. Solomon Raj.
https://www.loyolapress.com/our-catholic-faith/family/catholic-teens/religious-art/how-jesus-has-been-pictured-throughout-history?p=1 - accessed March 25, 2018.

172 "Come Lord to us to stretch Your hand, And receive us to Your home, the deathless land. This we ask You, O God incarnate."

It is amazing that such omnipotent Creator calls us His dear children. Solomon then talks about the Son:

> Our Lord Jesus Christ, to wipe away our sin and the curse
> ... Became incarnate and the earth rejoiced.
> ... Who died for us on the cross and rose again from the dead.

The creedal confession was appropriately expressed above. Solomon praises the Holy Spirit, Who is the Lord and comforter, "Who makes us wise in life and leads us along the way / Guiding us now with none else to lead." In the original song in Telugu, there is a clear mention of Solomon's hope of glory when he writes on Jesus as the only adequate one to take us to His own abode on the last day (*tudi dinamandu tanadagu neravu jerpaga jaaluvaadu*).

ii) Geetha Malika

This collection was Solomon's translation of his 44 Telugu lyrics into English, published in 2010 - with 11 of his '*Songs from Sambalikan*' appended. The three-fold theme glanced in the previous section will be gazed upon in detail, as these foundational doctrines were interspersed throughout the songs.

The Father God

The Creation (No. 18) is a *bhajan* with some of the divine attributes of God:

O, Lord, our King and our God,
You alone are our shelter
From generation to generation

The lines below confessing relationship with Creator God form the Chorus:

Before the hills were ever made,
Before the earth was given its shape,
For ages and ages, You have been our God;
From generation to generation, You are our Lord.

The wonder of His creation and vanity of mortal life are depicted in following stanzas.[173] In the light of this revelation, Solomon makes a prayer at the end for grace to be wise stewards of life:

Lord, teach us to fear You,
And lead us with You in the paths of life.
Give us grace to serve You while we live
And receive us at the end into the realms where You live.

The Incarnate Son

Almost three-fourths of the songs deal with the theme of the Incarnate Son, touching a five-fold dimension of the Incarnation:

On His Name:

In *The Name of Jesus* (No. 19) Solomon praises His Name, which is sacred. This song in Telugu was chosen as Andhra Pradesh Convention[174] Song for 1974, and is included in Andhra Christian Hymnal.[175] With fitting tune and profound meaning, it became popular, being used in churches till today. This song declares that Jesus is the way, the only way to everlasting life:

For us to see the other side of life's journey
And cross the ocean of death
Jesus is the only way.

Having risen from death 'to give us His own life' … He 'Gave to us His own name'. Being our eternal contemporary,

173 O, God, You will beckon us to Your side
As our mortal abodes go into the clay
Like the green grass that sprouts in glory at dawn,
The human kind flourishes by Your grace for an hour.
But soon, in the next hour
They wither away and droop to the earth. (Psalm 90).

174 Andhra Pradesh Conventions were the biennial conventions held at Krishna River bank in Vijayawada by the Andhra Christian Council, for Telugu Christians of all denominations.

175 (No. 699) 2008 edition, Published by Prabodha Book Centre, Vijayawada.

Today our King and Keeper stands with us
As we walk our way along with Him
We sing praises all the way to Him.

In '*The Ray of Hope*' (No. 28), the Lord is shown as 'the hope of our ancient fathers' and so a prayer to Him:

Once our fathers walked in paths of tribulation
They never lost hope in their hearts
But with great courage and faith
They walked ahead and reached their goal.

The 'paths of tribulation' through which 'our fathers walked' might very well be the social isolation and ostracism of ancient times.[176] Solomon identifies with the precious faith of his fathers, and presents a picture of the prophetic vision of all creatures living together in harmony:[177]

You lead all people in Your fearless path,
Till the rulers of this earth bow down before You,
And all creatures live under the rule of love.
His reflections are enlightening.[178]

On His Birth

The Love Song (No. 8) envisages the purpose of the divine Incarnation: "To quench the flames of sin and curse, / To help to cast away the dread of death." Christ's Crucifixion is mentioned before the Incarnation. This may be to emphasize the purpose of the Incarnation - He was born to die![179]

---

176 Solomon must have been aware of the debilitating impact of caste system and the evil of 'untouchability' of those bygone days – when Christian and 'dalit' students were seated on separate benches. And he recollects how the predecessors had withstood the onslaught of social evils, and had persevered to see a new day 'where the mind is without fear, and the head is held high' – as envisioned by Rabindranath Tagore!

177 Isaiah 65:25

178 "Caste oppression is like a self-made prison. Liberation is much broader than destroying caste system. Part of our oppression was our laziness, our lack of 'entrepreneurial' nature." Solomon's thinking is different from Dalit theologians, but also liberative (See his Buddha image in batiks). He however, does not express his personal views on Dalits and their plight. Personal interview on 20th April 2010 at St Luke's Lalit Kala Ashram.

179 It was Bob Mumford who reminded that the cross was in the heart of God from the beginning, which was graphically seen in the very structure of the camp of the people of Israel during their journey in the wilderness. An aerial view of the camp of the different tribes, whenever and wherever they halted, clearly looked like a cross, which was a gentle reminder to God the Father of the inevitability of the Cross in the fullness of time.
See Spirit-Filled Life Bible for a diagram of the cross with relevant details. p. 193

In *The Morning Star* (No. 9), Solomon addresses the Star of Bethlehem, and pleads it five times: "Cast out the darkness and show us the way / … Lead us on till we draw near". Solomon then talks about the King, Whose birth the star points to, and Who had condescended Himself. It's all done in the third person singular in the third stanza and the fourth stanzas. Thinking about Him in a meaningful way, though in the third person, must have brought Solomon all of a sudden into the very presence of the Lord, wherein he could not but talk to Him personally in an intimate I-Thou relationship: "It is not possible, Lord, to offer gifts to You / Nor to try and earn Your favor ever / So I give my heart to You and worship, my Lord …"

In *My Eyes Do Glow* (No. 10), Solomon testifies, 'my eyes glow with joy' because of the Incarnation of Jesus.[180] In the last stanza, he extends his worship in grateful adoration and rejoices in the mystery of incarnation: "To Jesus who is born on this earth / To the Lord who has pitied our plight."

Descent from Heaven (No. 15) is another lyric on the wonder of the Incarnation. As Jesus made His dwelling among us, Solomon wonders how He transforms us. Solomon finally makes a plea to the Lord to visit us once again: "To make the withering earth / Bloom again with Your life-giving light / Shed Your rays on us again / Lord to seek and save us." Karanam Balasubrahmanyam Pille aptly remarked about a particular line in the last stanza wherein Solomon invokes the Lord to visit us once again 'since we went astray from Your path': *Daari tolagina mammunu veduka / Mariyokapari itu rave Deva.*[181] This, Pille remarks, reminds us of the Lord's parable of the lost sheep wherein the incessant longing of the Good Shepherd for the lost is well described.

'The Blessed Incarnation' (No. 16), is another lyric on the Incarnation. A beautiful invocation is found in the Chorus:

O merciful Lord, adorable God
Robed in righteousness and Prince of peace
Jesus our King worshipped by the Universe.

Solomon ponders about the various facets of the blessing endowed upon humankind by the Incarnate Lord: "…watching over the humankind. / … To fill the earth with endless peace / … To set to rest our woes on the earth." There's no wonder Solomon concludes: 'Who is there but You to show us the way?'

180 He left His heavenly home
To seek and save the sinners …
And therefore my eyes glow with joy.
The glorious Lord and the true Word
Came down to the earth as one like us;
And therefore my eyes glow with joy.

181 'Sahabhavana' in *Gaana Kusumaalu*, (2002:xiii).

'The Abode of Our Lord' (No. 21), portrays how life is transformed as one would approach the abode of my Lord: Lighted heart, flower in bloom, and quickened foot are symbols of a new life in God. All this is possible because, "The King Himself stooped down to earth …"

'The Baby Jesus' (No. 22), is another song on the Incarnation. Jesus is twice acknowledged as 'The ruler of the heavenly realms'. The purpose of the Incarnation is expressed in unmistakable terms: "to save us / To lead us on the path not straying / And take us safely home."[182]

'The Three Kings of the East' (No. 23), is another song on the Incarnation. Solomon graphically narrates the course Kings of the East have taken in paying 'homage to the King of kings' and declaring 'Him as the heavenly King'. Solomon then goes a step forward in personal application. Solomon aptly invokes personal devotion and takes the opportunity to worship the Lord seeking His perennial blessing:

For us to bring to You our body and mind
To offer them to You at Your holy lotus feet
With these our gifts to make devotion.[183]

'A Light to Lighten the Earth' (No. 24), is another exercise of Solomon in portraying the outstanding blessings for humanity with the dawn of the Star of the Lord. The refrain sums up the whole message: "As the brightest light shines in the sky / The gloom of the earth was cast away."

The broken hearts of the oppressed race
Got redeemed from nagging doubt and great despair …
The fear of death has been driven away.

Solomon describes the night that brought a total transformation to the destiny of humans when Jesus was born - in four stanzas of *'The Holy Night'* (No. 31) - on the earth, in the skies, in Mary's heart, and to the destinies of humans:

Silence ruled the whole creation
When God Himself became a man and was born on the earth.

182 In the last stanza, Solomon who witnesses 'The golden circle surrounding His head' - the nimbus we see in Christian art works - declares that it 'Is the great and glorious crown, To tell us that He is the King of kings', that He is indeed 'the ruler of the universe'!

183 Solomon tells elsewhere the traditional story of the wonderful golden chest he saw in KÖLN Cathedral in Cologne, Germany where people believe, the relics of the three wise men are kept.

A great star ... in the sky
Hosts of angels came down to earth
To sing praises and wake up men

... The mystery still lingered in her mind
The Holy Spirit still ruled in her heart

But the darkness of sin has fled in flight
The curse on mankind rolled away then...
When God Himself came down to the earth.

Jesus is portrayed as *The Son of Man* in this song (No. 29); yet, He is called: 'Merciful Lord, conqueror of death, The way of life and Savior divine'. For this reason, he prays to Him: 'Show Your mercy and save us, Lord!' In the second stanza, Solomon envisages the meaning in terms such as - incarnation, death on the cross, and cleansing from His blood. Finally, in view of the incidence of sin and the resultant curse and death, Solomon praises the Lord for what He has done: 'You opened the gates of eternal life!'[184]

In the song, *The Lord of the Children* (No. 37), Solomon portrays how children identify with the Incarnate Son of God, Jesus. They call Him their 'companion', their 'everlasting friend', their 'commander' and their 'ruler'. They also have Him as 'the leader on the earth leading us', 'the wayfarer walking with us here', 'the master showering His blessings' and as the one who 'shows us the path of righteousness'. They have a solid base for such an intimate relationship with Him.

'Nativity' (No. 39), is another masterpiece on the Incarnation of Jesus Christ, with the beauty of Incarnation pictured in a new imagery.

... Was born in the manger the Savior, our Lord
The incarnation of the Logos and the Son of God.

... Indeed He came to the earth as God's greatest gift
To reconcile God to man and stop the rift.

... Of the womb of Mary the blessed Mother, thrice virgin
Immanuel, that is God with us, humble, loving and lowly.[185]

184 For us humans You came to the earth
You died on the cross and rose again
By the blood which flowed from
Your side You cleanse us from our sins, O Lord!

185 The idea of Mary being thrice virgin comes to Solomon from Eastern Orthodox icons and their theology. They wanted to emphasize the particular doctrine that Mary had no other children. The artists, when they made the picture of Mater Theo (Mother of God), put three stars on her image to suggest that she was virgin before, during, and after the birth of Jesus Christ. Solomon, however, was not thinking of that doctrine here.

Finally, Solomon elucidates the purpose of Incarnation making a grand proclamation: "… to win the deadly fight / And reach the heavenly realms … / And by His advent to the earth / He has driven our fears away." Solomon affirms the doctrine of Trinity, when he states that we ever live with the Father, Him and the Holy Ghost.

> "The heavenly Guru by His light has put our fear to flight
> And He beckoned us to join and walk with the heavenly hosts
> Till at the end we ever live with the Father, Him and the Holy Ghost."

An alternative rendering of the above song is *The Brilliant Baby.*[186] The purpose of the Incarnation is beautifully enunciated here. Jesus, the matchless image of the glorious Creator is also portrayed as the great forgiver. Solomon portrays how the Desire of Ages further came to the earth. Sent as God's great gift, He came to give us heavenly gifts, and to declare the day of redemption and 'show the Father's mercy':

'*A Light to the Gentiles*' (No. 40) is another song on the event of Incarnation. The transforming impact of Incarnation on the whole creation is aptly expressed:

> "… The earth became lighted up
> Death itself became mortal
> Curse moved away."

The two-fold purpose of the Advent of Christ is seen in that it affects both the life on earth and the life after death.

'*The Song of the Angels*' (No. 41) is based on the familiar passage of Scriptures, wherein reverberates the twin purpose of the Incarnation:

> "Glory to God in the highest
> And Peace and well being
> To God's blessed ones on the earth."

The refrain singing "Glory to God in the highest" at the end of each stanza not only adds beauty to the song, but also gives a reason to glorify God. The words of this song, with which the angels announced the birth of Jesus, are heard today in all languages of the earth, where God's people worship Him. In the three stanzas of this song, Solomon gives three distinct reasons for ascribing Glory to God in the highest in a fitting manner.

On His Crucifixion

Eternal Life Flowing out of the Cross (No. 5) is a panegyric on the riches of the cross. Solomon poses six typically different questions in each of the first six stanzas, the answer for all being an emphatic NO. But in the last stanza, we see a resounding

186 *Geetha Malika*, (2010:147-148).

YES as an ultimate ANSWER to all the NO's of life - all because of the cross! Though the way of the cross is sorrowful, Solomon writes,

> "… only there can we find
> The water of life to quench our thirst
> And the life force to restore our dying souls.

This ultimate answer in the cross satisfies all the questions Solomon very searchingly posed in each stanza of this song.[187]

'*The Pillar of Sacrifice*' (No. 26) is another song on the Cross of Christ, expounding all that it had wrought for the humans. The chorus points the listeners to the premises of crucifixion, and they are enabled to ponder the miracles done through the cross experience of the Lamb of God as enumerated in each of the five stanzas.[188]

On His Resurrection

In '*The Resurrection Song*' (No. 12), Solomon enunciates the purpose of the resurrection from the dead in simple but profound terms: "To give us life and from death to save / Now and forever that life is ours in deed." Though this is basically a Resurrection Song, Solomon loses no opportunity to envisage the purpose of His Incarnation! Finally he extols the uniqueness of Jesus on account of His atoning sacrifice, and victory over sin and death!

---

187 … Where is the ray to brighten our path?
Where is the song to make our hearts glow?
… Where do we find waters to quench our thirst?
And save us from the dread of parching death?
… Where is the bloom to sooth our tired body?
And where is the healing wind to our sickened soul?
… Where are the soothing wasps of wind to cool our hearts
And to renew our hope?
… Where is the possible shelter?
Wherein to hide our heads?
Where do we find a little light,
To lead our steps slowly along the way?

188 In the world … cursed with sin
And where it was thrown in the abyss of death
There dear Jesus …
Laid His life and died on the cross …
In agony which no one had ever did suffer
He died for us and yet He lives forever …
Through His death to give us heavenly bliss
And bring to us God's forgiveness …
He came to bring us to God again
And to bliss with which He always fills …
Jesus our Lord brought His great salvation
And between God and man a great reconciliation.

Another song on Resurrection is '*Sing with the Conqueror*' (No. 14). A 'wonderful story filled with glory' - this note rings out at the end of every stanza and dispels every fear. In the second stanza, he extols the cross and all that was wrought for humankind. The last two stanzas are full of imagery. The following lines liken the glorious event of resurrection to 'a wonderful bloom, Spreading around His great perfume' - as Jesus rose up discarding the mortal body. In the last stanza, we see the picture of the '*sleeping worm*' (Chrysalis), which wakes up in turn, 'Breaking the prison' wherein it lied dormant before. And this, he says, is the reason for rejoicing: "He rose again to life and has ended the strife / Therefore we sing and the ends of earth will ring."

On Walking with the Lord

There are many songs, which portray the Incarnate Son and Solomon's intimate relationship with Him. In '*O Son of Mary*' (No. 2), Solomon addresses Jesus as 'Lord Jesus, Son of Mary'. He sees Him as 'matchless Light' and pleads Him, 'Have mercy on us.'[189] In the next stanza he amply admits the divinity of Jesus. Solomon closes this song with beautiful Biblical imagery of the vine and the branch.

In '*Prayer of the Woman of Samaria*' (No.3), Solomon presents a three-fold confession of the Samaritan woman: First, about her ignorance - that she did not know Him and discern His ways though He was 'declared to us by the Holy Scriptures' and was 'full of glory and the essence of all the Scriptures'; Second, about the futility of her quest - that she 'became thirsty and wandered around broken cisterns' to quench her thirst; Third, about her life's fulfillment - 'I find rest to my bruised body, I find now the living waters of life, While all along I was among the broken cisterns.'[190] The original title to Jesus in Telugu version of the hymn is deep in meaning. He is called *Nigama Vedya*, 'One Who was announced in ancient Scriptures'.

In '*The Anniversary*' (No. 11), Solomon describes the determined walk of a disciple with Christ. The chorus is filled with thanksgiving and praise to the Lord 'Who kept us, And guided us along the way ... A response of gratitude at the milestone of every New Year:[191]

---

189 'Son of Mary' is an expression not so frequently used in Protestant literature. But like the title, 'Son of Man' used by Christ Himself, Son of Mary here is an expression of the humanity of Christ, as the well-known term 'Son of God' tells us about the divinity of Christ. Solomon freely used that epithet here, but demonstrates his distinctive faith by pleading Him directly for His mercy. In all this, he seems to be emphasizing the humanity of Jesus, yet he acknowledges His divinity by saying, "We bow our heads before Your ever shining Countenance".

190 Here is an allusion to the Biblical account of the people of God hewing them out 'broken cisterns' without turning to 'the fountain of living water (Jeremiah 2:13).

191 We walk with Him leaving the old behind, / We cast our cares on Him to bear for us; / ... We know this is a new path for us with Him / And ask the Lord to keep us from temptation. / We've decided to walk with Him and never to turn back, / We will not lay down the banner from our hand.

'The Living Waters' (No. 13), written in a classical literary style is about one's walk with the Lord. Solomon speaks to himself about the futility of searching for living waters in places apart from Christ - questions posed for personal reflection.[192] This is an expression of vain search for eternal joy in the wrong places. There are some bold proclamations made about Jesus too: "... But only Jesus the blessed Son of God / Can shower His mercy and quench our endless thirst.[193]

'A Child's Prayer' (No. 20), is about children's walk with the Lord as they have a sure opportunity for identifying with Jesus, celebrating His birth every year with joy, and being taught that He loved and received the children without hindering anytime. So children too can come boldly into the presence of the Lord with confidence and this song is such a beautiful exercise.[194] Children having 'I-Thou' relationship with the Lord is wonderful; approaching Him since He 'once walked, As a little one like one of us' is beautiful. Even in their faltering mumblings and tumbling steps children are conscious of a 'companion'. With their innocence and honesty they pledge their lives to walk with the Lord, and to 'walk with righteousness'.

'A Child's Covenant' (No. 27) is a song that talks about children's walk with the Lord in a covenant relationship. As soldiers of Christ, and with a sincere commitment, they pledge: "We walk ahead holding His cross in our hands/To conquer the evils of the earth /And to win the war against Satan." Their obedience to the call of the Lord helps them walk faithfully with Him: Identifying themselves as 'the sheep of our Lord' they were assured of His unfailing providence. The imagery of Psalm 23 is skillfully reflected: "We shall never be in want". The imagery of 'playmates in childhood' is applied to the children and Baby Jesus, giving them an opportunity to 'learn from Him mercy and love'. Solomon then uses the imagery of armor and soldiers to portray the commitment of children to the Lord.[195] We see that commitment to the Lord requires commitment to His Word - abiding by His Word! And then as 'warriors' of a new order, they stand

---

192 Why do you seek water, my soul,
In the dried up wells? ...
In broken cisterns, my soul?

193 This song has a similar pattern as one in the Telugu hymnal, *Yesuni premanu nemarakanu yeppudu dalachave yo manasa* (Meditate upon the love of Jesus, O, my soul, without forgetting). Andhra Christian Hymnal, Song No. 173 written by Dorasami Arogyam.

194 With You we hold our hands, Lord / And walk along the way. /
Our God, You fill our life with Your gifts / And do not caste us away Your dear ones /
O Jesus Who once walked this earth / As a little one like one of us.

195 The imagery of the 'sword' is taken from the Pauline armor of God (Ephesians 6:11-17).
We wear the armor of righteousness
And walk with Him in the holy path
Holding fast in our hands
The swiftest sword of His holy Word.

out bold. In this hymn, we see Jesus as the Commander of 'little children, soldiers of Christ.'[196]

In *'The Refugee'* (No. 32), Solomon presents a superb piece of *Bhakti Sahitya*, which demonstrates the intimate 'I-Thou' relationship between a devotee and his God.[197] The first three stanzas describe in intimate terms God's loving care for the devotee, and Christ as the only Savior. God is given the epithet of gift-giver. As prophet Isaiah declared,[198] God's care and comfort surpass those of a mother and father. The lyric ends with a deep desire that depicts the devotee's commitment to such a God: "I desire to abide with You / Both here and hereafter ..."

'My Sole Refuge' (No. 33) gives the key for union with God - nothing but the sacrifice of Jesus - His body broken for us, and His blood, which is shed for us. Solomon extols Jesus as 'the giver of life', Who alone is his 'refuge' and Who will never leave him desolate. Sustenance for life here, and eternal life hereafter because of the supreme sacrifice of Jesus! 'Standing steadfast in the realms of faith' Solomon declares, "We worship You today without ceasing; / And conquer sickness and death, / And step forward with You in eternal joy."

'God's People' (No. 25) is a call to the nation of Israel to turn to God and seek 'shelter under the arm', since the Lord 'will never forget His promises made to you'. Solomon pleads God's people to 'know the ways of His truth, And seek the strength of the Lord'. Finally, Solomon invites 'all the nations of the earth' to 'Gather around His mighty throne, Pay your homage and at His feet do fall, ... worship Jesus Lord of all'.

'The Heart of Jesus' (No. 30), demonstrates author's anguish for people's dilemmas about Jesus. Citing different situations in the life of Jesus Christ, when

---

196 Referring to Christ, it is very rarely that Solomon talks about war, arms, and triumphant warrior and ruler, much less as army commander. This song is an exception. To him a loving master is a more important image. But it is somewhat natural for children to use the heroic imagery in gentle terms sometimes; and so we have this one song in this tenor.

There were a couple of hymns in Andhra Christian Hymnal with the same tenor, which were Telugu renderings from English: *Onward Christian Soldiers* by Nabeen Barring-Gould was translated into Telugu by Jacob Chamberlane (Hymn No. 362). *Stand Up, Stand Up for Jesus* by George Duffield was translated by John Haye (Hymn No. 363). There was also an original song with popular tune, *Yesuto ttheevigaanu podama*, jointly authored by A. C. Kinsinger and P. D. Subhamani in almost the same tenor (Hymn No. 521). These songs, which had been in vogue, must have spurred Solomon to pen the song under consideration.

197 Who else but You
To save me and keep me, Lord?
No one but You is the gift-giver of life ...
... You without hiding Your face to me
Have beckoned me to Your bosom.
... From You I get all I need
And You comfort me more than
My mother and father can do.

198 Isaiah 49:15

He said or did something in their midst, Solomon wonders whether the people concerned know or understand meaning of the Scriptures. Having posed different kinds of questions, Solomon states a couple of staggering realities at the end: "Some people cannot see even if they have eyes to see! / And some people cannot hear even if they have ears to hear!"[199]

The last song in the book, '*The Disciples Song*' (No. 44) is taken from *Kim Kartavyam*. It is a fitting finale for every disciple in his walk with the Lord, envisaging one's fulfilling experience: "Lord our hearts are lighted / As we, Your great countenance behold." Being overwhelmed by this, the disciple longs for unbroken fellowship with the Lord in life and in eternity.[200]

The Hope of Glory (At The End of Life's Journey)

In *The Light in My Heart* (No. 6) Solomon prays God to "Let the light in my heart, Glow brightly To declare Thy path, And to people Thy word" - that he may go with God in full faith and to know the wonderful truth revealed to our ancestors and preserved for us in the Scriptures. Grace for life's journey as seen above, and assurance of eternal bliss as given below are the two-fold concern of Solomon in this song. Solomon longs for God's never-ending light to be his repose at the end of life on earth. This he calls night signifying the hope of resurrection that follows, since a new dawn always follows the night. And he longs to keep singing His praise in a never-ending song throughout the deathless eternity, which is symbolically expressed as the nightless day. Solomon extols God in all the various renderings of this song as '*Light in My Soul*' or the '*Light in My Heart*' and this is a well-known, well-sung lyric.

Solomon has done two alternative renderings for this song and some distinctive thoughts are expressed. In *The Light in My Soul*,[201] Solomon pleads with a yearning:

> For in Thy path of love I go,
> And that path to others I show.

---

199 Has this world ever known the heart of Jesus Christ?
Has the human race ever seek [sic] the meaning of the Scriptures?
... Did people understand what He was saying?
Did the world know this is the fulfillment of the Scriptures?
When Christ rose again from the grave and stood
In the midst of the disciples did they know that it was true?

200 Can we ever forget You, our beloved?
And can we depart from Your blessed feet?
We do not want to go where You're not;
With You we have all that we want.
... Have mercy, O Lord and leave us not,
And we steadfastly will cling on to Thee.

201 *Geetha Malika*, (2010:145).

Lord of life, You let them see
In my eyes Thy great mercy, the lamp of love.

At the end, when darkness (of death) comes to hide his face, Solomon prays: "Stretch Your arm and gather my soul / For all my woes at last to heal ..."

Another rendering of this song, *'Pray, Put a Flame of Light in My Heart*[202] is a two-fold prayer for both life on earth and life hereafter. With the revelation of God as the 'Lord of light' Solomon wastes no time but prays to God. This prayer for life on earth reveals his consciousness of mission of life, and need for equipping himself for such a task:

... let the flame in my heart brightly glow
So I may give light to all people.

Concerning 'life hereafter' Solomon pleads the Lord: "When the evening of my earthly stay draws near, / Receive me to Your bosom, O Lord / Receive me to the deathless land and the nightless day / To the very place where You ever abide."

In *The Lord of the Children* (No. 37), Solomon portrays how the children identify with the Incarnate Son of God, "Treading this earth like one of us little ones ..." The children talk of Him as their loving host who gives them robes of righteousness and everlasting life - demonstrating an unusual assurance of the future when none but the Lord takes them into His home!

Other Themes

Finally, a couple of other themes such as **life's pilgrimage**, and, **mission of life**. *'The Pilgrim'* (No. 17) is an invitation to the pilgrim who is "tired and broken hearted, and utterly lost' and whose life grew weary, and whose journey had become dreary. Solomon extends a consoling conversation and continues to minister encouragement to the pilgrim. Solomon also addresses the questions the pilgrim confronts on the way and tries to ponder and communicate feasible answers. The unique identification marks of Jesus are presented beautifully and anyone can 'Look for them and see that it is He'. Again, Solomon raises another question concerning the utility of the search, which might be racing in the mind of the pilgrim, and provides a reason enough for following Him! Through the last lines Solomon proclaims a twofold deliverance from sorrow and pain, and a two-fold cover all because of His mercy.

'Who Else but Jesus?' (No. 38), Solomon portrays how the merciful Lord proves to be a faithful companion and comfort in life's journey and beyond:

Who is the God who makes me stand
In the heavenly realms ...
Who is the One who leads me on day by day ...

202 *Geetha Malika,* (2010:146).

Wiping away the agonizing fear of guilt,
Bringing down the loads from my shoulders …
To keep me company in my earthly journey …
To put His merciful hand on my bruised head,
To carry all my woes and wipe away my tears ...

Who is adequate to help in all these daily chores on earth and beyond? Solomon declares: "Who else is there but the Lord Jesus?"

'*I am a Deer*' (No. 42), is based on Psalm 42 and envisages the way for life's pilgrimage. The great affirmation of the Psalmist is reiterated in the chorus:

Like the deer thirsty for cool waters
So my heart gets thirsty for the love of my Lord.

Solomon extols the blessings of fellowship: "There is a feast to my heart … / I will not find anywhere. / All my doubts and fears / I shall now put in His ears / My Lord … Shall never send me in vain." Solomon finally proclaims that He is unparalleled: "Where else shall I get the peace? / And where else my rest increase?" It is interesting to note that Solomon presents his 42nd song with a similar note found in 42nd Psalm!

In *'The Song of the Flowers'* (No. 43), Solomon compares little children with flowers or flower plants - a beautiful image familiar to Indian children. Unity and friendship are imperative for our existence. And a desire for consistent daily growth is essential for existence on planet Earth.

God has a purpose for everyone whom He has created and this is the **Mission of Life**. To know it and flow in it brings fulfillment to life. God's purpose for our lives also includes making us His instruments to lead others to find their destiny. *'The Story of the Little Lamp'* (No. 7), is a specimen to this. Solomon attains such a self-realization:

In the midst of the raging winds and the rising storm
The Lord has kept me like a lamp to shine.

… To cast away the darkness of the night
The Lord has kept me to shine.

… There is no shadow ever to face
Where the Lord has kept me to shine.

With such a sense of life's vocation, he gives call to fellow travelers to march forward without wavering on the way!

In *'The Early Dawn'* (No. 35), Solomon enunciates in simple terms his conception of the mission of life. At the dawn of a new day, 'I stand at Your door seeking to know Your will'. The insight that dawned upon him is well expressed in the following lines:

"... A way to help others who are in need
That is what today is for me ..."

With no regrets for the bygone past, and with no slackness that puts off things to an indefinite future, Solomon exhorts that 'now is the time' to fulfill the mission of life: "... Only today is the wealth in my hand."

'The Incarnation of Mercy' (No. 34) is a prayer for God's mercy adequate for life and eternity. For too long he desired His matchless treasure of kindness but now he comes to Him in prayer: The fear of death can be quenched by an unshakable assurance of eternal life. The longing for 'the whitest robe', which He alone can give, is free of all filth and dirt of this mundane world. A supplication is made to fill each realm of his heart and his thoughts always 'with an abiding peace'. A final plea concerns breaking of the rock of his heart 'so that tears of regret freely flow' and wash away his sins. Solomon desires nothing but 'a renewed heart' and 'the raiment of righteousness'. Here is the beautiful imagery of water gushing out from rock as when Moses struck the rock.[203]

In *'My Father's House'* (No. 36), Solomon demonstrates how he could overcome the fears of life and the fear of death, because he has the Lord as his 'light and salvation' and his strong fortress. He boldly declares: 'I shall not fear any danger'. Staying in the Lord's house, hiding in the bosom of the Father, and abiding with Him without fear - this Solomon considers as 'the endless Fortune'. Therefore, he longs to 'abide in the courts of my Lord' forgetting himself, 'Giving thanks to Him' and singing His praises in a thousand tongues.

This '*Bhakti Sahitya*' is attested to by a couple of scholars in theological and literary fields respectively. Bishop Peddi Victor Premasagar, in addition to his sincere appreciation for all the merits of this Bhakti Sahitya, brought out an instance where we find similarities with the writings of Isaac Watson.[204] Job Sudarshan aptly discerned the striking similarities in Solomon's Songs with Rabindranath Tagore's *Gitanjali*[205] for their short passages and deep meaning. Nobody knows how many other songs have flowed from the pen of Solomon. It is hoped that this study will stimulate interest for further research.

iii) Songs from Sambalikan

A manuscript in English with 11 songs by Solomon at Sambalikan came to light in recent research explorations. Written with some musical notations in the late

---

203 Numbers 20:11
One of Solomon's woodcuts is titled 'Moses Hits the Rock'. As Moses smites the rock, there were waters gushing forth to quench the thirst of the day. Here Solomon symbolically talks of the rock of his heart and the waters are the tears that flow from a broken heart. Published in *"The Bible and the Technologies of the Word"* ed. by Joseph Palakeel. Bangalore: Asian Trading Corporation, (2007:54).

204 Compare Song No. 9 with Watson's song in Andhra Christian Hymnal (No. 212).

205 Abhinandanalu, in *Gaana Kusumaalu,* (2010:ix).

1980's during Solomon's stay at Sambalikan as an artist-in-residence. Feliciano, the head of the Sambalikan was a Catholic expert in Western Music and wanted to give harmonic tunes to these hymns but it was unaccomplished. This collection of songs was fortunately published in the Appendices of *Geetha Malika*. The whole luster of this collection springs forth from the depth of theological themes embedded therein and the rich imagery - Biblical and indigenous. An analytical review by the researcher on the themes of these songs was published in the Journal of Contemporary Christianity.[206]

The Wonder of the Incarnation

Solomon has been a minister of the Gospel all his life, and has taken every opportunity to extol his Lord. In '*The Wondrous Jesus*' (No. 2) Solomon ascribes the highest honor to His name: '*Blessed thrice Thy name shall be*'![207] To say the word *holy* three times intensifies the idea to the highest level. The holiness of God is indescribable in human language.[208] Solomon sees the Lord as '*Blessed thrice*' and '*Shining like a brilliant star - Brighter than the sun and moon*'. He further exclaims that '*it's always noon*' wherever He is! Though he delights to praise the Wondrous Jesus, he recognizes the transcendental dimension: "Saints and angels do applaud / In the realms we cannot see." He further yearns for a '*darshan*' of His fullness, with a longing to fly to His bosom and live with Him forever.

This transcendental God visited the planet earth, and Solomon depicts the transforming power of the incarnation in the lyric, *The Holy and Profane* (No. 6). He envisions bridging the gulf between the sacred and the profane, when "*the Word had become flesh - To redeem the human race*". The Dichotomy disappears when "*all matter great and less / Was made holy by His grace*". This transformation is well illustrated by the Sacrament of Lord's Supper in that the ordinary elements of wine and bread become '*a meal divine*' when He blessed the wine and broke the bread; which is "*Strong to nourish and strong to save*". Solomon thoughtfully presents a new hermeneutic of the Sacrament! What a difference between our divided perspective versus the divine perspective!

In *Who is the Cause?* (No. 8), Solomon extols the incarnate Lord as the great eternal Source. In all the stanzas, the first four lines he raises questions, which lead one and all to the Source.

> Who for my sake has crossed the hell?
> Who is the source of lasting life?

---

206 *Geetha Malika,* (2010:151-164).
Moses Kumar, B.S. : "Songs of Solomon from Sambalikan: An Analytical Review" in *Journal of Contemporary Christianity*, Bangalore, 2014 (Vol. 4 No. 4).

207 This expression has an allusion to the three-fold 'Holy' in the angelic adoration, orchestrated in balance by the Holy Spirit, both in the Old and New Testaments. "To say *holy* twice in Hebrew is to describe someone as 'most holy'.

208 Isaiah 6:3, Revelation 4:8 (NKJV) Nelson's NKJV Study Bible, (1997:1121, 2172).

Who gave to me a story to tell?
Who brings me to the end of the strife? ...

Solomon introduces a refrain in the last two lines of each stanza, with a slight variation in the second one. This refrain not only gives the answer to the series of interrogatives in the preceding lines, but also makes a bold proclamation with personal application: "Jesus the Lord and He is my song / Keeping me cheerful as I go along." The variation in the second stanza enhances the scope of the proclamation even further with an alternate ending - Not just '*as I go along*' but '*all the way along*'! This is indeed '*a story to tell*'! There is a great hymn by Mungamuri Devadas written in the same vein. Aware of this hymn and being pretty familiar with this type of writing, Solomon skillfully followed the pattern even in English. The resounding answer to each of these questions is none but the Person of Jesus Christ! [209]

The Irresistible Call

The third song, *I Heard the Shepherd*, points to the Caller, none other than the Good Shepherd.[210] This song employs the beautiful Indian imagery of the shepherd, often portrayed with his flute. Solomon calls Him '*my Shepherd*' as David of old did in Psalm 23. He heard the call of his Shepherd: This call is not to entertain or exhilarate, but to solicit an implicit obedience '*to follow Him*'. Obey he did, in response to this irresistible call, mingled with love supreme. Solomon further extols His supreme love, as he gazes into the depths of His *bleeding bosom.* Solomon testifies of '*His sweet anointing*' that saved him '*from fall and fainting*', and the outpouring of '*all His love*'. This fills him with such unshakable assurance that he confides:

Now always I hear Him singing
Day and night great joy He's bringing
Casting out my fear and pain
All His love for me outpouring.

---

209 *Naakinta Protsahaanandambul* (Who is the Cause for me that I could get such encouragement and joy) - all the questions posed soliciting an eternally unwavering answer.
The Hymnal, Hymn No. 348
Sundar Rao, R.R.: *Bhakti Theology in the Telugu Hymnal,* (1983:108).
Who is the firm foundation for my *bhakti*,
and who raised my voice in the hymns?
Who bears the weight of my sins,
and makes friendship with God?
Who else, but Jesus who is crucified on the cross.

210 One of the seven *'I AM sayings'* of the incarnate Lord, as presented in the Gospel of John, presents Jesus as the Good Shepherd. This has been one of the fond and frequent themes of Solomon's art and verse. This song employs the beautiful Indian imagery of the shepherd, often portrayed with his flute. A flute, as we know, is a woodwind musical instrument, held sideways and played by blowing over a hole as its keys are pressed.

Here is an allusion to the prophetic picture of a singing God,[211] as seen in the Book of Zephaniah.

Another Song also deals with the theme of the irresistible call - *I Heard a Voice*. Solomon likens this voice to that of '*the wondrous lover*', which can never be disregarded. This call seems to be demanding an immediate and lasting response and so he responds: '*And then I told Him – I'm His forever*'. Solomon asserts His name to be blessed for reasons he knew best: "He never turned His / Face away from me / Mercy is His name / He always rains His / Showers of blessing / Night and day the same." As in the previous Song, the Caller is likened to a '*kindly Shepherd*'. It is indeed appropriate. Isaac Watts fittingly expressed in the concluding lines of his famous hymn on Crucifixion how "*Love so amazing, so divine - Demands my soul, my life, my all*". Solomon in a similar vein makes his self-surrender: "I made a covenant / To serve Him ever … / My life for Him I / Shall freely lay down …"

Love and Grace

The twin attributes of love and grace of God are portrayed by Solomon in two of the Songs. It is interesting, though, that the titles of these two songs sound to be the opposite poles - *The Stormy Skies* (No. 1) and *The Glowing Hearts* (No. 4). In the first song, *The Stormy Skies*, Solomon makes a couple of proclamations in relation to God's great love: "… 'Tis safe for them who know His keeping / And trust in His great love. / … It is but those who know His keeping / Can trust in His care and love." Before making these proclamations, Solomon shares his personal confession as a repeating refrain - in exercise of faith in the above proclamations: "I tell myself – the Lord is ruling / Whatever it looks like now." All this, in the midst of dark skies and razing clouds, '*when evening comes and darkness creeps*'! What an experience and what an assurance! When all is said and done, his eyes will close in sleep with great assurance and certain confession. This '*resting place*' in the midst of '*The Stormy Skies*' reminds us of the Psalmist's sleep and peace in the midst of distress.[212]

In *The Glowing Hearts*, we see Solomon with a prayer and a proclamation in relation to God's great grace. The prayer, at the start, is to the One Who '*livest in the brightest light - Far beyond the human sight*', Who is none other than Jesus. Though God's bounteous grace is ministered here in time and space, Solomon fondly anticipates the endless grace even beyond.

---

211 Zephaniah 3:17, (NKJV), Nelson's NKJV Study Bible, (1997:1530).
"The Lord your God in your midst, / The Mighty One, will save; / He will rejoice over you with gladness, / He will quiet you with His love, / He will rejoice over you with singing."

212 Psalm 4:8, Nelson's NKJV Study Bible, (1997:879)
I will both lie down in peace, and sleep;
For You alone, O Lord, make me dwell in safety.

Creation Redeemed

Two of the Songs deal with the theme of earth and environmental stewardship. In *The Mother Earth*, Earth is acknowledged as the Mother of all mankind; yet, it is rightly deemed as God's creation. We see here a poetic personification rather than a deification of Earth. It is amazing how the Earth fulfills its God-ordained purpose for ages, in submission to her Creator and His will. Solomon prays that God would teach us our responsibility in stewardship for the earth and for everything therein. This is not only our obligation, but also God's expectation:

> … Teach us, Lord! To love the earth
> Which to us has given birth.
>
> … You have made for us them all.
> May we look them with respect
> As from us this You expect.

What a piece of enlightenment and exhortation! Solomon reiterates that gratitude for everything in creation, and respect that emanates from such an attitude would go a long way in preserving the nature for posterity. In the concluding stanza,

Solomon expresses solidarity with fellow humans, as he confesses the corporate sins committed against Nature. He seeks not only forgiveness for the sins of the past, but also asks for instruction and wisdom that would aid future stewardship.[213]

In *The Weaver*, Solomon uses the imagery of the weaver and the potter in an endeavor to comprehend the amazing work of God in the universe and upon the humans. These common trades or tasks have been given a new status and dignity by means of using this imagery to describe the work of the Lord. The long and consistent process of a weaver's shuttle yields the joy of a work fulfilled, which He knows and sees, even before the start of the work. The first two stanzas in this song describe the human limitations as against God's infinite plan and design: "… How it turns out I do not know… / A host of hues come emerging / In various patterns as I stare / But the final shape to emerge / Is yet not known except to Him."

---

213 The impact of St. Francis of Assisi upon Solomon - forever it seems - is clearly seen in these lines, where he addresses River as Sister, and Mountain as Brother. Francis, we know, had personified the objects of nature affectionately as Brother Sun and Sister Moon, Brother Fire and Sister Water, Brothers Wind and Air, and Mother Earth and Sister Death.
http://en.wikipedia.org/wiki/Canticle_of_the_Sun - accessed January 18, 2018.
"We have sinned against the Nature Father do Thou please forgive Teach us how with every creature And with earth in friendship live Keeping safe its purity Giving for posterity." Quoted by Chilkuri Vasantha Rao: "Telugu Inculturation in Art and Literature" in *Planting in Native Soil,* (2014:126-127).

In the next stanza, the imagery of a potter's wheel is seen in relation to God's patient dealing with humans. The purpose of this ongoing process is to make a vessel as He conceives - a vessel usable and useful. Submission to Him and yielding to His touches is the key, whether we know the what's and why's or not.

At the Sunset: Forgiven!

A couple of songs in the collection touch base with sunset of life, and the required preparation for the same! *The Evening* deals with the final evening - the evening of life or the sunset of life. When it comes at last, here goes the prayer of that last moment: "Blessed Savior stretch Your hand / To receive me in Your land." And a final plea for forgiveness in the last stanza with due confession:

> O, my Savior make perfect
> All the pathways of my life …
> Since it was Your will for me
> Spotlessly for Thee to live.

The Lord is twice addressed as Savior in this song – as '*Blessed Savior*' in the first stanza, and as '*my Savior*' in the last. The '*Blessed Savior*' in the third person becomes '*my Savior*' in the first person in an inseparable eternal bond!

Forgiveness to Us! is a prayer that deals with forgiveness. Solomon asks the Lord to help him bear the pain, as he was heard amiss again. He asks the Lord to teach him to say a gentle word that would wipe the hurt caused. He further asks to hush up the soul, take away the hurt, and guard his lips in what he says. This Solomon needs so that he may watch his emotions before he reaches a deadly step. He seeks further help for self-control. In the last stanza, he asks for a two-fold relief:

> Lord, heal the wounds that I have made
> Set right the hearts that I invade,
> As now I ask, forgive my soul
> May You my rival too console.

The handful of themes discussed in the body of this essay give the reader an overview of the essential Christian message. Solomon wrote three songs about the Incarnate Lord, and two songs each on the following themes: a) Irresistible Call and Disciple's Response; b) Love and Grace; c) Mother Earth, Weaver and the Potter; and, d) The Sunset of Life and Forgiveness. Apart from other doctrinal themes, it is conspicuous that Solomon has exhibited such an enlightened realization about environmental stewardship. He seems to be a rare combination of classical taste and modern reflection. The whole collection of the Songs of Sambalikan is rich with imagery and word pictures, which aid greatly in communicating the message. According to Hanna Cheriyan-Varghese, another artist-in-residence at the *Sambalikhaan*, "Visual images reveal more of one's mind than words. That is why art has been used in education, contemplation, meditation and veneration in Christian tradition."[214]

iv) Paul Gerhardt's Keerthana Sahityam

Of late, the eye of Solomon was intently searching valuable resources in the area of Hymns of the early church and through the Reformation period. In the process, he was drawn to the *'Spiritual Songs'* of Paul Gerhardt (b. 1607 – d. 1676),[215] a post-Reformation hymn writer with hundreds of hymns to his credit in German. Many of these were translated into English and sung in the churches for centuries.

Solomon was not new to Gerhardt's hymns, as he had listened to some of them in the churches during his global itineration in 1980's. The message and the structural beauty of these hymns are remarkable. Solomon never thought of rendering them into Telugu during those bygone days. Now after some three decades, it is interesting to see him, in his nineties, do the present study on these Hymns. This first-ever Telugu rendering is a great contribution to the Telugu Church.

These hymns were originally translated from German into English, and now from English to Telugu. One wonders at the depth of their meaning, and the creative imagination and elaborate thought on the themes Paul Gerhardt touched. The Telugu rendering sounds almost like an original work. Solomon translates six of those hymns and this gives the reader a foretaste into the rich devotional literature of Gerhardt in particular, and of the Reformation heritage in general.

Gerhardt wrote some of these hymns during The Thirty Years' War. It is amazing to see a 'song' to the Lord in the midst of turmoil around, and it is unfathomable how Gerhardt was gifted to present the manifold themes of Christian Faith in such a voluminous and profound hymnody, even in such a disturbing

214 http://www.asianchristianart.org/art_varghese.htm - accessed April 10, 2018.

215 http://www.ccel.org/print/kelly/gerhardtsong - accessed April 10, 2018.

environment of warfare around. Ernst Bauerochse, a friend and colleague of Solomon Raj from Radio Voice of the Gospel, appreciates this maiden venture of Solomon on the Hymns of Gerhardt.[216] The unending thread of thought given for a certain theme is evidenced in most of these hymns of Gerhardt. Solomon has done a skillful rendering of these hymns bringing home to the reader the depth of meaning in the message envisaged.

A clear picture of the historical transition of singing in the Early Church, in the Middle Ages, and in modern times is clearly portrayed in Solomon's Introduction to this present work. When all is said and done, we have a rich treasure, as the following six hymns were rendered into beautiful Telugu for the first time:

1) Why Without, Then, Art Thou Staying?
2) A Song of Christian Consolation and Joy
3) Of the Appearance of the Angels
4) Now With Joy My Heart is Bounding
5) Scarce Tongue can Speak, Ne'er Human Ken
6) Now Spread are Evening's Shadows

Solomon's choice of the above six hymns out of hundreds is in deed a skillful choice, and they together present a cohesive and compact message for the reader in a simple and beautiful rendering. The fifth song is the only hymn Gerhardt wrote 'Of the Holy Trinity'. The first one is from Gerhardt's collection of hymns on 'Advent', while the third and fourth songs are from his collection on 'Birth of Christ - Christmas'.[217] The second song is from Gerhardt's collection of *'Songs of the Cross and Consolation'*. The last song Solomon translated is the last hymn from Gerhardt's collection of 'Morning and Evening Songs'. Solomon must have found some solace and preparation at his own evening of life spending time in meditation with this Evening Song. Solomon has faithfully

---

216 Ernst Bauerochse remarks:

> ... in 1943, I had to become a soldier and unavoidably became a prisoner of war in the year 1945. That was a bad time with much suffering from hunger and other problems. Now as prisoners, we received a small hymnbook, and one Sunday afternoon in 1946, I went into a quiet corner of our prison camp, opened the little hymnbook and asked myself:
> What was it that gave Paul Gerhard the strength and the faith to write hymns of joy and of thankfulness even during the horrors and troubles of the 30 years' war? The answer was quite clear from his hymns: It was the Christian faith, his trust in God the Father who loves us and cares for us, in Jesus Christ who died and rose for us, and in the Holy Spirit who - as he writes in one of his hymns - is a spirit of joy, of love, and of prayer.
> E-Mail: On Friday, 18 April 2014 6:35 PM, from Ernst Bauerochse to P. Solomon Raj <ernst.bauerochse@web.de>

217 The fourth song was tuned and released by Donald Church Hyderabad with the voice of Dr. Samata Prasad. (See https://www.youtube.com/watch?v=pr2AoOv9AX8)

endeavored to envisage the ageless message from Gerhardt's Hymns by means of this wonderful effort.

It is hoped that these Telugu renderings continue to bless the current and forthcoming generations just as the original hymns blessed 400 years ago. It is further hoped that this maiden effort would inspire many to fathom the depths in the riches of Christian hymnody and worship through the ages. Solomon introduces the Telugu Church in some detail to this rich heritage by this endeavor, and it is for the theologians and devoted churchmen of our times to move on from here to dig deeper into the historic heritage of the Church.

v) Greek Hymns

In recent times, Solomon has done a study of the Greek Hymns also. *Adi Kraisthava Sangha Kirthana Sahityamu: Greek Hymns* is a Telugu Translation of 40 Greek Hymns Solomon rendered into Telugu with a chronological account of Christian Hymns in Church History. With his inherent interest into Song tradition of the Church, Solomon digs deeper into the riches of singing heritage of the church, from the very beginning of her existence. There are two other works Solomon translated from English into Telugu:

- *Gerontia Swapnamu*
  (Translation of *The Dream of Gerontius* by John Henry Newman)
- *Suvarna Dhaanya Sampada*
  (Translation of *Golden Grains* by John Wright Follette)

For quite some time in his nineties, it had been his desire to write on the Miracles of Jesus Christ, *Yesu Kristhu Adbhutaalu* in the form of hymns, just as he wrote on the Parables of Jesus. A fair draft is still awaited! Not only Solomon wrote many songs and hymns, but he also knew the 'how' and 'why' of it - the theory and prosody of it! So we find beautiful essays on song tradition from the pen of Solomon, which are educational and enlightening, and which are furnished in the Bibliography. What a great teacher Solomon had turned out to be, even after ceasing his teaching and preaching exercises! Other accomplishments of Solomon will be briefly seen in the following section, amounting to his multifaceted genius.

Solomon Raj - As A Multifaceted Genius

Solomon Raj emerged as a multifaceted genius.. It is rare for an author in his late 80s to still publish books, as observed by Alle G. Hoekema. With his stern determination Solomon scaled many pinnacles and accomplished rare trophies - all with the help of his two little tools - his pen and his paintbrush. He had been at phenomenal ease in presenting almost each of his artistic creations with a matching verse superb in diction and profound in meaning. Added to this was his incessant *saadhana* in the realms of art and poetry, which had placed him and his works on higher pinnacles of global reputation. Having been into Christian art, Solomon had been influenced by the works of famous artists of the world, and was fascinated to adopt some of them - making his own creations. They are as follows:

- Andrei Rublev, one of the greatest medieval Russian painters of Orthodox icons and frescos. Solomon adopted his famous icon of the 'Trinity' and he made his own icon of this.
- Rembrandt Harmenszoon van Rijn, a Dutch painter, and printmaker, was generally considered one of the greatest visual artists in the history of art. Solomon adopted his 'Return of the Prodigal Son' and he made different pieces of art on this theme, in woodblock print, and woodcarving.
- Paul Klee, a Swiss German artist was famous for his "pure painting", an early term for abstract art. Adopting Paul Klee's art, Solomon did some works in batik as early as 1970's.
- Vincent van Gogh, a famous Dutch painter who created about 2,100 artworks, in just over a decade including around 860 oil paintings, most of them in the last two years of his life. He broadened his subject matter to include series of olive trees, wheat fields and sunflowers. Adopting his works, Solomon did some etchings and batiks on sunflowers.
- Among the Indian painters, Solomon was influenced by Jamini Roy, a Bengali painter. The characteristic feature of Jamini's art is people being depicted with huge eyes, with no lid, and resembling the so-called holy people who fix their attention on God. Solomon adopted this trait in some of his works, and like him Solomon did not create an exclusive art for an elite.
- Solomon was also impacted to some extent by the Ethiopian art. He visited Ethiopia three times attending Radio Studio Directors Conference at Addis Ababa. His fourth visit was during his Sabbatical from Suvartha Vani.

A brief survey of Solomon's other unique works is made in the following pages touching his latest and unique creations in art (namely, Icons, Triptychs and Brass Sculptures) and in poetry with hitherto untouched genres (namely, *Kandardhas* and *Vuyyala Paata*), sandwiched by his major literary work, "*A Christian Folk Religion in India: A Study of the Small Church Movement in Andhra Pradesh, with Special Reference to the Bible Mission of Devadas*" (his doctoral dissertation), and its sequel "*The New Wineskins: The Story of the Indigenous Missions in Coastal Andhra Pradesh, India*". Finally, Solomon's expansive volume of poetry in English as an octogenarian and as a nonagenarian (*Soliloquies in Solitude*) will cap it all to present Solomon Raj as a multifaceted genius.

i) Icons, Triptychs and Brass Sculptures

Icon simply means image. In popular parlance, it is vastly used in this computer age where we find them on the toolbar - each little symbol meaning something, representing a greater object and giving a quick link to that object. It is the same word used in the Greek Bible in the Book of Genesis when it says that God created man in His image. Interestingly, Paul uses the same word in his epistle to the Colossians as he refers to Christ as the visible image of the invisible God. The word icon is commonly used to refer to any religious picture big or small, done in any kind of material like paint on wood panels, or mosaics, ivory, or enamel, done in earth pigments and egg yolk. In church use and liturgy, icons are portable wood panel paintings usually ascribed to members of monastic orders for use in worship in orthodox churches.

Thus Religious icons were used as a form of prayer. They were not just 'art with a religious theme' but were deemed as 'sacred art' - as they usher the onlooker into the presence of the sacred! In fact, they were called 'windows to heaven or doorways to the sacred' as they are used by the monks for mediation. The technique of making an icon is rich with symbolism and significance wrapped with it.[218] Icons often are painted on high-quality wood, carefully shaped and smoothed - wood reminding of the life before the Fall. A linen cloth covers the wood with the twin purpose of protecting it and reminding us of the cloth Jesus was wrapped in after he died. Over the linen are applied coats of gesso, made from rabbit-skin glue and chemists' chalk - symbolizing the soul and life of the person.

The iconographer at work must be a personification of patience, who with undivided focus immerses with gladness in an otherwise laborious process. Primarily he cleans, smoothens and prepares the gesso to receive the image. The wood board is indented with raised edges and the center part is shallower. It is called *covcheg*, which in Russian means 'coffin'. The image is placed in this shallow space and etched into the gesso. A thin coat of clay bole (a mixture of clay and hide glue) is applied to the areas of the icon that will be gilded with gold leaf. The clay represents human physical nature. The iconographer breathes on the clay bole to vaporize it and immediately places the gold leaf on the damp area to apply gold. This process symbolizes the Spirit and reminds us of the breath of life in the act of creation. The gold itself symbolizes divine light and heaven. Icons often have gold backgrounds because the viewer gazes into heaven. The image is painted with a mixture of egg yolk, pure water, vinegar, and natural pigments. Many layers are applied, each with its own color symbolism.

Many other symbols are used in writing icons, which testify that icons are much more than what they appear to be. Icons are a visual form of prayer in line and color, seeking to tell us something true about the divine, and perpetuating

---

218 *Icons as Religious Art* https://www.loyolapress.com/our-catholic-faith/family/catholic-teens/religious-art/icons-as-religious-art accessed on April 5, 2018.

a long tradition of truths communicated visually rather than through words - passed on from one artist to the next! As was observed earlier, monks in monasteries had devoted their lives for spiritual cause and were committed to different kinds of spiritual exercises. Some of them as gifted iconographers had committed themselves to the vocation of producing icons as means of religious instruction that holds good for generations.

Solomon learned making icons and putting pure gold leaf gilding in England with some experts. There in 1986 they celebrated a thousand years anniversary of the Triumph of Orthodoxy, meaning the revival of making Icons in the churches. Solomon gives a brief but detailed description of icon making, as he teaches the prospective learners, which is appended. Solomon who longed for innovations in his work all along began experimenting on icons. Obviously Solomon was inspired by Rublev to work on this theme, and produced his version of the 'Trinity' as given below.

The innovative instinct of Solomon led him to create many other icons, and in no time he emerged as an iconographer of our times. The researcher has witnessed first hand how Solomon was patient at work in his Ashram, demonstrating the long process of making icons to the prospective learners, even in his early nineties.

A unique icon adorns his office, and another piece of the same theme given above is on permanent display at Hyderabad Bible College. It is unique in the sense of the theme and the people portrayed apart from the lines and the hues. The body of Jesus, after crucifixion, was being prepared for burial. The Synoptic writers didn't give much detail, except ascribing it to Joseph of Arimathea. John adds Nicodemus in the narrative, but never mentions specifically about any women. The women the Synoptic writers mention are a few, but Solomon imagines that those and other women must have joined, helping these men in the ritual. Solomon beautifully portrays this rare scenario of Jesus' burial preparation with two men and twelve women. Interestingly, there is a yellow halo around the heads of all - male as well as female.[219] Christian artists believed the halo to be symbolic of 'the light of grace bestowed by God'. Solomon must have tried to depict the feeling of reverence surrounding these persons here, who had the exclusive privilege of ministering to the body of Christ in preparation for the burial!

Solomon soon moved from icons to triptychs in course of time. A Triptych is a work of art (usually a panel painting) that is divided into three sections, or three carved panels that are hinged together and can be folded, shut or displayed open. The middle panel is typically the largest and it is flanked by two smaller related works, although there are triptychs of equal-sized panels.

A Triptych, in other words, is a picture or relief carving used as an altarpiece, and done with gold leaf or painted wood in the Middle Ages.[220] The usual Triptychs are done in the manner of icons, and these portable wood panel paintings are done in earth pigments and egg yolk generally ascribed to members of monastic orders.

219 A halo is "a ring of light that encircles something bright, or a ring of light over the head of an angel or other spiritual being, or a feeling of glory or reverence that surrounds a person or thing"
https://www.google.co.in/search?ei=v0zGWqSvF5KTzwK42proBQ&q=yellow+halo around+the+head+meaning&oq=halo+around+the+head&gs_l=psy- - accessed April 5, 2018.

220 https://en.wikipedia.org/wiki/Triptych - accessed April 6, 2018.

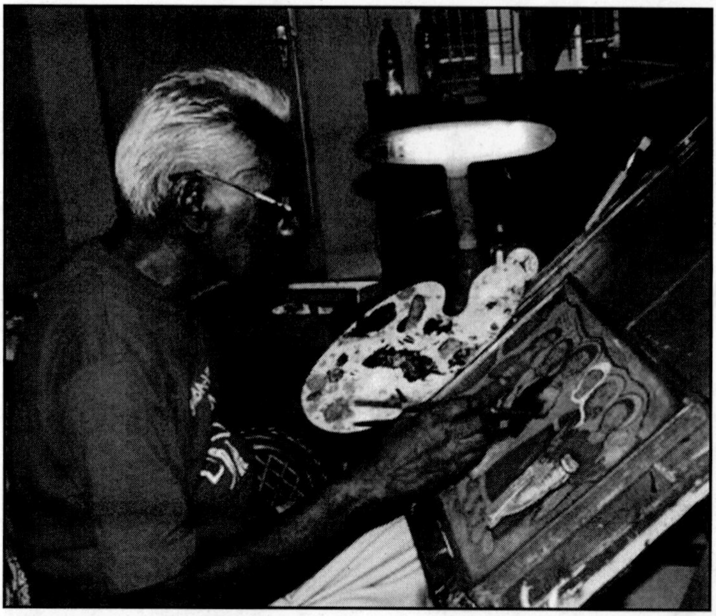

The three-fold nature of the Triptych reflects the religious symbolism of the number three. It is also observed that the three-act dramatic structure is evident in the application of the triptych format, with panels representing a beginning, a middle, and an end. Thus they show the progression of a subject, such as its growth or decline, or showcase three separate elements that are related and complement each other.[221] Solomon had to his credit many Triptychs, which are placed in many global centers. The researcher has a rare collection of Solomon's Triptychs, done mostly in his nineties. In this collection are found a couple of Triptychs on

221 https://www.thoughtco.com/triptych-drawing-definition-1123079 - accessed April 6, 2018.

Passion Week (reproduced below without the frames). Solomon seems to have embraced this theme dearer to his heart, and fondly depicts this event.

In the above Triptych are seen the scenes of the Triumphal Entry, the Last Supper and the Agony of Gethsemane, with an angel ministering. In the Triptych below Solomon moves beyond Gethsemane, to Crucifixion and adds the Resurrection.

Apart from individual works on Triptychs, *Biblia Pauperum* is the supreme example of a collection of Triptychs, of course done with wood block prints in black and white. Solomon later colored them.[222] The Triptych below is a specimen of the series, though not directly taken from his *Biblia Pauperum*. It follows the pattern of two types either end from the Old Testament with an ante-type from the New Testament in the middle. Here, the woman at the well was depicted in Indian imagery and peculiarly we find the woman at the pond! The works of Solomon are a testimonial for his gifts of focused attention, patience and unwavering commitment to accomplish the desired outcome, mostly in native setting.

Solomon had also done some brass sculptures following the lost wax method of the Hindu Temple sculptors. One of his classic works is given below. This brass casting of Christ was reproduced on the back cover of *Glad Tidings* published by Women's Missionary Society of the Presbyterian Church in Canada - depicting Faces of Christ from Southern Asia.[223]

---

222 An Analytical Essay by the Researcher on *Biblia Pauperum* with reproductions in color is due for publication on the website http://www.artway.eu

223 Vol. 62 No. 6, June/July 1986.

Apart from Solomon's trajectory of work in art and poetry, he presented many essays and articles in different academies around the world, some of which are published in Journals or Books. A list of these is given in the Bibliography. This list touches many fields of his interest, through his ascending stages of life, and irrevocably portrays the multifaceted genius of Solomon Raj.

ii) A Christian Folk Religion in India

This is the seminal work of Solomon with Birmingham University, U.K. under the guidance of Prof. Walter Hollenweger for his Ph.D. This was "A Study of the Small Church Movement in Andhra Pradesh, with Special Reference to the Bible Mission of Devadas". It was a classic contribution in missiology. In his foreword, Prof. Hollenweger refers to this book as "a milestone in modern church history" due to the importance of the new indigenous church movements that are growing across the globe. This is a detailed look at the Bible Mission and at Father Mungamuri Devadas, who founded it as a sect split off from the Lutheran Mission in 1938.

Solomon analyzes the factors that necessitated the emergence of small group churches like the Bible Mission. Devadas being a gifted poet had composed devotional songs sung in genuine Indian melody and meter, while the Lutheran church had few such songs. Most of their hymns were translations from western languages and had to be sung in the western style of music. The foreign character of the Lutheran Church became obvious in the form of their singing and worship, while that of Devadas' followers was fully indigenous. Devadas also had his own style of prayer, meditation, and worship, better adapted to the local mentality and manner than the official liturgical style of the Lutheran church.

The Afterword Solomon adds to the revised edition recognizes the pilgrim nature of the church, and as such "is seeking to find out the will of the Lord at every stage till it sees Him face to face someday". Solomon had given a mature treatment to the once rival group, making every effort for a judicious analysis of what happened before their eyes with the emergence of an inquisitive voice of Devadas. In his review essay, "*Towards a Renewed and Relevant Church*"[224] Siga Arles analyzed this doctoral dissertation and explored the role of an indigenous movement within Indian Christianity. As seen earlier, Arles identifies six themes, which will provide a helpful analysis not only for continuing developments in India, but also throughout the world:

- The Rise of Indigenous Churches – a Global Phenomenon
- The Cultural Unsuitability of the Western Church in Indian Soil

224 David Zersen and B. S. Moses Kumar: *"Planting in Native Soil: Studies in Gospel Inculturation"*, (Austin, TX: Concordia University Press, and Delhi: ISPCK: 2014).

- The Absence of Dreams, Visions and Healing
- The Church was Priest-Centred and Priest-Dominated
- The Priest should Equip the Saints - The Laity
- The Folk Church

Arles had been inspired by his thoughts and their relevance as a model for a younger generation of theologians and missiologists. He hoped that this work of Solomon Raj will become popular in theological colleges and be used as a textbook along with that of Robin Boyd's to impact current thinking and dreaming for a new shaping of the church in mission.

iii) The New Wineskins

This is "The Story of the Indigenous Missions in Coastal Andhra Pradesh, India" and it is a sequel for Solomon's doctoral dissertation above. This volume is from follow-up research, "looking more for breadth than depth" as H. L. Richard points out. This book is based on surveys of 73 "indigenous missions" or "new church movements" in the four districts of coastal Andhra Pradesh in South India. Broad perspectives on subjects such as the church, oral communication, lay ministry, leadership training, literature, the miraculous, stewardship and so on are introduced with examples and insights.

The difficulties in this type of research are openly acknowledged; many did not want to talk about their finances, and membership statistics are often among the least of priorities. Just the insights into the problems of this research make this an important book.

Two thought provoking essays are added in Appendices at the end in this Book. Roger E. Hedlund writes on "The Importance of the Study of India's New Christian Movements'. The other essay by Bishop Peddi Victor Premasagar is "Are Indigenous Churches A Silent Protest Against The So-called Mainline Churches?"

These two books are closely related, as even the subtitles indicate. The first is Solomon Raj's doctoral work under Walter J. Hollenweger in Birmingham, originally published in 1986. Raj, as an artist, adorns the covers of both the books with his works. H. L. Richard sums up his central thesis in both books as follows:

> ... the new church movements have developed due to obvious and glaring inadequacies in the traditional churches (generally called "mission churches" by Raj). The future of Christianity lies with the new movements, which he wants to encourage. Seeking to criticize will only drive the new movements further from historic Christianity; seeking to empathize might encourage the kind of dialogue between churches that Raj recommends (because the new movements do need help, and need to learn as well as teach).[225]

H. L. Richard commends the relevance of these two works for today's mission:

> Libraries of international Christianity need to hold these two important works on new Christian movements in south India. Students who want to understand the meaning of Christianity need to look beyond creed-based definitions to the grass-roots realities of the movements introduced here. The church international can only be grateful to Solomon Raj for presenting these important cases studies.[226]

iv) Kandardhas & Vuyyala Paata (Cradle Song)

Of late, Solomon has done his exercises at couple of the unfulfilled desires of his poetic thirst. *Kandardhas* is a novelty for him. Whereas he wrote hundreds of poems and even *satakas* of the *Kanda* and other nomenclatures all his life, he was fascinated to compose *Kandardhas,* and what he did he did very well. A *Kandardha* is a four-line *Kanda* poem with elongated lines with lyrical tune, and is to be sung as a song halfway. He has composed a good enough collection with 50 *Kandardhas.* This is in fact a poetic composition in Telugu of the Hebrew Wisdom Literature comprising the books of Psalms, Proverbs, Song of Songs and Ecclesiastes.

Vuyyala Paata is another popular rustic song with the repetitive word '*Vuyyala*' at the end of each line. '*Vuyyala*' means a cradle or a 'swing' and *Paata* means 'song'. This type of song is spontaneous and goes on and on, with ease and rhythm. Rural folks engaged in day's labor, mostly in agricultural enterprise, usually sing '*Vuyyala*' songs. There are some Christian '*Vuyyala*' songs also, mostly sung among rural churches with non-literates. All can join in singing easily, and thus they unite the folks and engage everyone's involvement. Solomon at last composed his '*Vuyyala*' song with some 50 stanzas, citing scriptural events or truths in those simple lines. It's all one song, with unending lines as time permits![227]

---

225 http://ojs.globalmissiology.org/index.php/english/article/view/113/326 accessed March 25, 2018.

226 http://ojs.globalmissiology.org/index.php/english/article/view/113/326 accessed March 25, 2018.

227 The verses related to Christmas were released by Donald Church Hyderabad in 2014. (See https://www.facebook.com/102113696560475/videos/1000902846681551/)

There was a saying about poetry in Telugu: *Kaadedi Kavitha Kanarhambu*! It means - Nothing is unworthy to be a subject matter of poetry! Likewise, in his incessant zeal for indigenization, Solomon adopts anything and everything as fit means - and he deems nothing unworthy! The essence of his every work seems to be his thrust for Incarnation of the Gospel - sharing the message of the Gospel in appreciably receivable mode!

v) Soliloquies in Solitude

An Anthology of Solomon's Poetry compiled and analyzed by the researcher in his latest investigation with the same title, it contains 127 poems in English written at random, as per the mood of his times and the corresponding musings, in his eighties and nineties. They are aptly styled Solomon's Soliloquies in his moments of Solitude:[228]

Early Poetry of An Octogenarian

The first part consists of 40 works, Solomon wrote from 2009 as an Octogenarian. This was initially titled as 'Hridayanandam', meaning 'Heart's Delight'. Solomon emerges, in his ascending stages of life, as a great poet in Telugu and English.

228 B. S. Moses Kumar: *Soliloquies in Solitude*, (New Delhi: Christian World Imprints), 2017.

It is true that 'man is a product of his environment', and as such we can locate the formative influences of a person in his surroundings – geographical as well as spiritual. The rural vicinities of the poet and the spiritual background he was raised in invariably reflect in his writings. This Early Poetry depicts a variety of themes - mundane, religious, and philosophical musings, mostly didactic. Touching things of every day life, which are a commonplace, Solomon draws his lessons of all times. We also can navigate through his journey of life, as he moves from the mundane to the spiritual and on to the philosophical. He is as famous for his pictures in art as for his word pictures. Whereas his earlier poetry was mostly reflective verse – reflecting on the works of his paintbrush, instant and spontaneous, the present volume, is also reflective - reflecting on his memories and meditations on life situations, or sitz im leben, as the Germans would call it!

The poetry on the mundane themes is a poetic exercise of ordinary emotions and natural expressions. The poetry on religious themes is a confessional exercise of one's faith foundations. And the poetry on philosophical themes is personal musings on existential issues and concerns of life. An analytical survey of Solomon's early poetry, in the purview of these three realms is in order at this juncture.

Mundane Themes:

First of all, the blessings of "*Deep Sleep*" and ensuing rest and relaxation are mused upon. As we 'rest a while' with eyes closed, we lay aside all our burdens. As 'a mantle of deep sleep' hovers on us, we need to 'stay a while' that way, anticipating a 'fresh dawn' – for, with a new dawn, we see a new path: "The past has gone, it does not stay / For you have now a new path to walk."

In a companion poem, "*Heavenward Way*", Solomon muses upon not only laying aside burdens but dreaming 'holy dreams' - dreams that are given by a holy God. It is in deed a blessing to 'sleep peacefully' (undisturbed) until we wake up, and see 'the glorious sun once again' - the sun that does 'wipe away your saddening pain'.

In the poem on "*A Friend*", Solomon bemoans how a long time dear friend severed his friendly ties in spite of the many cherished times spent together and the joys shared together. Forgetting the story, though not easy, subsides all questions and the poet emerges with a foundational finding: "… the bamboo flute / Does not sing the same sweet song always."

In another poem on "*Paper to Write*" Solomon enlists the uses of paper and the great 'story of paper' graphically. Then he mentions about 'Chinese made paper' and how he loved to use paper for his pen and the paintbrush over the years of his full life!

There are a couple of poems on water. In "*Digging for Water*", the poet narrates the futile attempts of man. All across the centuries there have been efforts to dig for water, successful and otherwise. Even with modern technology and know-how there are times with the same plight in certain places.

Another poem, "*Out From the Waters*", depicts the poet's personal plight as he crosses a fast flowing canal across a small wooden bridge, holding fast his grand mother's hand. Such bridges are often just the long palm tree logs across the canal. Having slipped into the waters and struggling for life with no skills of swimming, it's really a great relief to have survived. Ruminating upon childhood experiences in the lines of poetry refreshes!

Religious Themes

The call of God in one's life is irrevocable and irresistible. The initial moments of the call were captured in the poem, "*I Heard A Voice*": 'A voice still and small / Coming out from / Somewhere deep!' Though the recipient of the call wished in vain to write down the message, the fact of God's call was indelibly printed on his heart. Solomon in fact had a deep sense of God's call upon his life, and his subsequent obedience took him into many experiences in life and on to many pinnacles of achievement.

"*Faith and Works*" talks about the historic debate: "Is faith the fruit or is it the root? / Does faith precede or follow good works?" Solomon concludes that "If one can do good works all perfect" and "If we can do all that is needed without God", "Why a God"? and why "faith in such a God"?

Mere works of our human striving take us nowhere, but instead nurture in us a prideful "*Holier Than Thou*" attitude. Solomon projects the common proverb of a 'frying pan' that 'called the tea-pot black'. In fact, "the big man did not know that he was as bad as the other fellow" – "Like a man with a big log in his eyes / Sought to help another with a speck in his".

"*The Sinful Woman*" depicts the self-righteous contemporaries, when an anonymous sinful woman came to the Pharisee's house 'uninvited' to meet "the One who could wipe away her sins and give her a new life". She must be enacting the 'desired cleansing' in her life by what she did. Jesus declared His perennial appreciation: "What she had done shall be remembered" - not her evil past, but her redeemed present, "wherever the Good news shall be preached".

A couple of poems in this Early Poetry of Solomon are on Jesus' crucifixion. In "*The Blessed Pebbles*", the poet describes the 'forlorn and forbidden' pebbles as 'blessed pebbles' since they were 'moved with deep sorrow, wept sadly and wiped their tears' as Jesus "Came to that place called skull Carrying dreadful cross". The other poem, "*The Passing Experience*", presents the cross, the spear and the centurion. These are the "Sights we have in our memory's path". From here the poet moves on to our existential plight, where the cross and the spear can also be real for some of us. Though not manifested in a spectacular way they are silently endured.

The poem, "*Resurrection*", is written with rays of hope and assurance: Death is seen as 'final sleep', accompanied by an assurance of resurrection. Solomon expresses such confidence that after death, he shall 'surely awake', 'rise again' and 'jump out of the pit' and the source for such confidence is Jesus, the 'first fruit' of resurrection! He further declares that he shall not remain 'among the dead' and that he never would have a second death! Solomon claims that Jesus had 'sealed his promise with his blood' and that will be his second birth. This gives us the divine arithmetic - 'Born Once - Die Twice; Born Twice - Die Once."[229]

Philosophical Themes:

- 3 poems on birds and bees with philosophical musings:

In "*A Bird in the Cage*", the poet portrays the inherent longing of a caged bird for praise from the visitors - appreciation for its wisdom, beauty and goodness! Such favor found but for a while, but someone sometime is not pleased with us or with our performance, which brings us enlightenment: "life is a mixture of good and bad as well"! Alas, the caged bird did not have courage enough to take it, and "It got a shock and fell dead in the cage".

In "*The Sparrow and The Peacock*", the poet demonstrates how a sparrow envies a peacock, because of its beauty and the color. After all, the whole creation is marked by a rich variety of form and pigment. This poem teaches the need and importance to be content as we are created and endowed with. The sparrow learns this lesson only with the fowler's attempt to catch the birds with his nest, and when the peacock becomes a prey and the sparrow could escape. Therefore, "thank God for the way you're made to live" and "never seek for more fancies and grieve".

In yet another poem, "*Honey Bees*", the poet narrates the daily chore of the bees - Buzzing all around the trees and dipping into the flowery womb. But as they do their daily chore faithfully, they are making the trees multiply. Faithful commitment to our tasks accomplishes larger ends, knowingly or unknowingly!

- 6 poems on trees and flowers with philosophical musings:

In "*Luxury of A Lovely Rose Garden*", Solomon depicts a pretty rose garden and the "joy of sweet flowers and their flavors [sic]. The odors are alluring and as much as one wishes to spend there forever, there dawns the reality at last – "life is both sun and rain in some measure"!

In another poem, "*Transitory*", the poet presents the transitory nature of everything in creation, under the sun. The poet walks along the fields by a lovely pool, and gazes upon a lotus. Solomon finds great joy in the scene of the lotus in full bloom with green leaves all around. Beyond this fascinating experience, he confronts the stark reality of its transitory nature, which was frustrating. The poet perceives that all lovely things should one day go. "Nature had been designed so, for us to enjoy new things from time to time."

In "*The Sorrowing Banana Stalk*", the poet narrates the soliloquy of a tall banana stalk, which bemoans its plight, "standing all day in the watery mud", and "To become mother, bear fruit just once, and then to be cut up, cast out by the

229 http://www.bible.ca/ef/expository-revelation-2-11.htm - accessed May 26, 2018.

fence" and fully forgotten, giving her place to someone else. The pain intensifies and agony aggravates when the banana stalk compares with the mango tree how it stands year after year with its wide wings, every summer decked in golden flowers, giving its sweet fruit perennially.

The banana stalk resents the perennial fruit-bearing potential of the mango tree, making it much needed for the "Bees to visit and birds to live", and even humans desiring its cool shade. The 'One above' responded, after hearing this inner grumbling of the banana stalk and decided to turn all the bananas into big mango trees. And the outcome was neither desirable for mankind nor conducive to the order of creation and nature. People did not want only mangoes just in summer days but they crave also for the banana fruit year round.

In the poem, "*Lotus Flower*", the poet extolls the Lotus, the queen of flowers, for all its rich symbolism. With its status as the national flower of India, it brings to mind "symbols deep and sublime" and its course itself demonstrates great possibilities for humans to rise from the lowest depths to the highest heights. Doing a thing three times indicate intensity and symbolize significance. The Lotus receives a three-fold salute for it symbolizes the answer for the three-fold petition of mankind, as found in Upanishads, and as recounted by the poet: "You remind me of new life from deadly gloom / To leave the darkness and rise towards the light / Is to reach the wisdom's heavenly height." And the poetic Muse takes the poet to imagine the presence of Lotus all over the universe including the Blue Nile River. The poet also finally pens in this poem that Lotus was the new material for his paintbrush as well.

The poem "*Love the Trees"* portrays the poet's love for the flora and fauna of his rural birthplace. He reckons and loves trees as his friends, for "they keep company with us in all kinds of winds". Solomon remarks: "It is hard to imagine a tree-less earth; Trees are with us from our very birth". This small poem is like an ode on mango trees! "I like to sit under my mango tree"! The poet further describes how he cherished eating mangoes. He could not but declare the rich variety of mangoes and their peculiar tastes. Some of the household names are on his lips – 'name after name'. "We await the season for the mangoes to come / And we want to taste all of them or at least some".

One last poem of this period captures his steps on the sea beach, in the woods, and upon the haystack. This poem "*Alone!*" presents the addresses of the places he frequented in his childhood, and which he recollects now with philosophical reflection. Having been immersed in the beauty of the season and the grandeur of the location, he often forgot to eat those 'fried nuts in the brown paper bag'. He ruminates - "in all this there is no lonely place / However much I wanted / For me".

- 4 poems <u>on day-to-day objects</u> with philosophic significance.

"*A Square Peg in A Round Hole"* is pregnant with rich didactic significance. The poet clearly conveys that it is hard – "To put kind words in an uncouth mouth

/ Joyful thoughts in a hapless heart / And with kind words to mend a fool" - like "trying to drive a square peg in a round hole". In "*The Kite*", the poet describes the common object in such a way that it brings out a common truth to the fore - essential for all mankind: "The string that holds together us both / Helps us to be together in truth". "*The Signboard*" speaks to the viewers and demands attention to what it says. The essence of the poem lies in the couplet: "I am not ashamed / If ignored". It is to the risk or disadvantage of the person that ignores the signboard. Little things mean much when they accomplish needed functions, facilitating human existence and inter-personal communication. "*Door Called Dwar*" is an analysis on door. This is pretty much like an ode. The primary purpose of a door is well expressed as a means "to keep us always in, and others out". Further, we invite friends with open doors. The poet talks of three types of doors, designed for three different purposes: the garden doors keep goats straying; bed room doors keep Toms peeping; and, doors of steel keep thieves out 'from mischievous drill'. The poet later talks about keeping the doors open to our minds, so 'knowledge advent may happen'. When our open hearts let our love flowing, our affection always will be growing. Open minds help us avoid prejudices, but open mouths cause conflicts. Finally, see how the wise men pointed to us the importance of knowing "when to open the door and when to shut".

- 14 other poems from this period on philosophical themes:
- 4 poems on abstract themes and experiences.

In "*Awake or Asleep*", we see an experience talking to a man in an indefinite status of awareness. Couple of observations worth noting: Some people see / What they want to see. It may be far from reality like everything appears dark to the one who sees with dark glasses. Some strange experiences stay with us longer, but others move on like a cloud. It depends partly on the person who keeps things within forever or lets them go! "*Light Sleep*", similar experiences are recounted. The things seen in such unconscious or subconscious status - "Is it all real as in real life"? Is it a lingering of a past experience or a forecast of things to come? The main question remains: "What is its meaning?" In "*Darkness*", the poet presents the answer to the question of 'loneliness' and exhorts that "I need some good company in deed". But the legitimate question now is whether we can know in advance that a particular company is good. The complexity of the situation is penned well. In "*Breath Control*", Solomon recollects one of the humorous experiences he encountered in his cross-cultural communication.

- 3 poems on the philosophy of life.

Solomon, in "*Life is Like A Train Journey*", likens life to a train travel. The train runs quick and 'people come and people go'. For some it is a 'happy journey' while others experience drudgery. Solomon observes the inter-personal exchange during travel, which is unpredictable: There may be a smile sometimes from someone, which is conducive for all to feel at home. The lesson of life, we may draw from this, is even if we do not receive a smile from our fellow travellers, we can take the initiative in exchanging one, which changes the atmosphere: Sow a smile and reap a smile! "*A Trimmed Quill"* envisages the message to not find excuses but rather endeavor with the entrepreneurial skills: "Never say for a moment / That you were not born / With a trimmed quill in your hand". To substantiate this invocation, Solomon presents couple of analogies: i) "The tree had no fruits when it is planted"; ii) A sword cannot cut till it is heated in the fire and beaten with a hammer. Thus "A work of brain is half brain and the rest is strain". In "*Seeking Support"* Solomon expounds the need to complement one another. Solomon enunciates that "weak souls seek support". It is well known that "a solid tree stands on its own … facing all the rain and strain". With this analogy, Solomon exhorts, "Giving and taking some help / Is not unwise / Like a mighty gun will need a cartridge / To hit the target right.

- 6 poems on the theme of virtues

Through the rural scenery of feeding the birds, Solomon portrays the virtue of gratitude in the poem, "*Thankfulness"*. The poet delights to welcome the birds in the morning under the porch. And as he threw some grains, crows, songbirds and others swarm around. To his dismay "they all took to wings and flew away" after pecking the grains. What delighted him most, bringing a solace, was the gratitude of the songbird: "singing sweet songs for me". In "*Love is Long-Suffering"*, Solomon describes the long-suffering quality of love with a simile. "It does not jump to its feet too soon / When things go wrong sometimes / Love takes time to think and do / Like the sun rises only after / The night is gone." In "*Love Reality"*, Solomon describes another quality of love, namely, reciprocity or mutuality: "Love is by definition, mutual / One gives it and the other receives / And the one who receives love / Does also give it back / Happily to the one who first gives" – in contrast to 'self-love' or 'selfish love'.

In a similar vein, Solomon condemns the selfishness or egoism in "*I and Others"*. Until we find an equal or one superior to us, the egoism in us desires to puff up: "I am the first and all others next … Only my opinion in the world is the best / No one can think as best as I can / But then came one better than him". In "*Company and No Company"*, Solomon, as the ancient wise man, exhorts the readers to: "Cherish the company of all your friends / Who come and join as the journey extends. But we need to "stop fretting when they depart". They may leave us just like they came to join. "Leave a sweet thought about every friend / Because all friendships are transitory". In "*Agree or Disagree"*, the poet confesses his immature thought "that all should feel, just as I do and not differ a great deal". This variety is the beauty of life even among a couple: It would be 'a dull creation' "If the potter made all pots the same, / In size and shape color and name".

- A final poem on Solomon's 'virtuous woman'.

Finally, Solomon is fascinated to describe his own story in the poem, "*Show Each Other the Way*". The biblical image of marriage with complementarity as its essence is etched well into the lines of this poem. This sounds to be mostly autobiographical: "Once I saw a lovely little girl pretty and fair / She loved me too and came with me her life to share". The theme of diversity is carried on even into this poem where he relates this dynamic from his marital experience: "She agreed with me in life with all things most often / But she had to differ with me now and then".

Solomon concludes that 'Individual differences' are a fact of life woven into the human fabric, but never a hindrance even in the 'journey of life together'! The eternal purpose of diversity to be the complementing agent and completing element is beautifully summed up: "Two of God's creation each in our own way / One always to show the other the life's way."[230]

What a pleasant delight ('Hridayanandam') Solomon must have had as he penned these poems as an Octogenarian! And what a pleasant delight they are to the reader, beside their didactic contribution!

Early Poetry of A Nonagenarian

As a nonagenarian, Solomon was experimenting into **Odes and Sonnets**. Just as King Solomon of old tried and tested everything under the sun, Solomon Raj too seemed to have that urge to search the plethora of wisdom. It is interesting to see that he penned some 15 sonnets. Sonnets are ordered poetry, and these Sonnets of Solomon signify Solomon's ordered life and ordered confession!

Solomon's 'Journey into Sonnets' began with a poem titled "*Sonnet*" - on his childhood exploits in the midst of picturesque rural settings. Solomon started his life in nice vicinities. He has friends and cattle for his entertainment. He was always late for lunch. They spent life happily, but with a sincere realization - He and his friends escaped proper tending. In "*A Village Boy*", he describes himself as a happy village boy - never caring for any thing! His attachment to the nature and the things around are portrayed with gratitude: "The earth, the sun, the wind and water cool / The calf and cow the grassy fields I love … / These are the gifts we all get from above". Solomon extols God for His 'sweet creation' and thanks Him as 'He made us prosperous'!

In another sonnet, Solomon shares his philosophical musings on "*Adwaitha*", which means Monism. The reasoning and questioning faculties are at their best as he contemplates about being 'united with God'. Is it a hereafter thing or 'here and now' thing? Solomon propounds the proposition of real 'oneness with God': True *aikya* should happen on earth truly / In prayer and constant meditation / This leads to the oneness with the Holy / God is God and man is nothing but man. Finally, it is desirable and feasible that "God is to be enjoyed like sweet

230 Mary Sarojini, the only sister of Balla Moses, whom Solomon married, and she was his tower of strength in all his endeavors and achievements in life.

sugar". Solomon questions: "what joy if man himself becomes sugar"? and states his preference in parenthesis: "(So I like 'I and thou' relationship with God / Rather than being lost in him)"!

He wrote another sonnet on "*The Alcoholic*" - a social evil of all times. The intoxication temporarily helps them forget all the cares and loads of life - an easy escape! Solomon addressed other social evils later in some seven poems. Thinking about the evil consequences, he addresses the alcoholic who drowns deep in alcohol, and forgets his shame. Losing sense, he immerses in all sorts of demeaning actions, earning nothing but a bad name. Solomon makes a plea in the following lines to pause and think about the value of life and then to mend the way. This addiction causes "pain to parents and the partner", with no peace on the deathbed.

In "*Early Rising*", Solomon brings out the utility of the primitive saying, "Early to bed and early too to rise"! "By this during day more work could be done". With changing times and changing habits, Solomon sees this an optional. He concludes that life needs to be lived happily instead of becoming drudgery. After all, "Early to rise is not a big gospel" and "To stick to this old rule is impossible".

"*Two Kinds of Friendship*", deals with Friendship, and distinguishes godly friendship with worldly friendship. It's always good to have God-fearing friends - for the outcome of counseling, prayer and fellowship and the fruit of love, peace and sainthood. Solomon warns about the 'worldly chatting' - 'Which create rivalries and sadness'. "Believers do bring glory to His name / Worldly assemblies are another game".

"*Giving and Receiving*" presents the Biblical message of 'giving' - even the supreme giving Himself of the Son of God! This sounds a 'confessional' proclaiming the tenets of Christian faith. Christian lifestyle of giving is manifested as "we help others in need". We know it is more blessed to give than to receive. Giving implies giving to God, and benevolence is giving to those in need! We see Solomon the evangelist at his best in the next stanza - responding to the challenge of evangelization and extending a call to his readers: "This great salvation, which we have received / We share with all nations and bear witness"! In the last couplet Solomon proclaims that God is the greatest Giver; no one can ever out give God!

In "*Joy with Children*", Solomon shares his philosophy about offspring. The phase of giving birth to children, and nurturing them - with the accompanying joys of playing with them, employing their skills, and feeling proud of them as they are growing - does not compare to anything! But later the poet acknowledges that it is not easy to supply all expected comforts or to help them to 'succeed in life'. For all these, God and only 'God should enable them'! 'This we should pray for and always desire' and can aspire 'from God only'!

The last sonnet in this current section, "*Tent on the Highest Rock*", takes the readers with Jesus on to the Mount of Transfiguration. Like Peter on the Mount, Solomon desires to pitch his tent on the highest rock! The determination of the poet is vivid when he spares no cost in claiming his mountain, 'the best and noblest' designed for his 'greatest joy'! Solomon further declares: "God for us sure designs the best / As He gives me a heart to seek / Although I pass the path hardest / Who can tell me that I am weak?" ... "Do I need an assurance still, To make it true that He's with me?"

There are a handful of poems from this time, significantly with Biblical themes and exhortations. In "*The Sinner and His Song*", Solomon laments about the 'Original Sin' - the 'sin nature' inherited from Adam and exhorts about the need for watchfulness by virtue of the promise of the sin-cleansing blood of the Lamb! "I keep erring", he recognizes because "Old Adam's seed is in my blood". Until the day we shall reach sainthood, we have to watch our pace. What a provision and what an assurance till we reach paradise, that sinners have God's promises in His blood: Hence as we live on earth in solace which the Lord gives, we shall 'get cure' for our disease, and our soul lives with Him. 'The Sinner and His Song' is the title of this poem and it is its message too!

In "*The Stroke Dealt by God*", Solomon expounds the blessedness of being struck by God, in view of the outcome of finding Him through faith: "This stroke is what our souls will truly need"! The five senses are the gates of our perception, and we keep getting sensory thoughts constantly - some bitter some pleasant through these doors. "They go only so far and then prevent us to view the glories of heavenly shores". Only the stroke dealt by God will take us to the place where we find Him through faith. We know well that "till the Lord will strike us dead in senses" we are "blind to what God wants us all to see, and deaf to what God wants us all to hear". This is very much like the strokes of an artist, which bring out hidden beauty and grandeur.

In "*Who is He?*" Solomon discusses about Who Jesus is - John the Baptist, Elijah, Rabbi, Scribe or Pharisee? The woman at the well could not easily tell Who He is. Nicodemus had perceived signs and miracles He showed. How do the people see Him? "Simon Peter once could see / By the prompting of the Lord" that He was 'Greater than all these' - the only Son of God! Solomon sums up his findings that He was not the forerunner or the chariot rider but He was the true Savior, and the ultimate purpose of the Incarnation is – 'to save you and me':

In "*Redemption from Pain*", Solomon deals with the problem of pain. The universality of pain is expressed well: "Pain is common to all humans / Sadness is the rule of life. / Crying is how life does commence / And all life's journey is a strife." Pain may be endured by means of forbearance and silence, but cannot be ended. When all is said and done, Solomon upholds the biblical truth, as enunciated by Jesus Himself, that "all pain is not God's wrath"! Ultimately, "there will be an end to suffering" - some day! "Man is not made just for weeping", but to see relief some day!

In "*Waiting for a Harvest*", Solomon deals with the dynamics of harvesting! He shares a personal experience when he labored on a barren field, seeking a generous yield under the cycle of 'sowing, growing and waiting'. Since his labor was on a barren field, some thought it was 'mere waste' while others thought it a 'bad taste'. When in despair, he left the field the Lord woke him up and said, "I should not give up". With a song in his heart he 'worked again in the same place' with the sun right in his face. The rewarding outcome is gladly recounted: "Working thus I prayed to God / To whom there is nothing hard / He sent clouds and rain along / That made the crop green and strong". When the harvest turned out plentiful, all his barns came breaking full. And he testifies and proclaims: "I knew God will give the fruit / If I worked and afraid not".

3 **other sonnets** Solomon composed as part of his early poetry.

In "*Love and Respect*", Solomon presents a compact treatise on the twin virtues of love and respect. These are to be natural and spontaneous, springing from within and 'flowing like river'. As a 'gift from God' the bond of love must be perennial - 'blessing both receiver and the giver'! Solomon beautifully portrays this virtue in the Canaanite Ruth who had freely shown it to Naomi, and submitted her life in love. As He was pleased by this, "God in His love has firmly sealed it / A seal that lead to the Savior's advent". Genuine love is extolled as 'God's own blessed gift'.

The sonnet, "*Brothers Living Together*", envisages 'Brotherly Love' as enshrined in the Psalter.[231] We see a picture of the Indian joint-family in the first stanza: "How good for brothers to live together / Under one and the same roof as it were / If the wives do not fight with each other / And share life's blessings always together". There are families who live with strife all the time, and there are families who live in endless harmony. Often the presence of the head of the family makes the difference! The picture in the family of God with 'unity in diversity' is portrayed: "How Christ-like to live in brotherly love / Coming from different realms whatever / Share with each other God's gifts from above / This is what a brother does to brother". The picture of the Trinity is elucidated in the next stanza, with Tri + Unity - God's oneness in three persons! This sums up the divine design for the church:

"So His people live as His one body /
Till they be with Him in heaven one day".

In the sonnet, "*When My Heart Went Astray*"**,** Solomon portrays the message enshrined in the classical hymn by Purushottam Chaudhury -'*Yehova Naa Morallalinchenu.*'[232] The first two stanzas are rendering of the imagery of a wild elephant that 'has gone astray' – 'trespassing all the way'! Solomon contemplates how 'the Lord my God subdued it so kindly' – "He with His goad had soon controlled my heart / Subduing my unwilling rude spirit" - 'when my heart went

231 Psalm 133:1 - *"Behold, how good and how pleasant it is for brethren to dwell together in unity."*

232 Andhra Christian Hymnal, Hymn No.16.

astray running wildly' like the strayed wild elephant! But for God's intervention in his life, he could not have found the rest he enjoys now! All the cares and stress, and, snares and temptations are gone! Under this ministry of God, the poet does find 'needed safety' in His home 'And stay with Him through all eternity'!

Later Poetry of A Nonagenarian

A little over half of the present anthology constitutes the later poetry of Solomon as a nonagenarian. This is classified, into three categories - on natural themes, existential themes and Christian themes. There are some 3 sonnets and at least 3 odes in this anthology.[233] An analytical commentary on the later poetry is in order at this juncture. There are 11 poems with natural themes, 22 poems with existential themes, and 36 poems with Christian themes. These are not watertight compartments but are a broad classification. Being a Christian preacher and theologian, Solomon's faith manifests itself in whatever category we may classify, as it is embedded in every line he pens.

- 11 poems on **natural themes**.

In "*The River*", Solomon graphically depicts the course of a river from the mountain pinnacles where it originates to the valley beneath: Trickle by trickle through the narrow clefts of the mountainside, hiding behind the stones and showing up again, creeping down in curvy lanes while other such small streams join it along the way. The river swiftly comes down along the mountainside, and as it reaches a sharp edge, it jumps off making a thundering sound into the gorge below - uprooting shrubs to drag them along its way, and turning around the rebellious trunks rooted firmly standing along its way; polishing the smaller pebbles, and breaking down some bigger stones; and, raising clouds of foams at last it meets the motherly belly of the deep mountain valley.

"*Crossing the River*" also describes the course of the river in a similar streak, but the last stanza portrays a personal cruise. The river creeps, crawls and jumps in its 'native wild fury' along its way, along the mountain slopes. Crossing hurdles, turning around big bumps of boulder, leaping into the valley, and raising a cloud of mist in the process, and a rainbow in the sky above - the river flows in to gentle plainly land. It grows slower and wider to left and right looking like a lake. Finally it calmly tends to further slow down - by the big earthen dams across, when it is easier to cross by sailboat. The poet exuberantly depicts his cruise. He hails from the delta of the river *Godavari* in Andhra Pradesh State.[234] Here

233 An ode is a kind of poem devoted to the praise of a person, animal, or thing. An *ode* is usually written in an elevated style and often expresses deep feeling. It is a poem in which a person expresses a strong feeling of love or respect for someone or something. It is otherwise described as a lyric poem of some length, usually of a serious or meditative nature and having an elevated style, and formal stanzaic structure. It is a type of lyrical stanza.

234 *Godavari*, the largest of the peninsular rivers, has its source at Triambakam, near Nashik in Maharashtra State. It flows a length of 1465 kilometers with outfall into the Bay of Bengal,

is a cherished experience of childhood: "Take a trip on one of the big sailboats / Laden to the brim with dry coconuts / Kept in course with a mighty big rudder / Going forward with the help of the wind / When it nearly reaches the edge / The boatmen held it and pulled to barge". Finally, "How happy we were to have crossed the river" is the end note.

"*Childhood Memories*" describes some of the early memories of Solomon, which he recalls often. Most of the poems in this section are on his Childhood Memories. The present incident was one of his play times with his grand mother in the rice fields of his native vicinities.[235] Once walking through the rice fields, he went ahead holding grandma's hand. Before he knew what happened, he slipped from the narrow footbridge into the flowing channel. Poor grandma waded into knee-deep water to save him. Solomon cherishes such memories all along: "Living in past memories is wonder".

In "*The Amazing Spring*", Solomon picturizes birds and the deer, the branches and the jasmines. He describes the response of his inner being in the following stanzas: His heart was rejoicing and his joy was surging while experiencing this memorable delight. His soul sings along and his lower chin drops for the 'beauty of the spring'. In "*Hatching Bird's Eggs*", Solomon vividly recollects another childhood experience. Young Solomon was "Sitting on the wooden munch / Under the shade of coconut palms" on a 'cool early dawn' in the ripe corn field. His job was to scare the stray birds because the crop was ripe. The 'open straw-bed' was rather warm. His younger sister brought for him a 'pot of cool rice water'. When she was sleeping still on the munch, and the faithful dog has gone to chase the intruding fox, Solomon decided to climb the tree nearby and hunt for birds' nests. He slowly brought one down with a few eggs to cover them up and watch, hoping they hatch in another twenty days. The outcome is obvious: "Bird on the tree and man on the earth / Are always better of course".

"Floating in the Air" is a short poem where Solomon recounts an experience in the dream. Sometimes in dream he flies in the air. It was exhilarating as well as frustrating: "And then I like to stay right there / But soon I drop to earth like a stone / And find myself on earth alone". Flying feeling gives a strand of joy, but 'then sadness comes like a broken toy'! The poem *"The Toothless Smile"* describes his childhood experiences. The toothless smile of a baby is the content of this poem. The poet, as he watches the baby, thought that she was cute and wise. The poet felt so happy within for such a sweet little new life and breathed a blessing, thanking God for making her life a song.

In "*A Lazy Summer Afternoon*", he depicts the plight when time does not pass so soon: "Wet all over the body / With a humid kind of sweat / Hard to sit, hard to stand / Not so easy to understand". No use even with two ceiling

very close to the native village of Solomon Raj.

235 Solomon calls them 'Andhra's fame'. In fact, this coastal Andhra Pradesh is acclaimed the 'rice bowl' of India - ever green with rivers, canals and water streams!

fans as they simply send some warm air. "Getting unrobed? But to what limit?" – the poet ruminates in the sweltering gloom of the hot summer afternoon. In "*Sugarcane Plantation*", Solomon graphically portrays the interesting process of sugarcane plantation and sugar plant. The sweet smelling sight of a sugarcane field is presented: "Rows upon rows the canes grow tall" until they yield to the cutter's sickle. At a safe distance the oven glows in big hot metal pan, boiling sweet sugar cane juice, which thickly simmers and then poured into cans for cooling. Thus goes sugar cane harvest - cut, denuded, sent to be crushed, boiled in big vats, and poured in blocks, and by this process black sugar comes. Solomon enjoyed all this with village boys. As they loaf around there, the worker kindly cuts a piece and throws at them to chew happily.

"Kondapalli Wooden Man" is an ode on a native artifact from a place called Kondapalli. This woodwork is personified and Solomon wonders who ever can forget this wooden man. Forest timber and carving tools coupled with the carpenter's skill have made us dumbfound filling our hearts with wonder. The eyes of the Wooden Man are like ours small and black, staring at us as we once look back, daily standing where they are kept with one's art ware. Solomon converses with it that its life is transitory as ours, made for some joy and then disappears but ultimately "contributing happiness in this world of wilderness."[236]

"Song to the Koel" is another ode on a native bird called *Koel.*[237] Solomon welcomes the dear *koel*, perched on the green mango tree. He personifies this native bird and declares that "nothing in the world stops your singing" the joyful spring song to us, humans - even dreadful winter rain, blowing eastern wind. He welcomes the *koel*, coming from the freezing north, to stay with us as long as she wants. The melody of her song is sweet and the music of her sweet song "Redeems us from sadness" and the poet praises the little *koel* as 'conqueror of misery'. Finally, the poet invites her again after her departure for the current season: "When you leave us here dear *koel* / You come to see us once again / To feed us with your sweet song / And to relieve us from our woes."

---

236 Kondapalli is a small town near Vijayawada and the name is popular for its soft wood toys, distinct on various counts - the material being used, method of making, look and feel and themes on which these toys are made. They have been famous for many decades. Few Rajasthani *karigars* (artisans) settled over here from 16th century and started making these figures. They are referred as Aryakhastriyas.

237 The Asian koel is a bird of light woodland and cultivation, staying in a dense thick forest with thick trees and bamboos. It is also found in shrubby areas with tall trees, woods, gardens and forest. It is a shy bird, seen alone or in pair. It has straight and swift flight with rapid wing beats. It is an omnivorous bird, feeding mainly on fruits and berries, feasting on the ripe fruits, and also feeding on insects, eggs, small vertebrates and caterpillars. Asian Koel is very vocal. It is often heard before seen: song of the male is a repeated *koo-Ooo- koo-Ooo- koo-Ooo.* The female makes a shrill *kik-kik-kik...* call.
https://en.wikipedia.org/wiki/Asian_koel - accessed November 20, 2017.

- 22 poems with **existential themes**, such as social evils, trials and troubles, solitude and companionship and Solomon's sunset years.
- The seven poems on *social evils*, are short but straightforward:

"*Black Coffee*" is a small poem where Solomon addresses the prejudices and predilections about 'black coffee'. Though he dreams of black coffee in the bed after being well-fed, he hates to see it in the morning for reasons not stated. It could be because of a forced wake-up too early than normal, or it could be because of its imperfect proportion of the components. Though others may like to drink, thinking that it keeps them awake from sleep, and relishing its bitter taste, he personally thinks that 'it is all a waste'.

In *"Houses to Live"* Solomon addresses the social evils of injustice and 'unjust distribution of wealth'. In deed, "a house to live is gift of God"! This some of us receive while some have no place to live. While some command spacious palaces, some do not even have a hut. Solomon proclaims that poverty is the child of injustice, though it is not poor man's fault! "Unjust distribution of wealth does make some people poor"! And complaints, sit outs, and agitations cannot provide the cure. In "*Wealth to Show Mercy*", Solomon evolves a new hermeneutic to offset the above evil. The biblical basis for this is the story of the poor leper and the rich man, who both died – but the former went the 'blissful side' while 'not so the other one'. The 'why' of it was answered in the lines: "... One was patient in his faith / The other did only know / To drown deep in worldly wealth." The summary envisages that wealth, besides other things, is given 'for us to show mercy'! Poor humans forget this, but at the end when they try to see, 'the door then shall be shut'.

"*The Bazar*", is just a narrative of a typical Indian *bazar* (market). You see 'crowds moving all around' the city roads in the dusty wind – shopping, loafing, sightseeing, even some lazy walking. How much more? It seems unending! *"Meetings and Conferences"* depicts the routine of 'meetings, consultations, conferences and agendas, chairmen, presidents, welcomes and farewells'. The procedural norm is stated that 'everything is to be done openly, collectively, democratically and sometimes ecumenically. 'Democratic discussions - Never one man's decision' - though we hold on to this norm, 'at the end, that happens as one man's way'.

"*TV Preachers*" presents the sad state of affairs with "Many anxious TV preachers now". The poet laments how they make him tired of the Gospel, which he loves: "They try to impress me with loud noise / What can be told in gentle voice." He elucidates their sad plight: "Throat is their tool and volume their trick / Hoping the listener changed and quick / But seldom have they a tool to measure / How much the listeners got of the treasure." The Gospel in fact is simple but we try to make it heavy, trying to feed the lambs with meat while they only need milk. Having been a preacher all his life, Solomon aptly points out: "Preachers seldom have learnt the skill / Of teaching people with more good will / Using our Lord's beautiful fare / Of flowers o' the field and the birds o' the air".

Solomon's last poem on social evils, "*Human Wild Beasts*", strongly condemns tragic crimes like rape. It is hard to see and hard to overcome the shock and shame it brings. "Some youth today have lost their soul and forfeited their shame, making all our poor conscience foul and bringing to us bad name". The poet bemoans "Rape and kill a poor virgin - In a fast moving bus: How sad and painful to imagine, and how greatly disastrous!"[238] We feel the pain deep in our heart and now believe that "man is much worse than the beast" which lives in the wilderness. "A blooming life nipped in the bud"! Our conscience can never stop grieving in agony and shame!

- four poems about *trials and troubles*.

In the sonnet, "*Troubles Come Together*", Solomon portrays the glorious purpose of troubles in one's life - 'troubles come together and not alone'. He likens them to the herd of camels from father Abraham's house, as Eliezer was sent in search of a bride for Isaac. A great illustration with a message is presented here. If only we show kindness and love to the camels, they take us home to the bridal palace. The noble purpose for which the Father sends the camels (troubles) is for us to get abundant solace, and "to be received with great royal acclaim!" This is surely great and good news to our life to face problems when they come together, to be prepared to face our own strife, and to ever win Satan in His name: "Defeat the foe with the sign of the cross / And inherit the great kingdom at last".

"*Camels are Coming*" is another poem with a similar message as above. When "Camels come in a long big row, we do not chase them away" but 'give them water' and show mercy, because "To God's home they know the way". Camels imply troubles, and they are from the father's yard. "He sends them to bring the bride, so that she comes happy homeward, and to his son be wedded". Solomon enlightens the reader that "trials and pains are the camels", and if we "treat them well with cool water" and "put on them the proper saddle", they will surely take you to the father. What you sow you reap, always even more! This is true of the scriptural law of giving. Solomon beautifully portrays this in the following stanza: "In return to the food to the camels / Get gold bangles to your hands / And to the others in the house / There are gifts too and garlands". Assuredly, trials like camels show us the way - the right path to the bride-groom's feet!

"*As the Wind Blows*" presents a simple and sound teaching on the Holy Spirit and His ministry to the believer. Solomon exhorts himself ('my soul') to follow the Lord's leading. The Spirit shows silently as the wind blows gently. Jesus likened the Spirit to the wind and this metaphor is aptly used here. If we keep

---

238 Enraged in his spirit probably by the 2012 Delhi Gang Rape case, the poet pens his strong feelings and convictions addressing the inhuman evils in a civilized society. Man becomes inhuman sometimes, committing tragic crimes.

proceeding in the Lord's path, the poet assures: "You will not falter in your step / Your goal you will not give up". As He sends His angels to keep you from dangers, and brings us to His home guiding, we need to lean upon His bosom believing, when perils do appear and sadness comes near. He is able and kind hearted; He knows where we started, and He will make our entire path straightened.

"God's Ways are Greater" is another poem related to the theme of trials. The poet exhorts us not to fret when things go wrong, and when there's no song in our mouth. God knows what is good for us and His plans are always great and true. When we show great desire to the earthly kingdoms, we do not see God's kingdom since our eyes are blinded. When Jesus died on the cross His friends thought it was a loss. Desolate they went again to fishing, their old bargain. Jesus then opened their eyes and showed them that His rule will rise. Blessed are they who perceive and receive His promises!

- four poems on *solitude and companionship*.

They lucidly bring out the individual benefits of solitude and companionship maintaining a desirable equilibrium. "*Blessedness of Loneliness*", is an Ode on Loneliness. Human beings crave for the twin gifts of company and communication. Without company they feel vulnerable. Surely, the gift of speech, which facilitates communication, is also a great gift to mankind. But we desire both of these only in small measure. Evil company can lead to tears and sharp tongue can burn like wild fire. They both appear harmless but soon the fun will disappear. Hence, Solomon advocates that one should sit silently sometimes, trying to hear the still small voice. This we can hear only quietly 'since we become deaf with noise'! Further, our souls do get richly sustained in waiting for God's presence, and the holy countenance of God can be seen only in the lonely places. *"Companionship"* extols the blessedness of communion and companionship. Human heart craves for company. Loneliness is vulnerable just as nature abhors vacuum. Solomon extols the blessedness of the gift of speech. Speech is the greatest gift to humans to communicate. A silent person is either dumb, or he is 'a sage in forest in silence'. We are told that God the Father is always in communion with the Son and the Holy Spirit, as the doctrine of Trinity envisages.

'No man is an island', and the gregarious instinct in man propels him to communion and community. Solomon portrays this universal need in the poem, "*Man is Not Made to be Alone*". Solomon beautifully picturizes the foolishness of denouncing friendship. The friend denounced thus did not say a word in response but this sears the poet sharply through his heart like a bitter sword. Learning lessons from his foolish past, the poet in a friendly way shared his love with a stranger lad in kindly mood, which made him really glad. From this experience, and the supreme example of Jesus Christ, comes the enlightenment that humans are not made or meant to be alone or groan in lonely burdens: "The good Lord made them to each other's concerns made known". In *"Then and Now"*, Solomon proposes the need for icebreakers for friendship in a couple of simple stanzas:

Earlier, he does not know the name of the stranger though he saw him going that way often but "Once I tried to stop you and ask the same / So as to be your friend every day". Now that the poet knows his name and since they became friends, "Life now is no longer the same / We shall be friends till the end".

- Finally, there are seven poems on his <u>*sunset years*</u>.

"*End of the Journey"* is a Sonnet and it is not the first time for Solomon to contemplate and write on the 'end of the journey.'[239] Solomon supplicates to the Lord as now his journey comes to an end. The ravages of time are expressed in the words, 'bruised and wounded' and 'sores and cuts'. Only the Lord can mend them as He comes to His door and His gate 'greatly renowned'. Solomon recollects the divine call in the prime of his life. The Lord asked him to go to work in His vineyard 'with tools and wares', and he obeyed the call never counting the cost, and the Lord has taken all his cares on Him. Having been impacted by the teaching of St. Francis of Assisi, Solomon acknowledges what he was enabled to do in the course of his ministry: "When there was sadness I tried to sow joy / And where there was strife I tried to bring peace / Where there was greed there real contentedness / Which *mantra* St. Francis too did employ". Even when he did not get commendation from people, he went ahead and labored all the same.

"Desirable Epitaph" is another poem Solomon wrote in 2013 related to the sunset years. The numerical significance of this seven-stanza poem is it denotes completeness or perfection. The exhortation and the enlightenment the poet envisages in each of the poem are edifying. He addresses this poem to an anonymous friend declaring, 'life is too short'. We make the best of it as we work hard in the given task, and show now our stewardship skills. Secondly, a great life lived and a high virtue only will last and be of great worth. Thirdly, he exhorts not to 'fall in sloth and slumber' as it will make life a waste. Fourthly, the poet exhorts never to stop acquiring wisdom, as it helps to charter our path and keeps us from sad fall. Fifthly, as we make friends in life we are to do it wisely. Sixthly, we see the exhortation not to be a lender or a debtor, but to live within our means, be thrifty and share our cup with the poor. Finally, the poet assures his friend to go in peace when the call comes, as he will see his reward in God, and the life he has lived in grace will be engraved on his epitaph.

"*Miracles"* presents a three-fold message envisaging the salient insights from Solomon's pen: First, Miracle for miracle's sake doesn't aid building up of faith; it is just like a crutch. Standing on faith is required for stability and growth: "He who wants a miracle crutch / Does not stand on his faith as such". Secondly, being content with miracles to the neglect of fulfilling His commands amounts to folly. 'Faith based on miracles does not stand' just 'Like a man builds his house on sand'. Finally, the injunction given by Jesus is to 'not rejoice that you can do

239 His anthology of hymns, *Geetha Malika* contains many lyrics on this recurring theme. Also in his Songs from Sambalikan, we find this theme.

miracles' as 'they will not benefit you'. Rather, we need to rejoice that our name is written in the Book of Life.

"The Call and The Journey" portrays the mystery and the miracle of God's Call and the ensuing Journey. The five stanzas are like ascents in the journey - obviously Solomon's testimony about the blessedness of obeying the Call of God. This is like a Psalm of Ascents in the Hebrew Scriptures:

> "When He said to me "come"/ I didn't know what I get"
> - the poet confesses.
> "But when I simply went to Him / What I saw was perfect"
> - No regrets!
> "He wanted me to leave / some comforts of my own"
> - a step in self-denial.
> "But what great blessings He could give / To me till then unknown"
> - divine surprises!
> "Great wine and living bread / More than I ever see" - amazing supply.
> "He kept in store to keep me fed / And make me rested"
> - divine provision!
> "Fellowship of great lords / And company of saints"
> - awesome communion.
> "I did get as I went forwards / royal rich garments"
> - robes of righteousness!
> "My mouth was filled with song / Right along all the way"
> – perennial melodies.
> "And I had strength right in my wing / To reach the clouds and stay"
> - rapture!

"Offerings" is another poem giving us Solomon's ruminations of the sunset years. When all the labors of life have ended Solomon reckons that he spent his life with the Lord thankfully. And as the time of rest becomes immanent to him, he calls upon Him to come and help. So he forgets all that belongs to self and peacefully waits to see His face. In the second stanza, as one enters the next destination, Solomon depicts the blessedness and the reward. We have 'no need for any worldly lust' as all our needs in Him are fully met when we reach our heavenly rest. What a reward is the whitest stone the Lord will give, with a name known only to those that receive! This we will never get in our strength alone! In the third stanza, Solomon describes how all the promises we have lived to see are coming to be fulfilled now for us - since the Lord has always been faithful! Then we begin to see in full the glory in which He ever lives, and the everlasting peace He alone gives. Finally, he yields himself to the Lord in gratitude for His grace, which is 'wider than all my strife', and His love, which is 'still greater all through my life': "That which I did and what I couldn't do / I remit humbly all, my Lord,

to you / And ask you to fulfill this for me … / And now I come forever your face to see".

"Old Age Comes" presents a beautiful description of old age and the practical counsel for this particular season of life. Solomon accepts the divine plan for man's existence and exit from life. Solomon welcomes old age, as it has come at last. In this state of life there won't be any 'hustle bustle' as 'You do not run now so fast'. A new lifestyle is ushered as you wake up at night once or twice, with late mornings. A new etiquette is in place as you 'take your time at the dining place', 'chew and swallow', as 'it is not a race'. It is no longer time to 'crack hard nuts' lest 'your dentures break in bits'. Let your food be soft and spicy and 'This is wise as you would see'! And it's more pleasant to talk along: 'Do not sit and keep silent' is the rule of the time and space. Further, a new trend of conversation with eagerness to share and share, as if it's their 'endless vocation': "Wisdom is what you like to share / Even if others do not always care / Where should your experience go / If you to others do not show". But a word of caution - not to welcome verbal duel, as it is a 'sure fuel to bitterness'! "Learn to say, Yes - always / Whatever the opponent says"! Finally, the whole counsel in fact is Solomon's soliloquy – speaking to himself and others too in the process! He sums up his counsel in the last stanza: "Look ahead to a peaceful end / People bid farewell and send / For a while if they remember you / Know it as an added blessing too".

"To Be With My Lord" expresses the 'blessed assurance' Solomon has, as a result of the life-long revelation he has received, and believed. In a similar vein, as the 19th century poet, Sarah Flower Adams penned it in the hymn, "Nearer, my God, to Thee", Solomon expresses his desire to be with his dear Lord, 'good shepherd and a sure guide': "I have his great promise and good firm word / Which long ago in his presence I heard". And he trusts in the Lord's promise and hopes to be "Singing songs in praise to God", as he lives there, with angelic hosts always in perfect bliss and joy forever.

• 36 poems with **Christian themes** are the cream of the collection dealing with manifold themes like Praise and Worship (2), Biblical Characters (4), Waiting upon the Lord and Healing (3), Shepherd (3), Liturgy (5) other miscellaneous themes (19).

- a couple of poems on <u>*praise and worship*</u>.

In *"Adoration"* worship to the Creator God is invoked. We sing praises profusely, and offer our worship to God our Lord. He created the heaven and the earth and the depths of the space, just by His Word. His name is holy and worthy of praise. Heaven and earth and the whole creation shall raise songs to him and adore him forever. Responding to him in adoration and declaring his might for ever: "Who keeps us safe by his staff and his rod / We declare his might with voices equipped".

"How to Worship You My Lord?" is another poem on praise and worship. The poet engages in a dialogue with God, in an intimate 'I-Thou' relationship. 'How

to worship you my Lord?' – he asks, and how to 'adore your lotus feet'? And, How to get His kindly word, comforting and sweet? There is a metaphor here where God's feet are called 'lotus feet'! The poet wonders what is pleasing to His heart as a gift from him to God, and with what offering he should start, and what is it that He wants from him? It is strange He never asks gold and silver or incense, and He never makes our task burdensome. The poet offers repentance and tearful heart, and reconciliation to His feet and pleads for confirming forgiveness. Again the poet wonders what offering He wants most. He feels that a willing heart and a loving soul are pleasing to His taste and that He never calls more than these! He feels it strange that God never asks a gift. Since he is a pauper, he believes that He surely lifts fallen souls to give praise and honor Him! He recollects his role models from historical and biblical accounts at this juncture: His servant Holy Francis (of Assisi) discarded his mantle robe, walked shoe-less with gunny robe and went to preach in sack raiment. And, a poor woman seeking grace and forgiveness washed His feet with her tears of deep disgrace and poured perfume as an adoring treat. *Bhakthi* is what the Lord seeks, he raises these as gifts to Him: an ear to hear and a mouth to praise, and seeking to walk in His path.

- four poems on three of the <u>*biblical characters*</u> - Jonah from the Old Testament, Thomas from the New Testament, and an anonymous woman popularly known as the Samaritan woman or the woman at the well.[240]

"Beware Jonah" depicts the eternal message that God cares when people perish. The poet elucidates the blessing of doing 'the task that the Lord has assigned to you' - here, "to take a ship going to Nineveh shore to call people to repent, turn to God". When He sent you to Nineveh, but if you ignore that job and take a ship to safe Tarshish, then God sends a whale to swallow you and bring you back to tell the Ninevites so men and all creatures return to God, and know how God cares for the people when they perish. Apart from a narrative, the poem is didactic, enlightening people of the ways of God!

"Doubting Thomas" as commonly called, was not an agnostic, but a saint and a great martyr. We poor humans always ask questions and experiential proofs. No one suspects sunrise or sunset, since we see them happen always with us, but rising from death no one really expects. In fact, only Jesus did rise again from death. Thomas wanted to see by sight, which in a way is quite unwise. For knowledge of God comes only through faith, and we will never need wisdom for that. So Thomas the doubtful never counted it a loss to ask visual proof to see Him. Ultimately, Thomas, one of the apostles himself died for Christ on Thomas Mount.

There are two poems on the <u>*woman at the well*</u> in this collection. "*Women At the Well!"* is a sonnet, where the poet addresses the woman at the 'solitary well' in

240 It is interesting to see that this woman and her story in the 4th chapter of John's Gospel are Solomon's favorite material for his art as well as for his verse. It is well known that his famous dance drama, *Kim Kartavyam* was woven around her story.

the Samaritan village. He engages her in a conversation asking about the thoughts in her heart and anxious soul as she came along the way with empty pot seeking water from Jacob's blessed well. He asks her if she is not content with the places to worship their creator and God, even the great Gerizim their holiest mount, and the kings and the great realms. The poet welcomes her to meet Jesus who comes that day there to her, and assures her that He can give her what she seeks - freedom from hunger and liberty - and that He will surely break all barriers. He wishes that He might be her great savior today, whom she knows as great Messiah.

In the other poem, "*O Woman at the Well*", the poet employs the conversational mode and talks with the woman at the well, who was standing alone and looking around. He asks whether she is looking for 'blessed commemoration of ancestors and their gifts' or searching to visit pilgrim centers. He clarifies to her that though she may have all these one-day, but still she is lost. He gently focuses on what she needs most and leads her to Jesus, Who will give what she asks: "Better know what it is that you need most / And know who He is now speaking to you / And ask Him He will give".

▪ We see three poems now on *Waiting upon the Lord* and Healing.

In "*Waiting Upon the Lord*", Solomon distinguishes between praying and waiting. When he prayed before God he confesses that he talked all the time, not He - asking Him for all he needs, but He has given all to him. So he resolves: "Therefore let me wait on Him / In silence to what He says". He often prayed and asked the Lord so he try and help himself. So far he is well and good; when he needs he asks for help. So now he resolves: "If I waited on the Lord / He will do what I cannot". He often tried to tell the Lord knowing not what He can give; he asked for petty things he needs, but He can give so much more. Therefore, he resolves now: "So let me now wait on Him / For He gives more glorious gifts". He did not tell Him in prayer that he wants to serve Him now; and that he will do His will for His sake, if He kindly shows him how. So now he resolves: "I pray and wait on the Lord / Till He calls and lets me serve". If now he waits on the Lord, he shall get his health renewed like an eagle flies upward - running and never tired. So finally he resolves: "Walking fast I shall not fall / He shall leave me not at all".

▪ There are two poems on *healing and health*. In "*Healing Comes from God*" a couple of insights are elucidated by means of participant observation. The poet sat with people in sickness, and in deep and acute pain. Some wept and wailed in deep distress while others simply moan. The poet observes that it is the sign of a weak heart to go over all misfortunes and cry in many words; It makes pain all the more worse. Medicine helps to make pain less and doctors have some cures. The essential message of divine healing is summed up in the last two lines: "In spite of all our loud complaints / Only God our health restores"!

The other poem is like a treatise on "*Sickness and Health*". Several truths are lucidly presented in this long poem:

1) Mortal body is made of clay breakable on any day, brittle and fragile just like a mud-made pot and shredded one day on the spot.
2) Though kept lovingly with all great care and nourished with good fare all the time, no one knows why it gets so sick and receives the painful prick, when it gets into such a bitter state.
3) As we all know, sickness strikes both the rich and the poor alike - sometimes lasting long and deep, and sometimes making shorter sweep.
4) Often we do not know what brings torment to our healthy wings, whether it is wind and rain or summer shine, or even dirt and unclean food.
5) Man had fought with sickness too long, when medical skill was not strong. Plagues and pestilences wiped the earth with coffins carried or bodies burnt. Men fled from the plague migrating, as solution to the problem looked vague. Men worshipped trees and brooks, giving floral homage, but looked helpless.
6) Sinfulness too is said to be the cause of sickness as we see: Forgiveness will restore the health and brings back healing wealth.
7) Forgiveness and prayer heal when sickness was coming on sinful wheels. God who tests our faith through pain brings us wholeness once again.
8) In the light of all the above, don't blame others when sickness comes. God wills our good always, and if we bear the pain God will make us whole again.
9) Silence and some forbearance sure can cure with God-given herbs; But when God's time has come to go we should be prepared also.

- three poems on the theme of a *shepherd*.

First of all, there is a seven-stanza poem "*You Shepherds*" - written as a seven-fold call to the shepherds of the Lord's flock. The first stanza is like a wakening call to the godly shepherds to be awakened, never once to cast their eyelid as their flock is out grazing, and the wolf is hiding behind the fence. In the second stanza the poet calls the shepherds to wear their staff and their rod in hand to protect their sheep always; to keep them safe from disastrous land; and to lead them through the safest ways. The third stanza exhorts the shepherds to walk their sheep to the cool fountain springs so that they drink their fill and feel refreshed. The fourth stanza urges never to leave the weakling lamb but to take it on their strong shoulder; preventing strain to its body and giving it a new song. The fifth stanza encourages the shepherds to stand by the sheep when danger comes near and to give their life as their owner, unlike the bondsman. The sixth stanza calls forth the shepherds to gather the sheep together safe into the warm shelter, when the evening shadows fall. After all, they know their voice and their calling. The last stanza points to the way of Lord Jesus Christ, the Chief Shepherd, who wants us to follow Him and serve Him, as we have listened to His voice.

Another short poem, "*The Shepherd*" gives simple but relevant instructions. A shepherd, while keeping little sheep must give green grass to his herd and take them to shade to sleep. He must then hold fast his staff and rod to draw the straying sheep, to drive the wolf abroad, and to keep the flock safe. He must walk before the sheep to call them by quiet call and lead all of them till they reach the safe stall. This is what Lord Jesus, the prime Shepherd has told and did for us - so we reach His household.

"*A Pastor's Duties*" is a five-fold exhortation, related to Pastor's duties, given in this five-stanza poem. As shepherds of the souls pastors have to do it carefully in intent, for, this vocation involves fruits that shine in the firmament. Apart from pastoral care, personal care is emphasized. Here is a great advise from the poet who has been a pastor to pastors: "Do a good reading of the Word / Never assume you know it all / The more you spend your time with God / The more power your sermon call". Then, pastors are exhorted to pray for their people everyday so that the Spirit prepares them well. As a result, their hearts will look for Sunday, and the pastor's harvest will be full. Then, the holy obligation to rebuke and set men right for God's sake is stressed. God forgives the poor soul that errs, but never forsakes any soul. Finally, pastors are exhorted to give respect to all their colleagues, as they need their prayers in their task. A saintly man believes this and will ask for this gift from God.

▪ five poems on *Liturgy, Church, Faith of Our Fathers,* and *His Call.*

The poem on "*Liturgy*" is a sonnet where Solomon extols liturgy, its parts and blessings. In a way, we consider this as a didactic sonnet for its educational value. Liturgy is a wondrous gift to the Church - in fact, God's great gift to divine worship, helping us to lift our hearts heavenwards and to sing and praise God with others' fellowship. What a great privilege to us is Invocation, calling the worshipper to heed God's Word. Then we have Confession and Absolution (pardon or forgiveness), which we need. It is a great bliss guiding us in worship. Then, end the worship with Blessing from altar or Benediction. Step by step we are guided in the act - with the angels and saints from near and far, as our hearts start the heavenly journey. The last couplet sums up the design and the destiny of liturgy: "Liturgy indeed is a part of our life / Nourishing our souls to eternal life".

The poem on "*The Church*" is enlightening, with the meaning and nature of the Church well portrayed. What the Church is and what it is not are elucidated: "The church is not a building / … The Church is a place with people living / A 'church-like' life for others to see". The Church is not a place to seek glory, honor and the foremost seat. But our Lord had really taught servant-hood and a meek life. The Church is not meant to announce our great works of righteousness like the old Pharisee did once foolishly - telling God much of his godliness. The church is a place to get free and abundant forgiveness by God's grace, remission for all our sins, and then to be counted in His holy race. The publican who had cast down his head in remorse and shame and knew that he was indeed forgiven.

So, we should all do. The church is for worship and praise, thanking God for all that He gave and to raise our both hands to Him - imploring Him to kindly save.

▪ a couple of poems in the series on the *faith of our fathers.*

The first poem, "*Faith of Our Fathers-1*" declares the heritage and proclaims the present resolve in five different situations, as found in the five stanzas. The Faith of our Fathers is great and mighty. And the resolve, first of all, is to fight with Satan, and to give witness to the Lord's Name as long as we live in the world. The resolve in the midst of four other different situations is expressed in the following stanzas: When we are hungry and poor, we care for the man next-door, robe the naked to cover his shame and comfort him in Jesus' Name. When the rich oppress us, we want to bear such patiently. When in the world we have no name, we have the Name of Christ. When we are denied all comfort, we take resort with the faithful, living outside the village bounds but hearing always the heavenly sounds. We are not sad for all we missed, for reward is promised. All that we see is a bubble, but we have a heritage stable.

The second poem, "*Faith of Our Fathers-2*", presents the need for His continuing help in the midst of different challenges. There is the same refrain at the end of each of the four stanzas: "Faith of our Fathers guiding us / Help us to be true to Thee". As we pass in the sinful world, and as we see darkness all around; When we were hungry and poor, He has taught us to show mercy, and, when we call the helpless to our door, to give them a morsel taking pity. Our ancestors were unlettered, counting on fingers of their hand, and, losing their lands for loans battered, without a shelter to sit or stand. Faith of our Fathers, hope, and trust kept us alive through all the strife; bearing the cross in patience, we must go on seeking a better life!

"*When He Called*" is a short poem that portrays the wonder of His calling! It seems to be the personal testimony of the poet, as well as the experience of many who have responded to His call unconditionally. Four essentials of this calling are described in the four stanzas respectively. First of all, he could not see why, when He called him to come, but when he simply went to Him he did not need to try the reason. Then, when He wanted me to leave some comforts of his own, he did not know that He could give more than the world had shown. Again, He kept on board much ahead - the richest wine and ample bread better than I ever seen, even Manna from high heaven. Further, the nearness of the Lord and the fellowship of the saints was his share and he could go forward with the blessed sacraments.

▪ 19 poems of Solomon, on *different miscellaneous themes*.

"*You Give Darshan Before I Seek*" reminds us of the prophecy from the Book of Isaiah.[241] The poet wonders how the Lord is already there even before he sits to pray, and clearly says He is not so far away. Again, before some words come to

241 Isaiah 65:1 "I revealed myself to those who did not ask for me; I was found by those who did not seek me".

his tongue, the poet hears His soothing words and sees the comfort He brings. Whereas the poet just seeks Him with some desire in feeble faith and lingering doubt, His countenance burns his heart like sure fire and fear goes out. 'How can I have some doubts again?' - the poet declares when His love to him is so clear.

"*Second Plan*", enlightens the reader on God's second chance when we fail or lose the given opportunity. There is always a second chance with God. And second plan God shows us isn't bad if we see it like God sees it. May be we were glad in the first plan, but the second can prove better. When we accept it without murmur, we then can see the wonder. The poet exhorts not to seek always the good old place if it is not God's desire for us. Should we aspire for Bithynia comforts and its solace? If we want to do God's will, we shall ask His guidance and be still. Go to Troas and wait and stand, and God sends someone with a plea to bring the Gospel to Western land. That is God's plan for you. If you accept it, you will not be sad; for, it is what God wanted for you. Therefore the second offer exceeds in excellence in God's providence.

"A Fool's Prayer" is another poem with didactic message. A fool may pray hours long but it goes only roof high. A broken clock will make a big decoration but its cry will be dumb. A still small cry, or a repentant moan sounds louder than you hear, but it reaches inner parts of heaven where the Father will surely hear. God looks for man's inner mind and hears his repentant cry. And those who seek His mercy will find and will get reply surely.

"The Story of the Ladder" communicates couple of lessons. You don't need a ladder to climb the hedge-high bush because you are taller to step on it. The two lessons we have are clear, if we really want to discern: One is that you are greater than the bush with heart and soul to seek your God and follow Him as He would wish for us. And the other lesson is that "if there is a will there is a way".

"Ears to Hear" is an eye opener for one and all. The wisest man can get it wrong some times when he reads the scripture. The certain way to get it right and to get all the needed guidance is to seek the help of the Holy Spirit. Strangely sometimes we get the message, but it is not always so. 'He that has ears to hear' will never make it wrong. There are some symbols in the Holy Writings that need to be discerned. And the Spirit, if we seek, will surely lead us into Truth.

"What Do We Seek?" presents different people seeking different things from Jesus! There are a handful of accounts of the Gospel narrative. First, the woman with issue of blood touched His garment's end lightly. She did not ask any worldly good but wanted her sickness to end. Secondly, the man at the temple born blind did not know what he should have asked, but went as told to the pool to find a wonder and he received sight. Thirdly, the paralytic at the pool who lied there for several years obeyed Christ's call carefully and his disease disappeared. Jairus came to ask nothing but new life for his daughter who died. Jesus kindly granted him that and Jairus was satisfied. The good Roman centurion did not think he was truly good but asked Christ to just heal his man and Christ the merciful did. All

these people only wished to get health and healing, but they did not seek loaves and fish, which we may easily forget.

"Seeing and Hearing" points to a picture that is hanging on the wall, to solicit all that it makes us recall. The age-old problem of pain is addressed with philosophical musings: "What is it that keeps the wall from fall?" All the red bricks, all the water, cement and mortar - Do they keep it without falling forever? What can ensure its permanency in the midst of threatening wind, rain and storm? This is the song of human pain - the eye to see and the ear to hear! Rocks do not have any of these and they cannot hear or see.

"Daily Prayer" is a panegyric on prayer! The daily prayer is like milk for us to nourish the inner man. So we never fret to sit in prayer but sit and talk to God at length. In prayer we sit with Christ side by side and drink deep His love and the bliss. We ride on the big cloud of Jesus' love till we touch the glorious hem of heaven. We see the countenance of the blessed Lord and rejoice to hear His loving voice. Our soul responds willingly to His word making us completely deaf to this world. What a joy to sit silent and pray, and cast away all our cares and concerns.

In *"Song of A Little Lamp"* Solomon shares his heart-cry all through his ministry years - 'Let me shine and show the way!' He wrote a lyric in 1970's on this theme, *Naaloni Premajyotini Velunganeeyumaa* - which was a 'hit' of all times. Apart from translating this song like others, he gave two alternative renderings for this particular lyric - expressing his heart's desire in different words. This is echoed again now in this poem, even in his nineties! In roaring darkness, raging wind, to stand and show His light the Lord has kept me firm to stand and to declare His might. The stormy winds do rise and rage, but they 'cannot quench me', the poet says. His purpose is so strong and wise and His plans endure forever. The wayfarer will find his path again and reach the safe haven at last when he forgets all the pain. Sinners who have gone astray will see his light to find the way and cast away all fears and succeed. Hence the resolve: "So let me shine and show the way / To those who need the light / Till at the end they all may stay / In peace, forget the fright".

In *"Pilgrims"* the poet portrays the blessedness of the pilgrims to the Holy Land. Blessed are the pilgrims who hold some relics in their hand, with memories with us for a long time. The poet fondly remembers great places like Constantinople, holy sites the saints have walked in the past, and places lived by many faithful people. They built cathedrals and made holy icons to let the faith live with us through the ages. The articles of faith were defined there and the true faith was well proclaimed, laying clear memories for our guidance through long ages. In the last stanza, Jerusalem, the long lasting city and other interesting places for us are fondly remembered. As kings and emperors had gone to witness and commemorate sites of blessedness, the poet invites us all to bless the name of this holy land, where our blessed Lord Jesus once did stand!

In *"Flowers in the Forests"* the narrative sounds autobiographical: "One does not know what is good till he takes a start"! Once a man in the clan of teachers, himself being a teacher, thought he was happy and at full ease, enjoying with his young pupils, reading from books, and climbing trees. But he realized that he was in wrong, and that he did not know he was destined to a new life, a new challenge and a new command. Was he now to take it up or not - this specific role to play in life's theatre? Life never comes unchallenged; the road ahead is not always smooth and flat, but fields to plough and forests to mend. The teacher's son knew it only slowly. And one day he found entirely a new place, new people to live with, and new tasks and challenges to face! He was destined to watch new plants coming to growth - not dry forests, but flowers in blooming. He saw the path threatening at start. While going steadfast he felt sure and slowly found it pleasant as it gave him joy that endures. In fact, 'one does not know what is good till he takes a start'!

"Endless Labor" envisages the essence of life and its 'endless labor'. We see many nuggets of wisdom in this poem: "Life is not all freedom but some discipline! / God has not made just as I – but also we! / Your freedom to hit will end where my nose begins!" All these rules of life really end where our safety begins. One lives a long time and sees a little more. He gathers much experience to his store. Yet, the reality is that "he can lead the horse to the water, but he cannot really make it drink". Many prophets died with a broken heart, and many gurus tried to impart their best wisdom. But life is not a bunch of rules stopping the flow; Life is "a matter of an ear to hear and heart to obey". The poet thinks when the Lord made this world, He made a place for good and evil. It is not easy to tell those two apart: "After you have tried to make the world good / And have labored to set the good from bad apart / And saw only small progress in doing that / Then you call it a day, leave it to God, and depart.

"Your Merciful Visit" is on the visit of God, whom Solomon calls 'my beloved Lord'. The first couple of stanzas depict the glorious visit of God in the sun and under the moon. Having taken His morning bath in the rays of the morning sun, the Lord comes in glorious light 'to bring greetings to me for the day'. Then, in the rounded fullness of the moon, He comes 'to let me bask' in His peaceful glow. Even in the swiftly running lightening path, which gives him a taste of His endless power, the poet testifies that the Lord appears and disappears, filling his heart with endless awe. Finally, the amazing love of God that counts us worthy of His visit is exalted in the last stanza: "O Lord, how to tell Your wondrous love! / While resting Your wings in the widest realms, / You still deem me worthy to make / Your countenance briefly to shine upon me".

"Our Enemy Fear" exposes our enemy! Fear is the enemy of mankind from times immemorial. It kills our intention to the right act, makes us numb, and paralyzes our mind from firm decisions. Fear made Jonah to run away from his task; drove away Jacob to flee from his home; Lot's wife fearing her loss looked back; and with fear of death Peter tried to leave Rome. Fear warns us from coming

pain. But often it is fear of the unknown that drives us repeatedly to despair, like the ship going down even before the storm. Christ said to His disciples – 'Fear not': "Set your hearts steady and your minds in peace / When storms rise and thunders roaring heard / It is I who is coming to you walking on the waves".

"Do Not Despair" propounds the faith to see God's wonders. Solomon exhorts not to despair or to fret, for, the Lord is with us always: "If you fall in deepest pit / He will lift you now from it". If you have strayed like a fool into the deep forest, He will come in search for you and bring you to safety. When stormy winds blow on you, He will stand beside you. So rain or wind or roaring storm will not dare to harm you. He who rose from death clothes you firmly with everlasting life. When His people had to cross the Dead Sea and its huge high mass, He raised his hand and showed the dry land through the sea. If you need to see God's wonders where you are: "Cloudless eye and wholesome ear / These we need to see and hear".

"He Called Me" presents a call to salvation. Once the poet was in the wilderness searching for peace but God showed kindness upon him and called him. He thought he knew the way to life but he knew not he was blind. In the thickness of his hard strife he thought that he found the way. Just like a long lost son in his sins, his soul has died. At last he found that he was wrong and bitterly cried aloud. God then like a good shepherd came and found him roaming in the wild. He risked His life to bring him home as His child. Who can forget such a great salvation tale? Night and day on the mount and vale he would tell for his joy and for the Lord as well.

"The Wanderer" is the story of two wanderers. The first one was wandering in a wilderness - lost and deserted! He could not find the way - not even a beaten track or a trodden footpath. As he did not know what to do and where to go, he found a man also like him looking out to find a way. He approached him seeking some help to get out of this hopeless wicked wilderness. The other wanderer then said to him that he was also like him, looking for a way out. Therefore he had suggested to him to try and find the way himself and that he shall do the same himself.

"*Teach Me Forgiveness"* is a plea to the Lord to teach. And it is appropriate to come to Him for this, as He alone is competent to teach us forgiveness. This five-fold plea is simple and sincere. The poet asks the Lord to teach him to forgive as He has forgiven; to teach him to ignore insult whoever has done; and to help him to forget injustice done to him, just like it was done to Him on Calvary. As we are all sinners - both his opponent and he - if we ask tooth for tooth, there is not His love in us. It is time to see Jesus who humbled Himself and became a servant sent by God to bear our sins and to grant Salvation. It is not easy to forgive as it is a 'hard virtue'. So, let us all learn to forgive at His feet that we walk in His footsteps till we meet Jesus in heaven!

"Calm Down, Friend" is a single stanza poem conveying a profound piece of counsel. The two-word *mantra* is to "Calm down". This friendly advice enables one to compose his calm and be strong and determined in the midst of insult or ignominy. It is not your only lot!

As Henry Van Dyke pointed, poetry tends to be descriptive as well reflective.[242] This collection of Solomon's poetry is both descriptive and reflective with many bits of wisdom in his sunset years. It is hoped that this would bless the reader, through its didactic contribution.

Solomon's art works had been enjoying continuing appreciation from many quarters of the globe. His meditations that went with the art have been found very meaningful. Apart from his multi-ethnic, multi-linguistic and multi-cultural audience from other faiths, several of his batiks, woodcuts and etchings have appeared as title page illustrations, posters and cards around the world. Thus, though he seemed to be 'Displaced', giving service in the Lutheran Church for only 5 years, he was 'Not Misplaced'; in fact, being deputed by the Lutheran Church he was 'Well Placed' in an international, inter-cultural and inter-denominational arena where he served for over 45 years, enriching the wider body of Christ. The findings of Solomon's Evangelistic Innovations beyond the familiar, beyond the current theological jargon, beyond the normal confines, and beyond his times will be explored in the Conclusion.

---

242 Henry Van Dyke et al.: *Poetry: Descriptive and Reflective Verse,* Kessinger Publishing, LLC, 2010.

5

Evaluation

The way we live as Christians, our attitudes, our practices, the way we understand Christian doctrine, our prayer life – all these are affected by the great consciousness shift taking place . . . All that till now has underpinned our western culture is in the melting pot. These are not comfortable times."

(Adrian B. Smith)[243]

'Innovation' means 'introduction of something new' – a new idea, method or device.[244] It is "significant positive change. It's a result. It's an outcome. It's something you work towards achieving on a project."[245] Looking to the Latin roots of the word, "in-nova-tion" literally means "in a new way."[246] Innovation in fact takes one 'beyond the familiar' and 'beyond the known' into new vistas and horizons! The good news of all times is an eternal constant with nothing to add, nothing to modify or nothing to remove. But its proclamation across the mosaic of culturally pluralistic contexts demands for relevant communication processes and meaningful methods, and requires innovations in tune with changing times and climes.

This great salvation, which we have received
We share with all nations and bear witness

---

243 Adrian B. Smith: *Tomorrow's Christian,* 2005.

244 https://www.merriam-webster.com/dictionary/innovation - accessed April 9, 2018.

245 http://scottberkun.com/2013/the-best-definition-of-innovation/ - accessed April 9, 2018.

246 http://asq.org/learn-about-quality/innovation/ - accessed April 9, 2018.

O this message all over be proclaimed
And the Lord's kingdom on earth shall progress.[247]

Beyond the Familiar

Solomon seems to have imbibed a new sensitivity of the Spirit, as he watched in his young adulthood, how the Holy Spirit worked in the life and ministry of Mungamuri Devadas. Solomon witnessed a new level of relevance and meaningfulness in the new religious movement amidst the hitherto known and the familiar. His inquisitive mind stirred within as he began to think and evaluate the traditional methods of evangelization in vogue, especially those imported from the West. He was determined to be different but the question was 'how'? He knew how the Reformation had divided the Church, and brought a 'Protestant' element on a global scale into her history. And now he was watching how another division was imminent on the regional and probably national scene with new teachings of the emerging 'revivalist' in the AELC.

He must be looking for a new option, as an ordained minister, that would allow him fill the old wine skins with new wine, avoiding further division, but invigorating the clergy and the laity with the challenge of new potential and possible options. One of the Five Solas of the Reformation, 'Sola Scriptura', along with others, must have taken deep roots in the heart of Solomon, and he guarded himself to stay true to the Scripture. In this vast and exploratory study of Solomon Raj, the researcher has come across nothing contradictory to the Holy Scriptures in what he contributed either in writing or in art. With a ready willingness to be corrected, Solomon has emerged one of the most teachable persons, maintaining a beautiful balance in his faith and conduct:

"I still exercise my thinking along such expressions for precision in the context of culture and faith and I am willing to change my ideas where it is necessary to do so".[248] A study is in order as to how he tried to interpret the Gospel in the cultural idiom, in diverse literary forms and current art forms.

i) Presenting the Message in the Cultural Idiom

One of the contemporaries of Solomon in the Lutheran Church was Dr. Bathineni Venkata Subbamma, an Indian woman theologian and scholar, known for founding Christian ashrams. The phenomenon of Christian Ashrams and *Bhajans* was adopted even into some of the Protestant mission churches of the times. Solomon mentions in his seminal work three better-known Christian Ashrams - *Kristukula Ashram* started in 1921 at Tirupattur, *Kristhu Shishya Ashram* near Coimbatore, and Stanley Jones' *Sat Tal Ashram* in the foothills of the Himalayas. These are the Protestant Ashrams with a different emphasis than what we have

247 Solomon's Sonnet on 'Giving and Receiving', *Soliloquies in Solitude,* (2017:109).

248 P. Solomon Raj: *Memories of An Artist,* Unpublished article, p. 3.

seen earlier in the Catholic Ashrams. Solomon also mentions about the Ashrams of Dr. B. V. Subbamma run for a week or ten days in the Lutheran Church, which attracted many Hindu women and new converts for a period of prayer and reflection. She was recognized for her analysis of introducing and planting Christianity from a cultural perspective. In 1968 she founded a Christian Ashram at Rajahmundry with the goal of helping women in education and training nurses, social activists and leaders. She focused on introducing Christianity to Hindu women, believing that an indigenous approach brought understanding and integration of cultures.[249]

People want to hear the good news in their cultural garb - in their idiom and in their imagery. Solomon was one of the pioneers in presenting the Gospel in the cultural idiom of the people. The previous Chapter enumerated at length the methodological dynamics of Solomon Raj in presenting the Gospel. Solomon proved himself to be a lover and promoter of fine arts such as song and dance. With the opportunity of serving as Director of *Suvartha Vaani*, Solomon penned many lyrics and hymns, which were put to music, broadcast on the radio, and became household songs fondly remembered till today. Apart from popular songs, he composed many songs with classical music, and in his nineties he experimented *dandakas* and even *vuyyala patas*.

Solomon earned his popularity in 1970's with his kuchipudi style *yaksha gana* (dance drama), *Kim Kartavyam* enacted in Ravindra Bharati auditorium for the first time. It was a break-through in Indian Christian circles. Using the *kuchipudi* style, a famous local form of Hindu dance, Solomon created a unique form of communicating the Christian message.[250] There were many comments and criticisms about the appropriateness of presenting the Christian Gospel through the medium of Hindu dance and drama. A reputed Christian poet, Molatrati Vidyanandam, however, judiciously assessed, in his book on Aesthetics,[251] the unique place of *Kim Kartavyam* in the history of Indian Christian art. It was upheld a new milestone in the progress of Indian Christian Fine Arts, ushering a new era. The order of SVD (Societus Verbum Divinum) in Mumbai under Fr. Prokach and Fr. Barbota also made similar dance dramas at that time with Christian topics. The Jesuit dancer Dr. Saju George still has a dance ashram today near Kolkata.

---

249 https://en.wikipedia.org/wiki/B._V._Subbamma - accessed February 24, 2018. Her seminal work "*Christ Confronts India: Indigenous Expression of Christianity in India" was published in 1973 (Madras: Diocesan Press). Her other monumental work, "Christian Ashrams: Years (1968-1993)" was published after two decades in 1993. Other masterwork, "Open Doors: New Patterns of Church Growth Among Hindus in Andhra Pradesh" (Pasadena, California: Fuller Theological Seminary) was published in between.*

250 B. S. Moses Kumar: 'Liturgical Interests and Lyrical Innovations of Pulidindi Solomon Raj, *The Yobel Spring*, Vol. 2, (2014:434).

251 *Soundarya Kala*, Hyderabad: CLS, (1978:181-182).

Later this dance drama was enacted in other cities, and was acclaimed an appropriate adaptation of indigenous methods of Gospel communication. And Solomon penned many other dance dramas, and together published 5 such works with the title, *Kim Kartavyam* in 2001. Many Catholic and Protestant Church leaders have recognized the validity of this means of Gospel communication. There were forewords in this Book from the Catholic Bishop of Vijayawada, Joseph Tumma, and AELC President, S. W. Schmitthenner commending the work of Solomon Raj in presenting the Gospel message in the local cultural idiom.

ii) Interpreting the Message in Diverse Literary Forms

For long, the message of the Gospel was bound to the ecclesiastical languages such as Greek and Latin, and it remained 'Greek and Latin' for the common people with diverse vernaculars of their own. One of the blessings of the Reformation was printing the Word of God in due course in the languages of the people, such as German, English and so on. The Bible Translation Explosion has brought the Word into most of the languages of the people in the world. In each language, there will be different literary forms, and these can reach the respective sections of the population with which they are familiar and comfortable with - broadly speaking the intellectuals and the commoners.

The Gospel reached the common people among the lower strata of society in India in general, and Andhra Pradesh in particular, from where Solomon hails. Historically, there had been many efforts to take the Gospel to the higher strata of society. Solomon did his part profusely and proficiently in interpreting the Gospel Message in diverse literary forms. It was acknowledged that when people were apprehensive of a Christian dance drama in a public auditorium, when *Kim Kartavyam* was first enacted, the moment the program started with a prayer in Sanskrit, all the audience were spellbound, and that had ignited unceasing and rapt attention to the very end - contributing to the success of this maiden effort by Solomon.

Other literary forms Solomon maneuvered in his voluminous writing exercise may be elucidated below. The first five works of Solomon in Telugu are majoring on five different literary feats or creations:

- *Puja Mandiram,* meaning 'Temple of Worship' was written as a *dwipada kaavya,* verse in couplets. It is a poetic expression of I-Thou relationship between a devotee and his God, and Solomon as a poet describes his heart as a 'temple of worship'. This has great appeal among people of all religions with a bent of *Bhatki* (devotion), and draws the devotee closer to the presence of God.
- *Veda Vinodini,* meaning 'Scriptural Amusement' was written as a *Samasyapurana Kavyam,* answering the riddle, and it is a *Sataka* with 100 metrical Telugu pieces. This is a unique creation. Last line of each stanza poses a riddle from the vast expanse of Biblical stories, and the

answer is filled in the preceding three lines. It is first of its kind in Telugu Christian literature, presenting good humor and amusement in the acquisition of Biblical knowledge.

- *Eeshodaharanamu*, meaning 'Illustration of Jesus', is a *Udaaharana Kaavyam* (Illustrative verse) - an illustrative poetic exercise in portraying Jesus with a metrical poem and two songs, each addressed to Christ. It is a captivating call to Jesus in each of the seven case endings (*Sashtyanthas*) of Christ's name in Telugu language - each in one verse. As such, this is a very rare and high-class literary feat in Telugu.
- We have seen at length about *Kim Kartavyam* earlier and it is another literary form Solomon had chosen to write the message of the Gospel.
- We have also seen that Solomon has written songs and lyrics for radio broadcast, and some 44 of them were published in the book, *Gana Kusumalu* (Song Flowers) - communicating the essential doctrines of Christian faith in song. They were released at different times as gramophone records, cassettes and CD's. This work is a culmination of Bhakti flowing through the twin stream of *sahitya* and *sangeetha* - beautiful verse in melodious tune - refreshing many a wearied soul as they sing or listen to these songs.[252]
- *Daiva Gnana Siri* and *Upamana Malika* were two other poetic works Solomon composed in his nineties. *Daiva Gnana Siri* was an anthology of 157 poems on various Biblical themes. Intended to be a *Sataka, a* collection 100 metrical compositions, Solomon ended up with much more, which a testimonial to his incessant thirst for more! The addition of 29 poems written as *shashtyantas* makes this anthology a rare combination of his love for poetry and his love for devotional verse. Of the seven prepositions in Telugu literature, the sixth one (*kin, kun, yokka,* etc.) when applied to God, it becomes a word of worship, praise and prayer. These words used with the sixth preposition in poems, describe Christ's attributes and works, and these are poems of praise. When it is common to write six of such *shashtyantas* addressed to the Patron of a particular poetic work, Solomon Raj profusely added 29 *shashtyantas* in praise of his Lord!

The ever-innovative mind of Solomon Raj spurred him to pen a couple of *dandakas*[253] in profuse praise of Jesus Christ and as gems in the gallery of Telugu Christian literature. These may be learnt by heart by devotees, and used in praise of Jesus Christ for His glory and for personal edification.

252 B. S. Moses Kumar: 'Bhakti Sahitya from the Heart of Solomon Raj', *Geetha Malika,* (2014:94).

253 *Dandaka* is a prayer to different gods, and there are many *dandakas* in Telugu literature addressed to different gods. It is a literary style of poetry in Sanskrit and Telugu languages.

- '*Upamana Malika: Parables of Lord Jesus*' is a collection of Solomon's Poetry on Parables. It is an outflow of the Lord's teaching of the parables in simple and beautiful verse in Telugu. The thrust of each of his writings had been *didactic*, and Solomon now turns his eyes on some twenty parables – not as narrative, but with an interpretative treatment. The poet very skillfully introduces or summarizes each of the parables with his profound reflection making this work a reflective poetry. Solomon, a communicator all his life across cultures, communicates profound Scriptural truths, with an unusual ease and an unending elegance in Telugu verse. Countless truths are communicated as words of wisdom, adding didactic value to this writing. In the process of enunciating parables, we often come across a 'conversational mode' whereby he reasons with God on what seems a puzzle from the human end, or affirms God on things that sound justifiable. This conversational mode further ensures an intimate 'I-Thou' relationship with God.

Solomon didn't put his pen down until he wrote *Kandardhas* and *Vuyyalapatas* lately, interpreting the Christian message all along in diverse literary forms, and now in the so far untouched genres.

iii) Depicting the Message in Current Art Forms

Solomon was gifted to express the Gospel message not only in diverse literary forms, but also through different media of art works. They range from woodcuts and batiks to etchings and icons. The works of Solomon Raj had been inspiring countless audience and impacting hundreds of individuals around the globe. While his meditations which went with the art were translated into German and Dutch languages, the pictures with the verse have been reproduced in magazines and periodicals in either of the above languages as well as in English, as these pictures with the meditations have been found very meaningful to Christians in many countries. An Evangelist in his own right, he communicated the Christian message - not just to the Christian community, but also to the wider human community, through his innovative art! A new paradigm of evangelization is initiated which continues to inspire the emerging generations across the nations. Solomon justifies his innovations stating as follows:

> "Thus I think everyone, through this sharing of cultural idiom, one [sic] will experience the gospel in his own brush like everyone heard the gospel in his own tongue on the Pentecost day."

With the publication on art, *Living Flame and Springing Fountain* in 1993 he emerged as an artist theologian and acclaimed a prophet and a contextual theologian. The German edition of this work was published five years earlier. Each of his works in this collection, poetic or pictorial, has been seen as "a living rhythm with light and delight' - reflecting and revealing his spirituality. His further work, *Fiery Wheels: Art Works and Meditations*, published in 2003, proved him to be 'communicator of the gospel in word, image and dance' The wheel symbol on the title cover and the message of justice originally appeared in Hans Ruedi Weber's book, *'Immanuel* in 1984. Ever since, it has been a recurring theme, and Solomon emerged as a champion of justice.

The message from Solomon's Liberation Series resounds from the time of their genesis, and it is observed that they would never cease to speak! Significant for their serial form with a dynamic message of all times, Solomon's *Liberation in Luke's Gospel*[254] and its sequel, *St. John's Gospel: A Gallery of Hieratic Art*[255] - both adorned with matching meditations in verse for each of the works - continue to convey not just a single message, but 12-fold and 13-fold message, each with its distinct message and appeal. Apart from these works, made available for posterity in printed page, there are countless works Solomon created in diverse art forms, invariably produced as means of communicating the Gospel message.

iv) Innovative Theological Proclamations

The very purpose of the 'Gospel' is to be preached and proclaimed to all of God's creation. The same message for ever but innumerable ways and means in which to communicate it to be relevant and ever applicable! There was no technique left untouched, and no method left unutilized by Solomon in his lifetime mission of sharing the Gospel. In his verse, we come across numerous theological proclamations - a study that can never be exhausted. For limitations of space, just a couple of poems are given below:

'The Living Waters' (No. 13):

> Jesus our Lord alone is the never drying spring To quench your thirst and give the fill, my soul! ... But only Jesus the blessed Son of God Can shower His mercy and quench our endless thirst.[256]

'The Refugee' (No. 32),

> Who else but You To save me and keep me, Lord? No one but You is the gift-giver of life, I shall never forget You.[257]

Other powerful proclamations are about 'justice', and environmental stewardship.[258] Ecological preservation was a genuine theological concern as seen in several of his musical compositions. 'Teach us, Lord! To love the earth / Which to us has given birth" - Solomon sounds to be a modern ecological saint,

---

254 *Liberation in Luke's Gospel,* 1996.

255 *St. John's Gospel: A Gallery of Hieratic Art,* 2010.

256 *'The Living Waters'* (No. 13)

257 *'The Refugee'* (No. 32)

258 *Songs from Sambalikan: Mother Earth / Weaver*

as Ch. Vasantha Rao aptly remarks.[259] Solomon in solidarity with fellow humans confesses the corporate sins committed against Nature.

The Bread for the World (*Brot für die Welt*) Meditation flag, (4x2 m., Stuttgart 2002), Poster on *Thirst for Justice* is given below. We see three main colors in this batik - blue, yellow and orange. We see the contrast between the blue of the river in the middle and the dry and needy ground around, which stresses the dryness of the land. All Living beings need water. Solomon depicts the thirst for water in these barren places on par with the cry for justice of people in desperate situations. He used many images and symbols of Indian culture in this work. At the top of the batik are factories, smoke and dying trees showing the artist's concern for ecology.

Peculiar scenes reflecting the situation in India are on the left: cattle and two women carrying loads. Jesus is shown as taking care of a refugee family and a man pulling a rickshaw. On the right Jesus is taking care of a prisoner whom he frees from his chains. At the bottom people are looking up, expectant and

259 *Planting in Native Soil,* (2014:127).

praying for the kingdom of God to come. Below their feet are seen some flowers and birds implying that the whole creation is also awaiting God's kingdom. At the top on the right, the hand of God is shown - coming out of a cloud, pointing to a fiery wheel, which symbolizes that God's justice is coming. In the middle of the picture a river runs from the top to the bottom representing the water of life, a life-giving stream. And in the water we see a man pointing to the fiery wheel. This is a prophet who draws people's attention to God's judgment. In the middle we see a reversed tree symbolizing that truth is like an upside down tree, with its roots in heaven and bearing its fruit on the earth. Jojanneke Dekker presents a beautiful commentary on this masterpiece, in her essay, 'Meditation Cloth by Solomon Raj: "The polluted earth, the refugees, the prisoner, the rickshaw coolie and the prophet are all thirsting for justice. With the prophet Amos (Amos 5:24) this batik cries out: 'But let justice roll down like waters, and righteousness like an ever-flowing stream'!"[260] What a comprehensive vision! What a timeless message!

v) A Twentieth Century Reformation

Solomon, witnessed something like the historic Reformation and its aftermath within the local Lutheran Church (AELC) ultimately resulting in a division and the emergence of a new denomination, called Bible Mission. Solomon, with his doctoral research under Prof. Hollenweger, the stalwart on Pentecostalism, must have also watched the charismatic movement in the later half of the 20th century which swept all over the world within the established churches, where the new dimension of spiritual life is experienced and preserved but with people staying in their own denominational churches.

He must be pondering about a different kind of 'reformation' that would initiate progressive change without disturbing the unity of the church. The given talents in writing and art, and his experience in Christian Education department of his church, and the wider expertise in audio-visuals and radio broadcasting he acquired working in ministries like CARAVS and Suvartha Vani, positioned him for his wider ministry with global impact. Exploring possible creative and innovative means of communicating the Gospel through song, dance, drama, and art had become his new vocation. He already impacted churches other than his own denomination in his State and the nation such as Baptist, Methodist, C.S.I. and C.N.I. before his global ministry as an artist-theologian. All his works in fine arts, and in the art mediums of woodcuts, batiks, etchings and icons had the sole objective of incarnation of the Gospel in Indian culture. He brought a new awakening among churches and institutions, and thus ushered a 'silent reformation' by tapping into the plethora of innovations possible in diverse and distinct cultures, instead of confining to the traditional modes and bygone methods of evangelism.

---

260 http://www.artway.eu/content.php?id=1315&lang=en&action=show - accessed March 26, 2018.

vi) A Prophetic Artist's Vision of the Church

Solomon not only portrayed what a 'prophetic artist' is but emerged as one envisioning the future of the church in India. He endeavored to present his vision of the future of the Church in some his writings. In Chapter 15 of his seminal work, Solomon categorically declares: "… the church in India is not going to be what it was in the past … It has to 'make its Easter', to use one of the expressions of Paulo Freire; it must die and rise again." The old concepts and attitudes bequeathed by Western missions should give place to new concepts and new understandings.[261]

Solomon concludes with the current status of the church in India, pointing out what else is desired:

> The people of India have heard the Gospel; maybe they want to see more of it in action among God's people. The people of India have seen the big institutions which Christian missions have set up; they may now want to experience the power of God working in the Church.[262]

In the 'Afterword' he added to the revised edition of his seminal work, he presents 'a perspective from 2004', where he left in his earlier assessment. The church as a 'pilgrim church' seeks to find out His will at every stage until she sees Him face to face some day. "And then all things will be perfected by Him who is the only perfection, and all our 'buts' and 'ifs' will disappear."[263]

In his latest essay, *The Future of Christianity in India*, published in "We, The Church: Studies in Mission and Evangelization", Solomon envisions the future of the church in India, in the midst of a drastically changing scenario:

> Indian Church today needs strong ecumenical move not only among the missions and churches but also with other religions – an inter-religious ecumenism. …
>
> If we become aware of some of these things and practice, there is no danger to Christianity in India. *Ghar Vapsi* movement or even discrimination and persecution cannot wipe away the Church. The State authorities may legislate against our public preachings and even our churches, but how can they prevent us from reading our Bibles and praying in our homes?[264]

261 *A Christian Folk Religion in India,* (2014: 271).

262 *A Christian Folk Religion in India,* (2014:275).

263 *A Christian Folk Religion in India,* (2014:278).

264 *We, The Church …* (2017:151-158).

Beyond the Theological Jargon

Though having a high academic profile, Solomon was not bound in the 'theological jargon' but moved out of it - practically promoting dialogue, dreams, symbolism and incarnation instead. A brief study of this is in order at this juncture.

i) Dialogue instead of Denominational Hegemony

Those were the days of denominational kingdoms reigning in their allotted geographic territories in Andhra Pradesh – each promoting their doctrine and way of life. Pondering from earlier times, Solomon could sense the hand of God among 'people who are different' from his Lutheran Church. He had a chance to see the emerging movement of the Bible Mission, and in his early career various faith confessions other than his. In fact he worked most of his time among people of different denominations, in an inter-denominational context.

He had a dialogue with everyone, which shattered denominational hegemony, seen in some quarters. He was accepted by all and ministered in all denominational contexts and churches, and had impacted many to think for possible options at indigenization. This dialogue has taken him across the nations and opened up many doors of opportunity for his ministry. This dialogue must have opened contacts and conversations with people he was studying, and he could come up with a wonderful study on '*A Christian Folk Religion in India*' namely the Bible Mission, which was his seminal work, and again with his study of over 70 different new church movements, as a sequel, in his '*The New Wine Skins*'. He even proposes an 'ecumenical dialogue' with people of other faiths and no faith for accomplishing our mission.

ii) 'Dreams' instead of Dogmas

The charismatic element of 'dreams' has impacted Solomon, and he seems to have been convinced about their scriptural validity, as Prophet Joel prophesied (2:28) that in the later days God will pour out His Spirit on all flesh, when: "Your old men shall dream dreams, / Your young men shall see visions". In Chapter 13 of his seminal work, Solomon deals with 'Dreams, Visions and Healing: A More Detailed Analysis'. This ignored element in the Lutheran Church of his days, Solomon recognizes, has ignited a fresh appeal to the masses through the Bible Mission, and he became comfortable with 'Dreams instead of Dogmas'. He pointedly remarks, [265]

> The pastors and leaders of the mission churches need dreams and visions; they need a new type of spirituality. Above all, they need to understand the visions and dreams, which are already there in their congregations.

265 *A Christian Folk Religion in India,* (2014:272).

This 'paradigm shift' would facilitate indigenization process and makes things relevant, instead of being dogmatic about doctrine. Sound doctrine should always have its place for the foundation of Christian faith and conduct, but the Spirit should have His place too in all that we, as His people, do.

Solomon cared for orthopraxy without ignoring orthodoxy. In simple terms, Orthodoxy means 'correct belief' and Orthopraxy means 'correct practice'. Of course, without correct belief, there cannot be correct practice. But just holding on to orthodoxy without orthopraxy is not useful. With such a perspective, Solomon in his writings and art works emerges as a Champion of the poor and the oppressed.

iii) Symbolism instead of Status Quo

Status Quo means the present situation or condition. There is no problem if it is good and desirable. When it is not so it is bad and undesirable. The problem is intensified when the situation is undesirable and is in a maintenance mode. Maintaining the status quo with an undesirable situation perpetuates that which is no longer desired. Much of what we do in the church is characterized by this predicament - maintaining the status quo.

Symbolism generates a new hope and a new meaning - reflecting our aspirations and desires. Use of relevant and significant symbols opens of new vistas and horizons in our destinies. Solomon, with a thirst for the innovative, was not content with the status quo of church ministry or practice, but began to maneuver the mine of symbols in Indian culture with rich meaning and dynamic message. In his works of art as well as in the word pictures in his writings, we see rich symbolism, with great message. The amount of symbolism in his works is inexhaustible, and there is a vast scope for such a study. The most significant symbolism is seen in Solomon's use of lotus.

iv) On to Incarnation of the Gospel

Solomon aptly advocates a Panoramic Vision instead of Parochialism or narrow-mindedness. He subscribed to the teaching of the adage: *'sarve jana sukhinobhavantu'* – similar to the Latin expression, *summum bonum*, meaning 'highest good' of all.

Starting his career as a teacher, he never ceased to be a teacher. He continued to be a teacher and a Christian Educator through his writings and his art works all his life. And his works had great didactic value, and ultimately he teaches the thinkers and theologians the sole message of '*Incarnation of the Gospel in Indian Culture*'.

v) Theological Proclamations

The essence of Solomon's theological proclamation is found in the three-fold chord of **Justice, Liberation and Ecological Stewardship.**

• Justice

Solomon made *'The fiery wheel'* batik in 1980 for the book, "*Immanuel: The Coming of Jesus in Art and the Bible*" by Hans-Ruedi Weber. This has been one of the classic art creations of Solomon Raj, which speaks about 'Justice'! Here is the theological proclamation on justice:

> The chariot wheels of God
> are rolling, rolling, rolling on.
> And you my brethren who became the victims
> of oppression, injustice and cruelty
> Weep not any more,
> for the chariot wheels of God
> are rolling, rolling, rolling over,
> and they are here already.

Another classic work already seen on justice is 'The Thirst for Justice' batik, a meditation cloth made for 'Bread for the Word' in 2001 (ca. 150x225 cm). The symbols of the river, the wheel and the prophet are connecting the need for water and the theme of God's justice. As Jojannekke Dekker significantly points out,

> It seems as if the thirst for water of the earth in these dry places is equivalent to the cry for justice of people in desperate situations. The earth thirsts for water, people thirst for justice. Justice like water is life giving and necessary for humans to survive.[266]

• Liberation

The Kirchentag in 1991, with its watchword 'The Spirit of God Liberates' inspired Solomon to do colored woodprints on 'Liberation in Luke's Gospel', as Jörg Muller chronicles. With this, Solomon, urging for 12-fold liberation for all humans, proclaimed the resounding message of 'Liberation'! A detailed analysis of this 'magnum opus' is seen earlier, but some of the theological proclamations are astounding, and below are given selections from all the 12 meditative and didactic reflections:

> For all that we know
> when God decided to become incarnate
> He chose to enter
> the womb of a woman.

This is God's irrevocable perspective of gender equality 'gender justice'!

> So give me the gift of Light …
> and let the universe be awakened

266 *Solomon Raj, Prophetic Artist in India,* (2006:66).

into that glorious morning
which shall not be darkened
by another night.

This is God's ultimate design for dispelling 'sin's sickening darkness'!

The redeemer will bring
justice to the poor one day
taking his place
with those who are oppressed.

This is God's grand 'finale' of His scales of justice – His 'solidarity with the poor and the oppressed'!

Whenever you share your bread
and part with your cup
there is always communion.

This is God's grand purpose of communion – the 'glorious virtue of sharing'!

When shall the east meet with the west
and north with the south
And when shall saints and sinners
shall [sic] share the kingdom of God?

This is God's celestial consummation – the 'grand conglomeration of saints'!

The more my sins
the more is my love
The more my love
the more is the forgiveness
I receive.

This is God's 'equation for divine progression'!

The poor and the hungry
the oppressed
and the downtrodden
the casteless and the cast out
shall hear the good news
of hope.

This is the just scope of the Gospel – 'ministering hope to the marginalized'!

We all need to be freed
from demonic powers
from demons that bother us today -
demons, may be,
of a different kind.

This is the divine deliverance from the subtle 'demons in disguise'!

> Goals and values shift
> desires and ambitions keep expanding
> and in the haystack of too many cares
> humanity lost the needle
> of life's compass.

This is the pivotal role of the needle of life's compass – keeping 'goals and values in perspective'!

> May we think of the hungry
> and the naked
> before we ask –
> What shall we eat,
> or what shall we drink.

This is the divine obligation for fellow humans - thinking of others before asking for self!

> We wait for God's liberation
> from suffering
> we wait for God's answer.

This is being part of God's answer, and being free from the 'peril of suggesting our own solutions'!

> We do not know all the answers.
> But we surely believe
> that death is the doorway
> to a new life
> more glorious and more wonderful.

This is the ultimate answer for the final station on earth – ushering into the 'doorway to a new life'![267]

• Ecological Stewardship

Solomon emerged as a modern 'ecological saint', with concerns for ecological stewardship. In the meditation cloth above, we also see on the top of the picture factories, the smoke there from causing pollution and consequently the dying trees. Solomon's concern for ecology is graphically manifested through this.

Again, there are a couple of songs from Sambalikan, dealing with the theme of earth and environmental stewardship. We close with Solomon's prayer, and make it our daily prayer as good stewards of God's blessings and resources:

---

267 *Liberation from Luke's Gospel* (1996).

Teach us, Lord! To love the
Which to us has given birth.
Sister River, Brother Mountain
Birds and insects big and small
Raining cloud and spring and fountain
You have made for us them all.
May we see them with respect
As from us this You expect.

Beyond the Normal Confines

Humanly speaking, we are invariably confined to limitations of time and space. Our work is confined to our location and life span. Only a few are destined to transcend the normal confines, and Solomon's work has attained such a perennial privilege. To impact when gone is something, but to be classed with preceding times is something else. The Internet has facilitated with all its advantages to see such pedestals of perennial interface.

'Journey With Jesus' is a weekly webzine published every week free of charge for the global church since 2004,[268] serving through scholarship, teaching in third-world seminaries, consulting, and promotion of Christian philanthropy. Their mission vision is characterized by six values - biblical fidelity, cultural relevance, critical inquiry, pastoral sensitivity, global awareness, and ecumenical generosity. These studies on different themes make ample use of the classical art works of all times.

i) Journey With Jesus - 'Transfiguration of Jesus'

There are three studies published on 'Transfiguration of Jesus', where Solomon's batik is presented with other artists of different ages:

- 'Listen to Him: Transfiguration of Jesus'[269] - Published for Sunday February 26, 2006.
- 'The Dial and the Switch: Recognizing the Moments of God's Special Visitation[270] - Published for Sunday February 18, 2007.
- 'If Asked, Don't Tell: Secrecy and Jesus'[271] - Published for Sunday March 2, 2014.

For some eight years the work of Solomon given above was used three times in line with other works on this theme. The first study of 2006 places

268 https://www.journeywithjesus.net/index.php?option=com_content&view=article&id=19&Itemid=132 - accessed April 4, 2018.

269 https://www.journeywithjesus.net/Essays/20060220JJ.shtml - accessed April 4, 2018.

270 https://www.journeywithjesus.net/Essays/20070212JJ.shtml - accessed April 4, 2018.

271 https://www.journeywithjesus.net/Essays/20140224JJ.shtml - accessed April 4, 2018.

Solomon's work along with four other works of Fra Angelico, Italy (1400-1455), Andrei Rublev, Russia (1405), Bertrand Bahuet, France, fresco, (1995-1996), and Duccio di Buoninsegna, Italy (1308–1311) - spanning 700 years. The second study of 2007 places this same work of Solomon along with three other works of Coptic Transfiguration Icon, Painting by Curtis Doll, and Painting by Frantisek Kupka - spanning how long we don't know, for want of detail. The third study of 2014 places Solomon's work along with two other works - Ethiopian depiction of the Transfiguration, and The Transfiguration by Mimi Ess - spanning how long we don't know, again for want of detail.

ii) Journey With Jesus – 'Jesus in the Temple'

Another work of Solomon, which was used by 'Journey with Jesus' webzine in two studies with other artists of different ages, is on 'Jesus in the Temple':

- 'The Hidden Years of Jesus: A Spirituality of Invisibility and Obscurity'[272] - Published for Sunday December 31, 2006
- Plunge Yourself Into Obscurity: The Hidden Years of the Boy Jesus'[273] - Published for Sunday December 27, 2009.

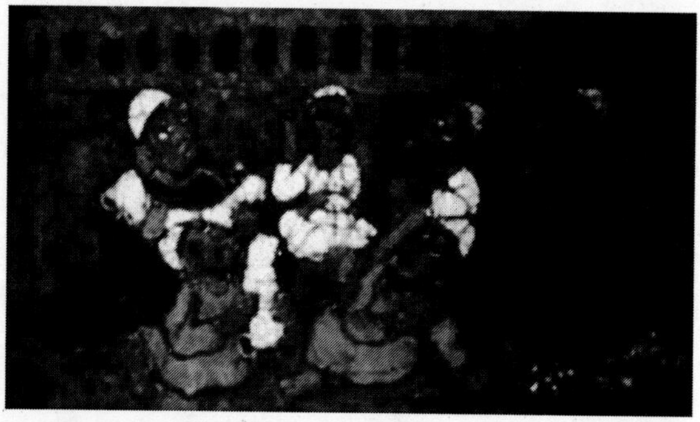

272 https://www.journeywithjesus.net/Essays/20061225JJ.shtml - accessed April 4, 2018.

273 https://www.journeywithjesus.net/Essays/20091221JJ.shtml - accessed April 4, 2018.

For some three years, the above work of Solomon was used two times in line with other works on this theme. The first study of 2006 places Solomon's work along with two other works: The Boy Jesus in the Temple by He Qi (China), and Jesus Among the Teachers by Jesus Mafa - spanning how long we don't know, for want of detail. The second study of 2009 places Solomon's work with the same two as above.

iii) Journey With Jesus – Resurrection of Jesus

Another work of Solomon, which was used by 'Journey with Jesus' webzine in one study with other artists of different ages, is on 'Resurrection':

- 'Believing the Believers: Public Evidence for a Mystery' - Published for Sunday April 8, 2007.[274]

The above work of Solomon was used in the study in 2007 in line with three other works on this theme: *Three Women* (Easter Sunday) by Romare Bearden (1912-1988), *Who will roll away the stone* by Hanna Cherivan Varghese, Malaysia, and, *Empty Tomb* by He Qi, China.

iv) Jesus Throughout History

Loyola Press, a Jesuit ministry, presents chronological examples of how Jesus has been pictured throughout history, beginning from circa 430 through 2000 A.D. Of the five works in this study, two works on 'The Good Shepherd' and 'The San Damiano Cross (circa 1100) were anonymous; one work was on Wedding at Cana (1998) by He Qi, and two were on Resurrection – one by icon painter Nana

274 https://www.journeywithjesus.net/Essays/20070402JJ.shtml - accessed April 4, 2018.

Quparadze and the other one by Solomon Raj. Solomon's work on Resurrection is the same as above (seen earlier in 6.3.3).

This image was originally created for Bishop Sam Amirtham of the Church of South India to accompany a pastoral letter at Easter. Solomon uses the message behind an ancient Upanishadic prayer to interpret the meaning of the Resurrection:

> At the top of the image is the bright sun, and below it is the lotus blossom which is a symbol of the movement "from darkness into Light / and from death into Life." The lotus moves from the dark clay at the foot of the water and rises into light toward the sun. This is the message of the Gospel. At the bottom of the image is the demon of death. Christ is shown rising triumphantly and trampling the demon of death, who is virtually under his feet. Raj borrows this symbolism from Hindu iconography, which often shows the god figures trampling miniature forms of the demon of death or the demon of darkness.[275]

v) Ongoing Revelation Through Art

Madeleine Beard has written the article with the above title, with Solomon's Transfiguration (seen thrice earlier on the website of 'Journey with Jesus' website in 6.3.1) in line with other works since 12th century, and shows how "the artists take us from public to private interpretation of text through art".

Looking at Transfiguration in art from the 12th century to the present is a conspicuous demonstration of the 'ongoing revelation through art'. The study

275 https://www.loyolapress.com/our-catholic-faith/family/catholic-teens/religious-art/how-jesus-has-been-pictured-throughout-history - accessed April 12, 2018.

brings to the pedestal the works on Transfiguration by Theophanes the Greek (late 14th century), Giovanni Bellini, an early Renaissance artist (15th century), Carl Bloch, a Danish artist (19th century), Tim Steele (20th century), and Alex Grey (late 20th century). Links given for each of these are unfortunately not accessible for some technical problem. Madeleine Beard further remarks:

Contemporary artist Solomon Raj paints an Indian Jesus, because "What is needed is not cultural isolation (the existence of many cultures without mutual contact) nor cultural universalism (i.e. the domination of one particular culture without freedom for others) nor uniformity but rather unity through the acknowledgment and interaction of diversified cultural identities and gifts.[276]

vi) Pentecost

Dr. Ralph F. Wilson, in his Collection of Artwork and Paintings of the Day of Pentecost,[277] presents six categories of works: Descent of the Holy Spirit paintings, Contemporary artists, Illuminated Manuscripts, Stained Glass Windows, Peter Preaching, and Collections. Among the Contemporary artists, Wilson sites the work of Solomon Raj, along with 14 other works, and 3 works of unknown artists. The Link given for Solomon's work on Pentecost is not accessible, so it is not known for sure which work Wilson must be citing. In fact, the researcher could locate four different batiks by Solomon from available sources, which are given below.

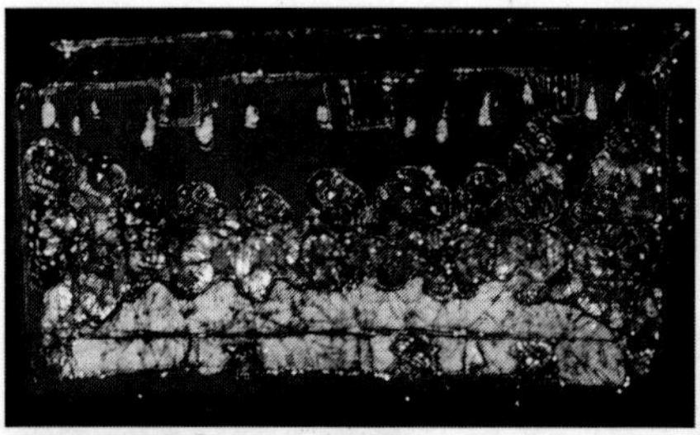

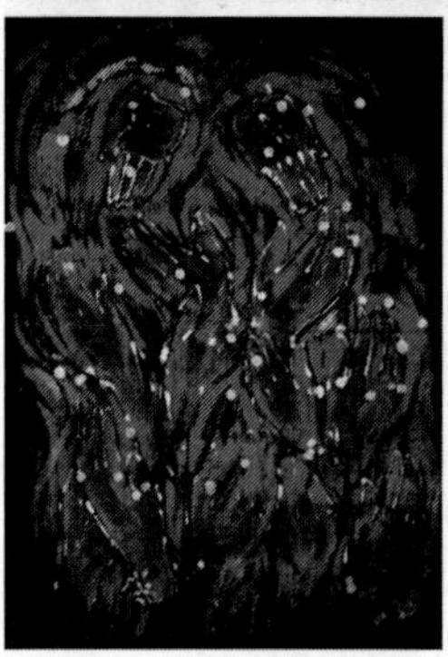

276 https://episcopal.cafe/?s=Madeleine+Beard+ongoingrevelationthroughart - accessed 6 years ago. Presently not accessible.

277 http://www.joyfulheart.com/pentecost/pentecost-artwork.htm- accessed April 12, 2018.

It is obvious that Solomon produced more than one work on themes that are dearer to his heart, and Pentecost seems to be one such theme of interest for him.

Beyond His Times

Having served across the globe for over half a century, Solomon returned to Vijayawada and established St. Luke's Lalit Kala Ashram. Though his house is about 100 yards from the Ashram, this place had become his second home. Until recently, when he was 95, he used to daily walk up to the Ashram, climb up the stairs two levels, as the Ashram was situated on the second floor. Here he was busy the whole day with his paintbrush or with his computer. As a nonagenarian, he did more work than ever before. It was Solomon's 75th birthday on February 21, 1996. After the celebration, all the guests were given a tour of the Ashram. It was here that the researcher was first exposed to Solomon's art gallery in general, and to his amazing series on 'Liberation from Luke's Gospel'. This triggered an insatiable quest for more for the next two decades, resulting finally in this dissertation. Solomon's work from here has been touching and impacting countless people beyond his times. In this section, a brief attempt is made to envision how Solomon's work and his impact may outlive beyond his times - by means of ongoing exhibitions, by his works on permanent display, by his writings, by Maria's batiks, by Chinese Biblia Pauperum, and by *Palm Leaf Prayers'* impact in 21st century:

i) Ongoing Exhibitions

i) A timeline for about half a century of Exhibitions of Solomon's art across the globe may be found at the end of his Festschrift. This source also records that there were "many others before this timeline in the U.K., Germany, Netherlands", et cetera. Beginning from 1966, the timeline goes on to the early decades of the 21st century, as listed in the Appendix. For about half a century, these exhibitions were held at West Bend, and Milwaukee in Wisconsin, in North Carolina, Washington D.C., at Austin in Texas, St. Louis in Missouri, Irvine in California, at Itasca and Chicago in Illinois, at Indiana, Toronto, and Ontario in Canada, at Munchen, Stuttgart, and Heilbronn in Germany, at Utreacht in Netherlands, London in UK, at Bethlehem in Palestine, at Quezon City in Philippines, at Yogyakarta in Indonesia, and at Vijayawada, Hyderabad, and Bangalore in India.

ii) It is learnt that the Dutch Missionary Society in Netherlands has a collection of his art works in a lending exhibition going around the country in white metal tin cases.

iii) As to the latest status, the researcher could obtain the following data from two current available sources: The only place that Prof. David Zersen knows where Solomon's works are held is at the Brauer Art Museum at Valparaiso University, Indiana, USA. Zersen points out that these works are not always shown, but they would be willing to bring out all the works they have to show, if researchers visit there. His younger son Augustine Jyothi Raj presents the latest donation of 140 art works of Solomon to Brauer Art Museum, in the presence of Prof. David Zersen in May 2018.

iv) Prof. Gudrun Löwner, heading the Department of Mission and Ecumenics since 2011 at the United Theological College, Bangalore furnishes the current status of Solomon's works in Germany:

The late Jörg Müller (Porta Westfalica, Germany) was the former pastor of the German speaking congregation in Bermingham, when Solomon Raj was also there. Solomon met him and his wife and they became his lifelong friends. They both were dedicated and faithful patrons of Solomon's art almost all their lives. After his return from Bermingham, Jörg Müller joined the VEM in Wuppertel, United in Mission, the mission body of the Westfalian Church in Germany and in this position he propagated Solomon's works till his retirement and beyond. Jörg Müller founded a friendship group, One World Art, and gave works of Solomon for endless exhibitions in German churches, academies and every two years at the Kirchentag meetings. Lately, they have donated their Collection of art works of Solomon Raj to the Evangelical Lutheran Mission (ELM) in Hermannsburg. They are in the process to catalogue the donation: they already made two public exhibitions of his works, and they are publishing in their monthly Journal some of his *Liberation* works.

ii) His Works on Permanent Display

Apart from countless works with countless individuals or families on all continents of the universe who treasure one or more works of Solomon, there are some recorded places where his works are on permanent display. The first such place was the Jesuit Missions Office in Nuremberg, Germany where much his work is published since 1984. Joe Ubelmesser acknowledges that the batik, which adorned the cover of their magazine for Christmas 1984, has been on the wall of their dining room since then.

The series of twelve pictures on Liberation in large original prints are on permanent display in many places in Germany, Netherlands, Switzerland, England and the U.S.A. The Evangelical Lutheran Mission (ELM) in Hermannsburg, Germany also has a full set of the Liberation series by donation of Dr. Jörg Müller and Mrs. Müller since 2017.

As Gudrun Löwner remarks, the batiks cannot be put on permanent display. She updates that the Neuendettelsau Seminary had some batiks hanging nicely in the chapel where they lost color and got dirty. In order to save them, they framed them and put them on permanent display in the staircase of the Theological Seminary in Neuendettelsau. It is the *Liberation* Series in batik. This must be priceless, as only the woodcuts of the *Liberation* Series are mostly known.

A great contemporary artist-theologian, Jyoti Sahi, has inaugurated Dr. P. Solomon Raj Art Gallery at Andhra Christian Theological College (ACTC), in the presence of Marco Olgiati, Switzerland, under the patronage of the then Principal, Chilkuri Vasantha Rao. Jyoti Sahi also presented a couple of his woodcut works to the Art Gallery on this occasion. Many works of Solomon are on permanent display here.

The Campus of Donald Ashram - consisting of the Sanctuary, Hyderabad Bible College and Joan's Haven - is adorned with much of Solomon's art. While the originals are kept in the Archives, framed copies of the *Liberation* Series and St. John's Icons are on permanent display in the halls and corridors of the Seminary. Also few original icons, a handful of original triptychs and the Bread for the World (*Brot für die Welt*) Meditation flag, (4x2 m., Stuttgart 2002), Poster on *Thirst for Justice* are on permanent display.

In May 2018, one of Solomon's sons, Augustine Jyothi Raj personally donated 140 art works of Solomon Raj, including two icons, to Brauer Art Museum at Valparaiso University in Indiana, in the presence of Prof. David Zersen, the art curator Gregg Hertzlieb, and other Faculty members. This Museum is home to a nationally recognized collection of 19th, 20th, and 21st century American Art. Along with displaying selections from its permanent collection, the Brauer Museum hosts a full schedule of special exhibitions and events. It was proposed to host an international exhibition of Solomon's art here in August 2020, duly cataloging all of his works.

iii) His Writings

Solomon has done extensive writings, published and yet to be published, as seen at length in the previous chapter. Whereas Solomon extensively had given his lectures and presented his essays in different Academies across the world during the prime of his career, of late, he wrote in a limited measure for the last one decade, contributing to Festschrifts of his esteemed colleagues and friends. Probably, the impact of his ideas will continue to flow through the family lines of the people for whose Festschrifts he has written. The titles of these essays are listed below chronologically, with due reference to their publication:

- *Christian Prabandha Literature.*

This is a brief survey of Classical Telugu poetical works on Bible themes with a special reference to *Vedanta Rasayanam*, and eighteenth century work of Mangalagiri Ananda. This was published in "Striving for Excellence: Educational Ministry in the Church", Essays in Honour of the Rt. Rev. Dr. Narendra John. Solomon makes a study of a classical work by a Christian poet of over two centuries ago. This is a rare dig, and not much research was done on this.[278] The Christian message is presented by this classical poetry.

- *In digenization of the Gospel through Art.*

This was published in "The Yobel Spring", a Festschrift to Rev. Dr. Chilkuri Vasantha Rao, edited by Praveen P. S. Perumalla and others.[279] This is one of the unique festschrifts of our times, in that it was in honor of a person at a young age

278 Bangalore: Asia Theological Association, (2007:393-409).

279 Delhi: ISPCK & ACTC, Vol. I, (2013:84-89).

on his fiftieth birthday; and in that the work was in two volumes. Solomon's life's message is presented in this work, which deals with the exercise of indigenization of the Gospel through art. This opens up further options of exploration into indigenization through different other means.

- *The Future of Christianity in India.*

This was published in "We, The Church: Studies in Mission and Evangelization", Essays in Honor of Bishop Dr. B. S. Moses Kumar, edited by Smitha P. Coffey and Donna Tracy Paul. In this essay Solomon categorically states:

> "Indian Church today Needs strong ecumenical move not only among the missions and churches but also with other religions – an inter-religious ecumenism ... The State authorities may legislate against our public preaching and even our churches, but how can they prevent us from reading our Bibles and praying in our homes?"[280]

iv) Maria's Batiks

Maria Clara is an emerging Christian artist of our times in Hyderabad, India. She is known for her Biblical art. Though her art styles originally included Abstract Expressionism, Surrealism and Figurative art, the influence of Solomon Raj upon her art is evidenced much these days, as she is into producing woodcuts and batiks. As part of her requirement for Certificate Course in Art and Critical Appreciation

280 New Delhi: Christian World Imprints, (2017:151-158).

with Jawaharlal Nehru Architecture and Fine Arts University (JNAFAU), Maria gave a Presentation on Dr. P. Solomon Raj. She points out how he discovered the possibilities of using visual arts as a means of explaining the biblical narratives and propagating the Gospel. She appreciates Solomon's batik on 'Thirst for Justice'.

Dr. Chilkuri Vasantha Rao expressed that he was "actually grieving when Artist Solomon Raj said he will not do Batik art anymore" but was appreciative of Maria Clara and remarks: "continuing this unique tradition of art is a hope in this generation and the generations to come".

Maria's very maiden effort on the wise woman of Proverbs is given above and 'the beauty of batiks' is undeniable! At this juncture, Maria acknowledges that Solomon Raj was her inspiration and that "he did take me through the process at his ashram". Maria producing her batiks and woodcuts began instructing many through workshops.

v) Chinese *Biblia Pauperum*

It is conspicuous that Solomon's 'Reproduction' of the medieval technique, in his *Biblia* Pauperum, instead of ending up as a monumental endeavor, turned out to be 'Reproducing' - inspiring following generations! In 2009, under influence of his work, Madam Fan Pu created her *"Biblia Pauperum"* in Chinese folk paper-cut art, according to principle of putting New Testament story in center with Old Testament story either side. In concise skillful style, she depicted the message by delicate drawings made from cutting and carving of shapes on paper decorated with colorful dyed rice paper.

Her work delivered the message of the Bible and the Christian Faith in Chinese artistic beauty. Each work has a theme Fan Pu selected from the scripture and she had incised each Chinese character for each piece of work, as seen in the specimen page of her work reproduced above. Each image was accompanied by a poetic meditation serving as a means for readers to encounter God through these meditations.

vi) Palm Leaf Prayers' Impact in 21st Century

Probably the earliest work of Solomon published in Germany in 1988 was *Palm Leaf Prayers* - containing fourteen wood block prints and linocuts by Solomon, with short prayers and meditations by Jörg H. Müller in German and English. Linocuts are a printmaking technique, a variant of woodcut in which a sheet of linoleum is used for relief surface. This early work of Solomon, published overseas, made him well known in Germany and many countries ever since in the West.

Dr. Müller was former Lutheran Pastor in Birmingham for the Germans, and a colleague and confidant of Solomon at the Selly Oak Colleges, who held countless exhibitions for Solomon in Germany in his presence and absence as well. He had the largest collection of Solomon's works with him. He and his wife, on account of ageing and health considerations, have lately donated their collection of Solomon's art works to Evangelical Lutheran Mission (ELM) in Hermannsburg. They are catalogued and two exhibitions were held. They are publishing his works in their monthly Journal. Müller preserved copies of all the works in his possession in ten folders, a total of 167.[281]

281 On the cover image above is a woodcut of crown of thorns encircling a scripture verse in Solomon's mother tongue Telugu, depicting the message of forgiveness: *"Be kind to each other, tenderhearted, forgiving one another, just as God through Christ has forgiven you"* (Eph. 4:32).

Solomon's earliest work, 'The Man of Sorrows' that won him awards is in this book.[282]

Two of his other works on the great theme of Jesus' solidarity with the cast-outs and the refugees - 'Behind the Barbed Wire' (1986) and 'Refugees in East

282 About four decades before 'The Passion of the Christ' movie directed by Mel Gibson was released, Solomon made this woodcut in 1969, clearly depicting the suffering Christ.

Pakistan' (1973) - are published in this collection. In the woodcut below, 'A Man wearing a crown of thorns embraces refugees in the India-Pakistan war'.

In the 1970's with the flow of Refugees from Bangladesh into India, this woodcut had great impact on many, promoting the cause and demonstrating Jesus' solidarity with the Refugees. Prof. Gudrun Löwner remarks that this masterpiece is continuing to be used, even in present times in Germany because of the current refugees there and immigrants all over.

It was a pleasant surprise to the researcher, on his recent visit to '*Divya Ashray*' in Varanasi, to see the impact of Solomon's earliest art on a new ministry of the 21st century in India under the leadership of Presiding Bishop Michael John. A beautiful sanctuary with indigenous symbols and images adorns this place.

Known as a 'Place of Hope' (*Ashaa ka Sthaan*), and a 'People of Promise' (*Pratignya ke Log*), this Divine Refuge (*Divya Aashray*) emerged in recent times as a community of Jesus' Disciples, consistently growing in the Spirit and in number. The campus of this sanctuary reflects native design and symbolism to the core – even subscribing to an all-acceptable vegetarian life-style, with no stumbling block to any. The imposing emblem on the frontal elevation is from *Palm Leaf Prayers* with rich symbolism. The Crown of Thorns and the fire of Pentecost speak of the suffering and death of Christ, His resurrection and ascension, and the decent of the Holy Spirit upon the Church. The three flames on the top are representative of the Trinity in Godhead.

The two *mudras* (hand postures) are taken from Indian imagery and tradition. The upward hand is the position of the *guru*, also seen often as *abhay hastha* of God (hand of assurance). The forefinger touching the thumb is symbolic of the divinity and humanity of Jesus Christ. The downward hand is seen as *dat hastha* (hand of giving) promising the devotee that He is the One who gives grace and

strength. The combination of the two hand positions indicates that Jesus Christ is not just one of many masters, or one of many incarnations of the divinity, but the one and the only *Guru*, the unique incarnation of God. Wounds on wrists identify both hands as Christ's and give the emblem the dimension of His saving sacrifice and triumph over death.

This whole message is embedded in the woodcut, 'The Source of Our Comfort' given above. The same emblem appears at '*Divya Ashray*' on the pulpit even more strikingly, in gold color - gold signifying heaven and divine revelation - as seen in the reproduction below:

There are four scenes from the Life of Christ again on all four corners, in the frontal elevation - signifying that the whole message of Christ must be shared in all corners. They portray Christ's essential four-fold mission as *rakshankarta* (Protector), *muktidata* (Savior), *mritunjay* (Victor over Death), and *punaragaman* (Second Coming). The first two of these works are also adapted from the woodcuts of Solomon's *Palm Leaf Prayers.* The work sited above on 'Refugees in East Pakistan' is used to present Jesus as *rakshankarta* and 'The Man of Sorrows' is used to present Jesus as *muktidata.* Two other new works are used to present Jesus as *mritunjay,* and His *punaragaman.* Having walked through Solomon's *Evangelistic Innovations* with a *Theological Perspective,* the ultimate findings will have to be summed up in Conclusion, ushering in a *New Paradigm of Evangelistic Means*!

Conclusion

Incarnation of the Gospel in Indian Culture has been the theme of focus in the present dissertation. Having stated and elaborated the problem, and having identified the resources that would help our reflection, this study has taken us through a panoramic view of the process in a historical perspective. In the backdrop of this ongoing exercise, a study of the life and work of one of the contemporary Indian Christian artist-theologians, Pulidindi Solomon Raj, was taken up. And an appraisal is made of his contribution in art and poetry, with theological and evangelical perspectives, in the cause of Incarnation of the Gospel in Indian Culture! The personality and oeuvre of Solomon as an artist, as a poet, as a lyricist and hymn writer, and as a multifaceted genius was explored at length. The evangelistic innovations of Solomon Raj from a theological perspective are analyzed in the process.

A true artist is not one who is inspired, but one who inspires others. It is an undeniable fact that Solomon Raj stands and stands high in the annals of Indian Christian art not only as an inspired artist but also as an inspiring artist. All through his journey as an artist, people from across many countries and cultures were impacted and inspired by the art of Solomon Raj. The last three instances under the point 'Beyond His Times' in Chapter 5 – namely Maria's Batiks, Chinese *Biblia Pauperum* and *Palm Leaf Prayers*' Impact in 21st Century - amply testify to the continuing inspiration and ongoing impact of the art of Solomon Raj! As Alle G. Hoekema remarks, Solomon holds a very special position among the Christian artist-theologians in Asia, and "his way of transmitting and transforming theology is exemplary to many theologians and missiologists in the West."[283]

The findings and analysis of the modes adopted in the task of Incarnation of the Gospel usher the future generations into 'a new paradigm of evangelistic means'! And it is verified that the Gospel can safely and effectively be presented in Indian context through the art and culture of Solomon Raj – with the specific

---

283 *P. Solomon Raj: Biblia Pauperum. The Poor Man's Bible,* Book review published in "***Exchange***" 38, 2009 (381-388).

modes of poem, song, dance, drama and art, in their various expressions! The three-fold challenge of Christian education is experimenting, engaging and enlightening, and Solomon has responded well to this challenge in his pedagogic mission as a Gospel communicator.

Experimenting

Solomon had been an educator all his life as a teacher, preacher, and as an artist and theologian. He is seen experimenting at every turn in his life and vocation. He never confined to a routine in his vocation. In his teaching assignment at the start of his career, he was open for learning and growing, and it had become his life-style ever since. He was already writing lyrics during this period. One of his earliest songs on the 'Lord's Prayer' (*Paramandali Maa Tandri*) was popular and was in use by many, including the non-literate adults of the congregation. When traditional catechism taught the Lord's Prayer through memorization - getting by heart, he composed this lyric, by which the Lord's Prayer stays forever in the hearts.

And he was already writing books on Audio-Visual Aids *(Drishya Sravana Sadhanalu)*, and Story Telling (*Katha Paddati*) - thus teaching these skills and mentoring rural evangelists and preachers beyond his own denomination. He went all the way to Allahabad for Agriculture Extension Training, when he was teaching at Teacher Training School, Rajahmundry. From the humble steps in art, which he learned at Damerla Rama Rao, he moved on in an ever-progressive manner with every art form ranging from woodcuts, batiks, etchings and icons.

When it came to writing, he began writing poetry and essays on varied themes of interest. He experimented writing Telugu poetry, in various literary processes such as *dwipdadas* (couplets), *satakas* (collection of a hundred poems), *vinoda kavya* (amusing poetry), *udaharana kavya* (illustrative poetry), *yakshaganas* (native folk songs), *shashtyantas* (poetry with preposition-endings in praise of God), *dandakas* (profuse praise of God in a non-stop recital), *kandardhas* (four-line poetry with lyrical ending) and *vuyyala patas* (swing songs).

He also wrote Christian lyrics and hymns in Telugu and English. As he wrote English poetry, he experimented writing even sonnets and a few odes. From early water color paintings at the genesis of his artistic venture, Solomon moved through ascending stages of his life - experimenting with wood-cut prints on rice paper, batiks, etchings and icons! This experimenting trait in Solomon continues to be an inspiration for many across generations. The potential and faculties God endows one are amazing and one should never cease to deploy such gifts and capabilities in the service of the Lord! What an example and what a challenge for ministers and servants of God - never to be afraid of failure, but to go on experimenting, and utilizing the Talents the Master has given!

Engaging

Engaging the learner is the second dimension of education, and Solomon succeeded in soliciting active engagers rather than passive onlookers with regard to his art creations. Every art tells a story, no matter the media, and it invites one to be part of something greater. As Sam Gunn points out, art must engage us and then captivate us "starting with something small that points to something immense". Solomon Raj, apart from enjoying his art with his own reflections, longed that "those who look at these pictures will bring out their own reflections in response to these pictures."[284] His longing has been fulfilled from time to time, as many people in different places reflected upon different works of his Series on Liberation in particular, and others works in general. It is a happy surprise when his longing was fulfilled in plenitude as The Lutheran Church of St. Luke, Itasca, Illinois celebrated their centennial in 2008 with Gerald Danzer's 'Meditations for the Twelve Days of Christmas' through these liberation prints of Solomon Raj. Solomon's message of liberation had refreshed many who have seen his art and verse, and it is hoped that they would continue to refresh the new generations, who are new to this great contribution, and that it would help communicate the richness and beauty of his message, challenging them to herald this message for those who need liberation in our times. Art is expected to be evocative rather than merely descriptive or prescriptive! The viewers respond to the pictorial presentation, as it invokes and invites a response. Each viewer responds differently, in tune with the message one comprehends, and as they respond, none is wrong or better.

Enlightening

Another dimension of education is enlightening - bringing new light where it is absent and where it is needed. Whether it is art or poetry, it is meant to be educational and enlightening. Apart from other things, Solomon had ably and appropriately maneuvered the 'Hymn Tradition' in Telugu language and literature. The repetition method of *pallavi* (chorus) and *charanam* (stanza) for the oral communication tradition may be seen with examples from the songs of Solomon Raj. The theology in his songs, the Indian imagery compared with the Western images in our church songs, and the whole idea of inculturation of the Gospel, or the 'incarnational theology', are the enlightening tools for the church. This may be illustrated by means of the English translations of some of his well-known songs demonstrating how they are used in India in songbooks of the church, the cassettes and radio broadcasting.

Solomon understood the place of images and imagery in multi-cultural backdrop in India, and utilized this resource fully well in presenting the Gospel! From the very basics of audio-visual teaching aids, he made a marvelous journey

284 *Liberation in Luke's Gospel,* 1996.

in producing many art works for the sole purpose of presenting the message in a graphic manner. The interplay between the word and the image has a great significance to us because the Word became Flesh in our faith. Solomon had highlighted the importance of the typological teaching of the Bible, which was so important in the ancient Church, and he made his own images to illustrate this. The three aspects of the challenge examined above serve as a touchstone for every endeavor at indigenization!

Rooting the Gospel in the Native Soil

The whole thrust of the three-fold challenge of Christian education, as depicted above, is 'rooting the Gospel in the native soil'! "Over the years, I was a pastor, a professor and radio producer," Solomon said. "However, my *Sadhana* - my personal discipline and avocation - was to root the gospel in the native soil of India." This 'sadhana' for over half a century had yielded much means through his great contribution, which ensured the end! David Zersen remarks:

> The Gospel must be shared in a way that it comes to find a home in your mind and heart, and in the culture of your society. It is the task of the preacher or the poet or the singer or the painter to find the way to allow the Good News about God's love in Christ to find a patch of ground and to blossom in our lives. When this happens profoundly, the dance or the song or the art that results from it reflects the joy of the life that experiences it.[285]

"*Each one with his own Brush*" - is the title of a book written long ago, by Daniel Johnson Flemming, on the topic of contemporary Christian art in Asia and Africa.[286] Flemming pleads that the gospel should be passed on in the language and the idiom of all the nations of the earth, in symbols of each culture so that each person hears the good news in a way he or she will be able to relate to it and accept it - like on the day of Pentecost each one heard the good news in his own tongue. This is also the meaning of the 'word becoming flesh' in all ages and in all lands. That is why the Christian artists in India today want to use the symbol language of their land and give to these symbols a meaning and significance. First of all when the artists use this language known to the Indian audience, the message is not looked upon as foreign to our culture. When each one of us uses the cultural symbols from our diverse cultural backgrounds, we are bringing a brick from our own distinct culture to build the universal household of our Lord. We are not really preaching several gospels but one gospel in different tongues - just like people of all lands can read the Bible in their own language today.[287]

---

285 David Zersen in *Now We are Free*, (2008:33).

286 New York: Friendship Press, (1938).

287 Solomon Raj: *Christian Art in India: Present Trends and Future Prospects,* Unpublished Paper.

i) Endangering

'The end justifies the means' is an adage, but not always appropriate or desirable. Through the detailed historical survey among catholic and protestant thinkers and pioneers, we have seen countless measures they adopted in expression of their faith and practice - some of them interesting, some inspiring and some merely enigmatic. Obviously most of them became obsolete! One thing to beware of is the 'peril of syncretism' – diluting the purity of the Gospel and demeaning its distinctiveness! This is another touchstone that helps preserve the pristine treasure of the Gospel handed over to us! Having seen various experiments and having heard the diverse ideas and propositions, and having spent several years with Solomon Raj and his multifarious works, the researcher could hear a 'ring of truth' about most of his attempts and endeavors, which could be well attested and endorsed by others who know the man and the manner of his contribution.

ii) Moderate in everything

This could have been the result of holding on to the 'sola scriptura' of the Lutheran Reformation, and heeding to the scriptural injunction to "be sober in all things."[288] Everything can be good within limits, and such bounds the Creator had set for all, in their best interest. In all that he did, Solomon seems to have kept himself on guard, and so are found no aberrations in what he wrote or what he depicted through his art! And he emerged as a mouthpiece of God, speaking for God and ministering to people of all nations and generations!

iii) A Global Christian

The Psalmist says, "The steps of a good man are ordered by the Lord!" and someone added: 'Not only the steps but also the stops'! Surely, the Lord must have ordered the steps and stops of Solomon, for such global impact through his contribution for incarnation of the Gospel in native cultures. Joe Ubelmesser attests to how "Solomon has lived his life - at least part of it - as a citizen of the world. He has done service for the Gospel in Africa, has studied art in the United States and lectured in England. And he visited his many German friends as often as possible."[289] Surely the Lord has enlarged his territory of influence to bring in a new awakening about the challenge of relevant and meaningful Gospel presentation. Solomon Raj thus emerged as a 'global Christian' with openness for every persuasion of Christian faith irrespective of denominational barriers or differences. This was well attested to by his in-depth studies of small church movements, in his seminal and sequel works on the subject, apart from other evidence.

---

288 2 Timothy 4:5.

289 Joe Ubelmesser: 'A Word about the Artist', *Liberation in Luke's Gospel,* (1996:7).

iv) A Bold Apologist

Some would further see him as a bold Apologist of Christian faith raising his voice in a very creative manner even against certain cruel interpretations of Christian faith and conduct. When the word 'harvest' was 'grossly misunderstood in some quarters', and people like Arun Showrie gave a cruel interpretation to this word, Solomon refuted it with his beautiful interpretation:

> 'Harvest' is a beautiful word. It brings to mind the fruit-yielding land, the labor involved and the long waiting on the part of the farmer to collect the fruit. The universe is like a fruit garden and the creator God looks for fruit from His creation. Human life is expected to yield fruit –fruit of friendship, peace, harmony and joy.[290]

Solomon laments that it was really shocking to see such harmless and gentle imagery of the 'harvest' distorted to give such a painful and unpleasant interpretation. When the whole Christian world was shocked at such misinterpretation, Solomon too was shocked but come out with a bold and genuine interpretation about the Christian use of the word, 'harvest'. Solomon Raj thus emerged as a bold apologist of the Christian message.

v) A Prophetic Artist

Solomon had a sense of destiny and he heard the call of God! He knew about prophetic art and talked about prophetic art. As Jean Shen postulates:

> Prophetic art is God giving us a "now" word. He is communicating now, sending a visual "speech" which must be responded to now. Thus it comes with immediacy and urgency and timing. When the art piece is seen, heard and read by those whom the Lord has been preparing to receive that word, this is their response, "Yes, Lord. I hear Your voice. I feel Your heart of love."[291]

Solomon not only wrote about prophetic art, but he became a prophetic artist himself, with the trumpet call for justice, liberation and ecological stewardship, as seen earlier! Solomon thus emerged and remains an Advocate of Justice, a Champion of Liberation and an Ecological Saint! He is in deed 'a theologian ahead of his time'![292]

Can Gospel be presented in Indian context through the art and poetry of Solomon Raj?

---

290 *The New Wine-Skins,* (2003:xvii).

291 http://jbrushwork.com/html/prophetic_art.html - accessed March 25, 2018.

292 Walter J. Hollenweger: 'A vision of the Church: A Tribute to Solomon Raj', *The New Wine-Skins,* (2003:xii).

Can we discern a new a paradigm of evangelistic means here?
Can we move from the rotten ritual to a fresh vision of the risen Lord?
Can we seek His justice and delight in His liberation?
Can we see a new day before the Day of the Lord?

The Gospel can be presented in Indian context through the art and poetry of Solomon Raj in our times. An affirmative answer for the above questions would determine the relevance and viability of the modes and means Solomon employed, in our times of globalization and social media explosion. His classical poetry such as *shashtyantas, dandakas, eeshodaaharana kaavya,* and *dwipada Kaavya,* draws anyone from the intellectual strata to the Gospel any time and any clime. The message in poems and the varied literary styles appeal to the intellectuals of any religion in urban or rural setting. The message of the Gospel through cradle songs (*vuyyala paatalu*), poetic lyrics (*kandaardhas*) and dance dramas (*yaksha gaanas*) appeals to the rural masses even today. And so with the urban slum dwellers and working class people. The only thing required is to discern which one to use where – the audience determines the genre?

Solomon's evocative art can never be outdated, as it continues to inspire people, in spite of their nationality. His artistic innovations and the media such as wood block prints, batiks, etchings and icons attract the attention of all. The message is clearly and sharply communicated through his different works of art. It is not that evangelism can be done only through Solomon's means, but that one is given inspiration and motivation to workout his own contemporary indigenous means. Using inexpensive tools for making lasting impact is possible through indigenous inventions.

Bibliography

Primary Sources:

A) **Books in Telugu by Dr. P. Solomon Raj:**

Raj, P. Solomon — ***How to Study the Bible***
Rajahmundry: Christian Publishing House, 1957.

" — ***Story Telling*** *(Katha Paddati)*
Rajahmundry: Christian Publishing House, 1957.

" — ***Audio Visual Aids*** *(Drishya Sravana Sadhanalu)*
Rajahmundry: Christian Publishing House, n.d.

" — ***Wild Flowers*** *(Adavi Poolu)*
Rajahmundry: Christian Publishing House, 1973.

" — ***A Theological Dictionary***
Hyderabad: St. John's Publications, 1977.

" — ***Christ, the King of Kings*** (*Raaraaju Kristhu*)
Hyderabad: CLS, 1978.

" — ***Pooja Mandiramu*** (The House of Worship)
Vijayawada: St. Luke's Lalit Kala Ashram
Originally published 1978, Hyderabad: CLS, 1999.

" — ***Veda Vinodini***
Vijayawada: St. Luke's Lalit Kala Ashram, 1999.

" — ***Eeshodaaharanamu***
Vijayawada: St. Luke's Lalit Kala Ashram, 1999.

" — ***Kim Kartavyam***
Vijayawada: St. Luke's Lalit Kala Ashram 2001.

" — ***Gana Kusumalu***
Vijayawada: St. Luke's Lalit Kala Ashram & Yesupadam Books, 2002.

" ***Luka Suvarthalo Vimochana Prasakthi***
(Telugu edition of 'Liberation in Luke's Gospel')
Vijayawada : Swarna Deepika, 2008.

" ***Daiva Gnana Siri: Prayers and Proclamations***
Vijayawada: St. Luke's Lalit Kala Ashram
Edited by B. S. Moses Kumar, 2012.

" ***Upamana Malika: Parables of Lord Jesus***
Jointly published by St. Luke's Lalit Kala Ashram & Andhra Christian Theological College Hyderabad: Vijaya Printers Edited by B. S. Moses Kumar, 2012.

" ***Paul Gerhardt Kirthana Sahityamu***
Vijayawada: St. Luke's Lalit Kala Ashram
Hyderabad: Vijaya Printers
Edited by B. S. Moses Kumar, 2014.

B) Books in English by Dr. P. Solomon Raj :

Raj, P. Solomon ***Palm Leaf Prayers***
Wuppertal: United Evangelical Mission, 1988
Reprint, 1995.

" ***Living Flame and Springing Fountain***
(Batiks and Meditations) Delhi: ISPCK, 1993
First Published in Germany, 1988
Lebendige Flamme – Sprudelnder Quell
Eds. Dr. Heimo Ertle and P. Joe Ubelmesser S.J.

" ***Liberation in Luke's Gospel*** *(Image and Word)*
Vijayawada: St. Luke's Dalit [sic] Kala Ashram, 1996
(Also Published in German & Dutch).

" ***The New Wine-Skins***
(The Story of the Indigenous Missions in Coastal Andhra Pradesh, India), Delhi: ISPCK, 2003.

" ***Fiery Wheels:*** *Art Works and Meditations*
Vijayawada: St. Luke's Lalit Kala Ashram, 2003.

" ***A Christian Folk Religion in India: A Study of the Small Church Movement in Andhra Pradesh, with Special Reference to the Bible Mission of Devadass***
Bangalore: Centre for Contemporary Christianity
Second Revised Edition (reprinted in India) 2004, and reprinted in 2009 duly updated and revised.

First published by Frankfurt: Verlag Peter Lang, Germany 1986.

" ***Biblia Pauperum: The Poor Man's Bible***
Bangalore: Asian Trading Corporation, 2008.

" ***Etched Icons, Art Faith and Culture***
Vijayawada: St. Luke's Lalit Kala Ashram, 2009.

" ***Geetha Malika***
Delhi: ISPCK, Tercentenary Publication, 2010
Editor: B. S. Moses Kumar.

" ***St. John's Gospel: A Gallery of Hieratic Art***
Vijayawada: St. Luke's Lalit Kala Ashram, 2010.

C) Articles Published in Books, Journals & Magazines:

Raj, P. Solomon *The fiery wheel*
In Hans-Ruedi Weber: ***Immanuel: The Coming of Jesus in Art and the Bible***
Grand Rapids: Wm. B. Eerdmans & Geneva: World Council of Churches, 1984 (19-21).

" *Father Devadass and the Story of a Folk Church in India*, In ***Dharma Deepika*** 1:1 (June 1995) (61-68).

" *Christian Art in India: A Survey of Recent Trends,*
In ***Ishvani***
(A Documentation Journal on Christianity and World Religions) Vol. XV, No. 3 (Sept.-Dec., 1997), (75-84)
Pune: Ishvani Kendra.

" *Artistic Creativity and Prophetic Gift*
In "Contemporary Christian",
Bangalore: Centre for Contemporary Christianity, Vol. 2, No. 1, August 2010, (10-19)
(Lecture presented at Heidelberg University, Germany).

" *Introduction* to ***"St. John's Gospel: A Gallery of Hieratic Art"***, (An Introduction to Christian Art and Icons), Vijayawada: St. Luke's Lalit Kala Ashram, 2010, (11-18).

" *Prologue* to ***"Etched Icons: Art faith and Culture"***,
(An Introduction to Icons and Etching)
Vijayawada: St. Luke's Lalit Kala Ashram, 2009.

" *Christianity among the Kammas and Reddys of Andhra Pradesh,* In ***"Christianity in India: Search for***

Liberation and Identity", ed. F. Hrangkhuma Delhi: ISPCK, 1998, (71-73).

" *Songs of the Pilgrim Churches - The Story of the Hymn Tradition of the Indigenous Mission Churches in Andhra Pradesh, India* (In ***"Dharma Deepika"***, Chennai).

" *Christian Song Tradition in India with Special Reference to Telugu,* In ***"Exchange"***, Vol. 29, No. 4 Brill, Leiden. Boston, The Netherlands, 2000, (353-360).

" *Christian Song Tradition in India with a Special Reference to the People of Andhra Pradesh Speaking Telugu Language,* In ***"Exchange"***, Vol. 31, No. 1, 2002.

" *Song Tradition of Telugu-speaking Christians: With* Special Reference to the Songs of the Christian Church,
In ***"Geeta Malika"*** Delhi: ISPCK, 2010, (3-10).

" *Images in the Bible,*
In ***"The Bible and the Technologies of the Word"***, ed. Joseph Palakeel Bangalore: Asian Trading Corporation, 2007, (210-220).

" *The Place of Images in Communication with Special Reference to Theological Education* (unpublished).

" *Icons in Worship and Renewal,* (unpublished).

" *Christian Prabandha Literature,*
In ***"Striving for Excellence: Educational Ministry in the Church"***,
eds. Siga Arles & Brian Wintle Bangalore: Asia Theological Association, 2007, (393-409).

" *Inculturation,* In ***"Dictionary of Mission Theology"*** ed. John Corrie, Nottingham, England: InterVarsity Press, 2007 (181-184).

" *Indigenization of the Gospel through Art,*
In ***"The Yobel Spring"***,
ed. Praveen P.S. Perumalla et al.
Delhi: ISPCK & ACTC, 2013
(*Festschrift in honor of Dr. Chilkuri Vasantha Rao*).

" *The Future of Christianity in India,*
In ***"We, The Church: Studies in Mission and***

Evangelization"
Gen. Eds. Smitha P. Coffey & Donna Tracy Paul, New Delhi: Christian World Imprints, 2017, (151-158).
(*Festschrift in honor of Dr. B. S. Moses Kumar*).

” *My Experiments with Art Expression,* In ***"Living Flame and Springing Fountain"***, Delhi: ISPCK, 1993, (83-102).

” *My Story as a Christian Artist,* (unpublished).
Passion and Glory of Christ our Lord from an Artist's Viewpoint, (unpublished).

” *Religious Perceptions of the Masses (Dalits and Tribals) and their Artistic Expression,*
In ***"Mission Today"***, Oct-Dec 1999, (304-313)
(Paper presented at the World Council of Churches Consultation in October 1995 at United Theological College, Bangalore).

” *The Influence of Pentecostal Teaching on Some Folk Christian Religions in India*, In ***"International Review of Mission"***, (39-46).

” *The Significance of St. Luke's Teachings to the* Contemporary Christian Communities in India with a Special Reference to Luke's Gospel
(Presented at Luther University, Wittenberg, Germany).

” *Father Devadas and the Story of a Folk Church in India*
In ***"Dharma Deepika"***, Vol. 1, No. 1, (61-68).

” *Kosuke Koyama: Is there anything we can learn from* his theological thought?
In ***"Contemporary Christian"***, Vol. 1, No. 3, (22-27)
Bangalore: Centre for Contemporary Christianity.

” *Bible Mission of Devadas,*
In ***"Oxford Encyclopaedia of South Asian Christianity"***, New Delhi: Oxford University Press, 2012, (85-86).

D) Papers Presented in Academies

Raj, P. Solomon *The Bible Seen through the Cultures of India with Special Reference to India's Art Forms*
(Paper Presented at Doshisha University, Kyoto City, Japan in 1991).

” *Christian Art in India, Present Trends and Future Prospects* (Lecture given at Academy Bad Boll, Stuttgart, KoWADiS), 1997
50th Anniversary of Indian Independence.

” *Story Telling In India: With a Special Reference to Telugu Language,*
(Paper presented at Loccum Academy, Germany).

” *The Influence of Indian Culture on the Church in India with Special Reference to its Art Forms, Image and Liturgy.*

” *Indian Church and its Response to Culture with Special Reference to Fine Arts and Literature.*

” *Indigenous Missions*
(Paper presented to Pastors from Netherlands at Henry Martin Institute, Hyderabad at the meeting hosted by D'Souza).

” *Dance and Musical Plays in Telugu with Special reference to their subject matter content.*

” *Kim Karthavyam – What is to be Done?*

E) **Unpublished Works:**

Raj, P. Solomon *Adi Kraisthava Sangha Kirthana Sahityamu: Greek Hymns – Telugu Translation.*

” *Gerontia Swapnamu*
(Telugu Translation of *The Dream of Gerontius* by John Henry Newman).

” *Suvarna Dhaanya Sampada*
(Telugu Translation of *Golden Grains* by John Wright Follette).

” *Yesu Kristhu Adbhutaalu* (Hymns on the Miracle of Jesus).

” *What I Owe Him?* (An Account of My Life Story).

Secondary Sources:

A) **Dictionaries and Encyclopedias**

Anand Amaladass SJ & Gudrun Löwner ‘*Solomon Raj*’ In ***“Christian Themes in Indian Art: From the Mogul Times Till Today”*** New Delhi: Manohar Publishers, 2012.

Roger E. Hedlund, Chief Ed. — ***The Oxford Encyclopaedia of South Asian Christianity***
Vols. 1 & II, New Delhi: Oxford University Press, 2012.

B) Books on Culture and Inculturation

Adrian B. Smith — ***Tomorrow's Christian: A New Framework for Christian Living***
Winchester, UK & New York, USA: O Books, 2005.

Peter Schineller, S.J. — ***A Handbook on Inculturation***
New York: Paulist Press, 1990.

Roger E. Hedlund — ***Christianity Made in India: From Apostle Thomas to Mother Teresa***
Minneapolis: Fortress Press, 2017.

R. R. Sundar Rao — ***Bhakti Theology in the Telugu Hymnal***
Madras: The Christian Literature Society, 1983.

Sunand Sumithra — ***Christian Theologies from an Indian Perspective***
Bangalore: Theological Book Trust, 1990.

C) Books on / for Solomon Raj & His writings:

B. S. Moses Kumar — ***Soliloquies in Solitude: Solomon's Verse in His Nineties Depicting Cultural, Natural, Existential, Philosophical and Christian Themes***
New Delhi: Christian World Imprints, 2017
Christian Heritage Rediscovered (Series) – 55.

David Zersen and B. S. Moses Kumar — ***Planting in Native Soil: Studies in Gospel Inculturation***
Jointly Published by Austin, TX: Concordia University Press, and Delhi: ISPCK, 2014
(*Festschrift in honor of Dr. P. Solomon Raj).*

Gerald A. Danzer — ***Now We Are Free***
Itasca, Illinois: The Lutheran Church of St. Luke, 2008.

D) Book Reviews:

Fuchs, Stephen — Book Review for *'A Christian Folk Religion in India: A Study of the Small Church Movement in Andhra Pradesh, with Special Reference to the Bible Mission of Devadas'*
n.d.

Hoekema, Alle G — Book review for *'The New Wine-Skins: The Story of the* Indigenous Missions in Coastal Andhra Pradesh,

	India', In ***"Exchange"***, Journal of Missiological and Ecumenical Research, Vol. 33, No. 1, 2004 (98-99) Brill, Leiden - Boston, The Netherlands.
"	*P. Solomon Raj: Biblia Pauperum. The Poor Man's Bible,* Book review published in ***"Exchange"*** 38, 2009 (381-388).
Lawson, Chris	*In Honour of Solomon Raj - Cross Cultural Communicator*, Book review on *"Planting in Native Soil: Studies in Gospel Inculturation"*, 2014.
Richard, H. L.	Reviews on *"A Christian Folk Religion in India: A* Study of the Small Church Movement in Andhra Pradesh, with Special Reference to the Bible Mission *of Devadas"* (and) *"The New Wine-Skins: The Story of the Indigenous Missions in Coastal Andhra Pradesh, India"* Published in Global Missiology, Review & Preview, October 2004, www.globalmissiology.net.

E) **Writings on / about Solomon Raj & His Writings:**

Anandan, K.,	*'Pulidindi Vamsha Gnani'* Telugu Foreword to ***"Daiva Gnana Siri: Prayers and Proclamations"*** Vijayawada: St. Luke's Lalit Kala Ashram, 2012.
"	*'Guru Vriddhulu – Gnana Vriddhulu'* Telugu Foreword to ***"Upamana Malika: Parables of Lord Jesus"*** Jointly published by St. Luke's Lalit Kala Ashram & Andhra Christian Theological College, 2012.
Arles, Siga	*'Towards a Renewed and Relevant Church'* In David Zersen and Moses Kumar: ***"Planting in Native Soil: Studies in Gospel Inculturation"***, 2014.
Challa, R. M.	*'Spirit of Christ – A review of Kim Karthavyam' (A Musical Program broadcast over All India Radio Vijayawada)* Excerpts from Indian Express, 30th Dec. 1978. In ***"Kim Karthavyam"*** by Dr. P. Solomon Raj, Vijayawada: St Luke's Lalit Kala Ashram, 2001, (vi).
Dekker, Jojanneke	*'The Tree Bearing Fruit on Earth, Rooted in Heaven',* In ***"Planting in Native Soil: Studies in Gospel Inculturation"*** Jointly Published by Austin, TX: Concordia University Press, and Delhi: ISPCK, 2014.

Dev, D. Sanjiva	*'Rhythmic Vision'* (*An Appreciation of the Art Work of Dr. Solomon Raj*) In ***Living Flame and Springing Fountain*** by Dr. P. Solomon Raj, Delhi: ISPCK, 1993.
Frederiks, Martha	*'Solomon Raj: Art as an Invitation to Relate'*, In ***"St. John's Gospel: A Gallery of Hieratic Art"*** Vijayawada: St. Luke's Lalit Kala Ashram, 2010.
Hardy, Michael	*'Solomon the Artist I Know'*, In ***Fiery Wheels*** by Dr. P. Solomon Raj Vijayawada: n.p., 2003.
Hoefer, Herbert E. (ed.)	*'Christian Art in India'* Madras: Gurukul Lutheran Theological College and Research Institute, 1982 (Gurukul Publication).
Hollenweger, Walter J.	*'A Vision of the Church: A Tribute to Solomon Raj'*, In ***The New Wine-Skins*** by Dr. P. Solomon Raj Delhi: ISPCK, 2003, (xi-xvi).
Jones, Arun	*'Translation, Inculturation and Conflict in South Asia'* In ***"Planting in Native Soil: Studies in Gospel Inculturation"*** Jointly Published by Austin, TX: Concordia University Press, and Delhi: ISPCK, 2014.
Joseph, Ravela & Bhanu, B. Suneel	*'Bibliography of Original Christian Writings in India in Telugu'* Bangalore: Board of Theological Education of the Senate of Serampore College 1993, (3, 20, 29, 36, 40 and 67).
Joseph, Stephen	*Introduction* to ***"Etched Icons: Art faith and Culture"***, Vijayawada: St. Luke's Lalit Kala Ashram, 2009.
Kuester, Dr. Volker	*'Renunciation of Inculturation as Aesthetic Resistance'*, In ***"Fiery Wheels"*** by Dr. P. Solomon Raj Vijayawada: n.p., 2003, (100-122) Also In ***"Exchange"***, Vol. 30, 2001.
Kumar, B. S. Moses	*'Bhaki Sahitya from the Heart of Solomon Raj'* Published in ***"Geetha Malika"***, Delhi: ISPCK, 2010.
"	*'Thirst for Vaividhya'* Published in ***"Daiva Gnana Siri: Prayers and Proclamations"*** Vijayawada: St. Luke's Lalit Kala Ashram, 2012.

”	*'Didactic Literature from the Pen of Dr. P. Solomon Raj'*, Foreword to ***"Upamana Malika: Parables of Lord Jesus"*** Jointly published by St. Luke's Lalit Kala Ashram & Andhra Christian Theological College, 2012.
”	*'Paul Gerhardt's Hymns: A Review of Telugu Rendering by Solomon Raj'*, Published in ***"Paul Gerhardt Kirthana Sahityamu"*** Vijayawada: St. Luke's Lalit Kala Ashram, 2012.
”	*'Liturgical Interests and Lyrical Innovations of Pulidindi Solomon Raj: An Experiment at Indigenization'* Published in ***"The Yobel Spring"*** Vol. 2 Edited by Praveen P.S. Perumalla et al., Delhi: ISPCK & ACTC, 2013.
”	*'Songs of Solomon from Sambalikan: An Analytical Review'* ***"Journal of Contemporary Christian"***, Vol. 5, No. 4 Bangalore: Centre for Contemporary Christianity, 2014.
”	*'Incarnation of the Gospel Without Cultural Baggage'* Published in ***"Planting in Native Soil: Studies in Gospel Inculturation"*** Gen. Eds. David Zersen and Moses Kumar Jointly Published by Austin, TX: Concordia University Press, and Delhi: ISPCK, 2014.
Lott, Eric J.	*'Dangers at the Well: Drawing on Indigenous Traditions'* In "***Planting in Native Soil: Studies in Gospel Inculturation***" Jointly Published by Austin, TX: Concordia University Press, and Delhi: ISPCK, 2014.
Löwner, Gudrun	*'Solomon Raj, A Christian Liberation Artist'* Published in ***"Sahrdaya"*** Jesuit Artists Association Bulletin, Vol. 17, September 2005.
Megumi, Joshida	*'Abundant Grace of God in Dr. P. Solomon Raj's Art Images'*, In ***"St. John's Gospel: A Gallery of Hieratic Art"*** Vijayawada: St. Luke's Lalit Kala Ashram, 2010.
Raj, P. A. Jyothi	*'My Tryst with Solomon Raj'* In ***"Planting in Native Soil: Studies in Gospel Inculturation"***

Jointly Published by Austin, TX: Concordia University Press, and Delhi: ISPCK, 2014.

Rao, B. Rajanikantha — *Review*
In ***"Veda Vinodini"*** by Dr. P Solomon Raj, Vijayawada: St Luke's Lalit Kala Ashram, 1999, (vii-viii).

Rao, Chilkuri Vasantha — *'Telugu Inculturation in Art and Literature'*
In ***"Planting in Native Soil: Studies in Gospel Inculturation"***
Jointly Published by Austin, TX: Concordia University Press, and Delhi: ISPCK, 2014.

Rao, T. Venkata — *'Solomon Raj, An Artist of the Bible Stories'*
In ***"Planting in Native Soil: Studies in Gospel Inculturation"***
Jointly Published by Austin, TX: Concordia University Press, and Delhi: ISPCK, 2014.

Roy, Sumita, — *Foreword* to P. Solomon Raj's ***"Geetha Malika"***
Delhi: ISPCK, 2010.

Sahi, Jyoti — *'Solomon Raj: Artist with a Cosmic Vision'*
Published in ***"The Yobel Spring"*** Vol. 1
Ed. Praveen P.S. Perumalla et al.,
Delhi: ISPCK & ACTC, 2013.

" — *'Solomon Raj and the Prehistoric Origins of Dalit Art'*
In ***"Planting in Native Soil: Studies in Gospel Inculturation"***
Jointly Published by Austin, TX: Concordia University Press, and Delhi: ISPCK, 2014.

Sudarshan, K. Job — *'A Pleasant Bridge Between Indian Culture and Christian Faith: A Charioteer of Christian Literature and Art Expression'* In ***"Swarna Deepika"***,
Telugu Christian Journal, January 20, 2006.

Takenaka, Masao & O'Grady, Ron — *'The Bible Through Asian Eyes'*
Asian Christian Arts Association
Oakland, Pace Publishing, 1991.

Ubelmesser, S.J., Joe — *'The Word of God Translated into Images to Contemplate'*, In ***"Biblia Pauperum: The Poor Man's Bible"*** by Dr. P. Solomon Raj
Bangalore: Asian Trading Corporation, 2008.

Zersen, David J. *'Planting Lutheran Seeds in India's Soil'*
In ***"The Lutheran"***, Dec. 2007.

" *'Introduction'* to ***"Biblia Pauperum: The Poor Man's Bible"*** by Dr. P. Solomon Raj
Bangalore: Asian Trading Corporation, 2008.

" *'Solomon Raj and his Johannine Icons'*
In ***"St. John's Gospel: A Gallery of Hieratic Art"***
Vijayawada: St. Luke's Lalit Kala Ashram, 2010.

" *'Solomon Raj's Batik Mission and Wood Block Gospel'*
In ***"Lutheran Forum"***, Summer 2014.
Also Published in ***"Planting in Native Soil: Studies in Gospel Inculturation"***
Jointly Published by Austin, TX: Concordia University Press, and Delhi: ISPCK, 2014.

F) Essays on the Internet

Beard, *Madeleine* ***Ongoing Revelation Through Art***
http://www,episcopalcafe.com/art/art/ ongoing_revelation_through_art_1.html.

Moses Kumar, B.S., *Liberation in Luke's Gospel: An Artistic Appreciation* and A Theological Analysis
http://www.artway.eu/content.php?id=1365&lang=en&action=show.

" *Solomon's Gallery of Hieratic Art in St. John's Gospel: A Thematic Appreciation*
http://www.artway.eu/artway.php?id=584&action=show &lang=en.

G) Unpublished Dissertations on Solomon Raj and his Works:

Cicilya, Marie Dominic ***"Dr. Solomon Raj: A Christian Artist"***
Dissertation submitted for the degree of M.A. in History of Fine Arts, Stella Maris College, Madras, 1995.

Dekker, Jojanneke ***'Solomon Raj, Prophetic Artist in India'***
A research on Dr. P. Solomon Raj's art as a medium of inculturation of the gospel in India,
(Master's Dissertation submitted to the Faculty of Theology, Utrecht University, Netherlands), 2006.

Mathew, K. Sam *A Study of Indigenous Symbols in Selected 'Batik Paintings' of Pulidindi Solomon Raj as Means of Communicating the Gospel in India*

(Thesis submitted to the Senate of Serampore College for the degree of M.Th.), 2009.

H) **Personal Interviews**

i) Interviews with P. Solomon Raj at Vijayawada from 2010-2018 (on April 20, 2010.

ii) Interview with Gudrun Löwner on March 31, 2010 at Donald Ashram, Hyderabad (12.30-2.30 PM).

iii) Interview with Dr. Jyoti Sahi at Andhra Christian Theological College, Hyderabad on February 6, 2012.

I) **Other Sources**

i) Personal Files of P. Solomon Raj.

ii) Letter of Dr. Jörg Muller to P. Solomon Raj dated 4th May 2012.

iii) Personal Correspondence with Dr. Jyoti Sahi.

iv) Personal Correspondence with Prof. Gudrun Löwner.

Appendix 1

Picture of P. Solomon Raj

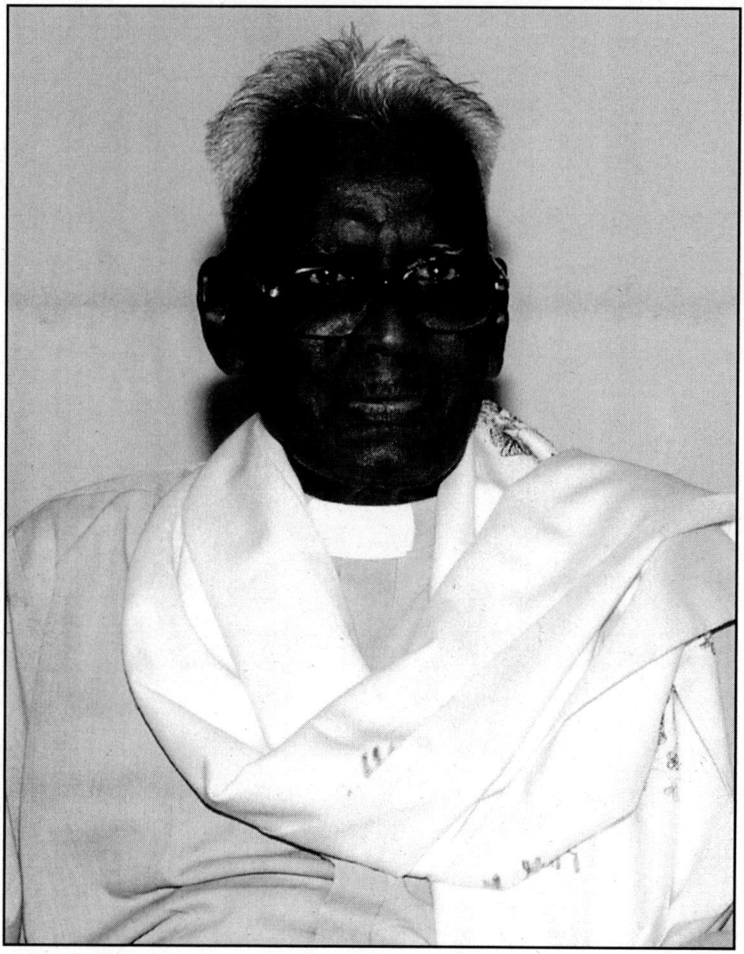

Appendix 2

Timeline of Solomon's Art Exhibitions

1. Bethel Lutheran Church, Muskego, Wisconsin, USA 1966
2. Andhra Academy of Arts, Vijayawada, India 1973
3. Ausstellungen, Munchen, Germany 1982
4. Kilainskirche, Heilbronn, Germany 1982
5. Midland Lutheran College, Mushbach Art Centre, January 1985
6. Lenoir Rhyne College, Carl Rudisill Library, N.C., USA 1984
7. St. Andrew's Presbyterian Church, King and Simcoe, Toronto, Canada, 1987
8. United Theological College Bangalore, India 1988
9. Thummalapalli Kshetrayya Kala Kshetram (Town Hall), Vijayawada, India
10. Asian Institute for Liturgy and Music, Quezon City, Philippines, March, 1992
11. PUSKAT Yogyakarta, Indonesia, 1993
12. Suvartha Vani Hall, Vijayawada, on Solomon's 75th birthday, 1995
13. Mission House Utrecht, 2002
14. Landan, Stuttgard, 2002
15. Uniting Missions, Utreacht 2002
16. Kraemer Institute, Oegstgeest 2002
17. McMillan Gallery, Austin Presbyterian Theological Seminary, Austin, TX, 2005
18. Dadian Gallery, Wesley Theological Seminary, Washington D.C., USA, 2006
19. Seminary Gallery, Fuerbringer Hall Library, St. Louis, Missouri, USA, 2006
20. Friend Art Gallery, Concordia University, Irvine, California, USA, 2007

21. Al-Khaf Gallery, International Center, Bethlehem, Palestine, 2007
22. Concordia Seminary, St. Catherines, Ontario, Canada, 2007
23. *Chitramayee* - State Art Gallery, Hyderabad, 16-21, September 2007
24. St. Anne and St. Agnes Lutheran Church, London, UK, 2008
25. St. Luke Gallery, Itasca, Illinois, USA, 2009
26. Annex Gallery, St. John Lutheran Church, West Bend, WI, USA, 2010
27. Garth Gallery, Fourth Presbyterian Church, Chicago, Illinois, USA, 2011
28. Parish Hall Gallery, St. Paul Episcopal Church, Milwaukee, WI, USA, 2011
29. Andhra Christian Theological College (ACTC), Hyderabad, India, 2011
30. Zion Bible College, Vijayawada (on Solomon's 91st birthday) India, 2012
31. St. Meinrad Archabbey Gallery, St. Meinrad, Indiana, USA, 2013

Appendix 3

Bibliographical Account by Gudrun Löwner

Brot für die Welt 2002	Brot für die Welt: Meditation flag, India, Dr. Solomon Raj 4x2 m., Stuttgart 2002
Brot für die Welt 2003	Brot für die Welt (ed.): Dürsten nach Gerechtigkeit, Begleitheft zur Meditationsfahne aus Indien, Stuttgart 2003, (with transparent foil of meditation flag)
Collins 2007 This book does not mention Solomon Raj, but is good for all inculturation questions.	Collins, Paul M., *Christian Inculturation in India*, Aldershot (Ashgate Publishers). The author also offers a very useful website:http://inculturation.chi.ac.uk where lots of pictures of churches, shrines and temples are visible. In the book are also 12 b/w pictures of Indian churches. It is an excellent book, especially about modern churches and the indigenization debate, very recommendable.
Hoefer 1982	Hoefer, Herbert E. (ed.): Christian Art in India, Gurukul Lutheran Theological College and Research Institute, Madras, 1982 (Gurukul Publication) (I think Solomon is also in this book, but all his contemporaries are).
Image	*Image* is a journal published by the Asian Christian Art Association and was started by Prof. Takenaka in Japan. It is still existing and a treasure trove for Christian Art in India. As there are so many articles, which are mostly very short, they are not mentioned in the bibliography, but it is worth to have a look.

Küster 2001	Küster, Volker: Inkulturations verweigerung als ästhetischer Protest, Das Werk des indischen Künstlers Solomon Raj in einem neuen Licht. In: ZMR 81, 1997, Part II pp. 153-163. In English: Renunciation of Inculturation as Aesthetic Resistance. The Indian artist Solomon Raj in a new light. In: Exchange, vol. 30, 2001, pp. 359-371.
Lederle	Lederle, Matthew SJ: Christian Painting in India, Heras Institute of Indian History & Culture, Bombay without year (few c.p., 102p) (Heras Institute). After the death of Lederle, Jyoti Sahi edited this valuable book.
Löwner 1991	Löwner, Gudrun: Solomon Raj – Christ & Künstler aus Indien. In die Welt für die Welt, 29. Vol. July/August 1993 pp. 26-31, also in English, Indian Christian artist: A Lutheran theologian from India, Solomon Raj is trying to express his faith 'in the visual idiom of my country'. In: One World, Dec. 1991, vol. 171, pp. 9-10.
Löwner 2007	Löwner, Gudrun: Christian Art in India, In: Indian Church History Review, Dec 2006, p. 91-106 in full form in German with pict.: Hat Kunst Religion verändert? Das Beispiel des Christentums in Indien, In: Koch, Michael ed.: Verändert der Dialog die Religionen? Religions begegnungen und Interreligiöser Dialog, Frankfurt am Main 2007, pp. 103-132 (Lembeck Verlag, Beiheft der Zeitschrift für Mission, vol. 9)
Löwner 2009a	Löwner, Gudrun: Christliche Themen in der Indischen Kunst von der Mogulzeit bis heute, Frankfurt a. Main 2009 (Lembeck Verlag, Christliche Kunst Weltweit, vol. III), pp. 165-172 (This is my main book on art, and these are his pages and 2 colour pictures)
Löwner 2005	Solomon Raj a Christian Liberation Artist. In: Sahrdaya (Jesuit Artists Association Bulletin), Vol. 17, Sept. 2005, S. 3-12.
Löwner 2000	Theologie mit dem Pinsel – Weitergabe des Glaubens durch Kunst Azaria Mbatha, Solomon Raj und I Nyoman Darsane. In: Mit dem Fremden leben, Festschrift Theo Sundermeier zum 65. Geburtstag. *Dieter Becker/Andreas Feldtkeller*, hg., Erlangen 2000, Bd. 2, S. 33-48

Löwner 2009b	Befreiung durch Kunst. Porträt des indischen Künstlers Solomon Raj. In: WELT bewegt Juni-Juli 2009, S. 8-11.
Raj & Müller 1995	Raj, S. / Müller, Jörg: Palm Leaf Prayer, Wood cuts and meditations, Wuppertal 1995[2] (Vereinte Evangelische Mission)
Raj 1993	Raj, P. Solomon: Living Flame and Springing Fountain, Batiks and Meditations, Delhi 1993 (ISCPK)
Raj 1997	Raj, P. Solomon: Christian Art in India "A Survey of Recent Trends". In: Ishwani, 15.1997, Part 3, pp. 75-84
Raj 1999	Raj, P. Solomon: Religious perceptions of the masses (Dalits and Tribes) and their Artistic Expression. In: Mission Today, Oct-Dec 1999, pp. 304-313
Raj 2003	Raj, P. Solomon: Fiery Wheels, Art works and Meditations, Vijayawada, St. Luke's Lalit Kala Ashram 2003 (St. Luke's Ashram Publication)
Raj 2008	Raj, P. Solomon : Biblia Pauperum. The Poor Man's Bible, with recent block prints and text, Bangalore 2008 (Asian Trading Cooperation)
Raj 2008	Raj, P. Solomon: The Etched Icons. Art, Face and Culture, Vijayawada 2008 (St. Luke's Lalit Kala Ashram)
Raj 2010	Raj, P. Solomon: St. John's Gospel. A Gallery of Hieratic Art, Vijayawada 2010 (St. Luke's Lalit Kala Ashram)
Sundermeier 2007	Sundermeier, Theo: Christliche Kunst weltweit. Eine Einführung, Frankfurt am Main 2007 (Lembeck Verlag) some pages about him and also coloured woodprint
Takenaka & O'Grady 1991	Takenaka, Masao/O'Grady, Ron: The Bible Through Asians Eyes, Asian Christian Arts Association Oakland 1991 (Pace Publishing). *One side picture in colour, opposite page meditation on the picture.*
Amaladass 1997	Amaladass, Anand SJ: Das indische Gesicht Jesu, Wie indische Künstler Jesus sehen. In: Weltweit, Weihnachten 1997, pp. 3-18 (Missionsprokur der Jesuiten in Nürnberg)

Appendix 4

How are Icons Made?

Take a piece of wood plank. Clean it well with spirit or turpentine. Take handful of animal gum (I use rabbit skin glue which is clean and free from dust etc.), and soak it in water (a pint of water). When it is soaked well, heat it and it should be the consistency of liquid gum. Paint the piece of wood first with this glue solution with a brush. Then take a piece of cotton cloth the size of the wood block, dip it in the gum solution you made, and spread the piece of cloth straight without folds on the plank of wood. Let it dry completely.

Then make more of the same gum solution (thin), and put zinc oxide powder and white lime (*sunnam*) in 1:3 proportion into the gum liquid and mix it well. It should be the consistency of single icing. With a brush paint the lime and zinc oxide solution on the plank, which is covered with the cloth. Make a thin coating and let it dry. Then rub the surface with sand paper and a piece of wet cloth, polish it smoothly. When it is done then put another coating of the zinc and lime solution on the top. Let it dry and then again wipe it with sand paper and wet cloth. Like this you have to make 5 to 6 coatings and you get a smooth nice surface ready to paint.

Then make your picture on the surface of this white block with pencil or trace from a paper drawing. Use a sharp needle and draw the outline along the drawing you made. This scratched line will be permanent. Then use pigment colors (these are special powders made from earth and precious stones). You buy them in art stores. To mix the colors you have to use egg yolk (yellow of the egg, not the white) a little distilled water and a drop of vinegar. This egg yoke solution only is used to mix the powder colors, and make your painting slowly on the whitened board.

There is a special way of making icon pictures because the old monks used the designs and painting methods faithfully. There is very little change or creativity in the icons, but they are always copied from the great old masters. Therefore also there is a tradition that Christ himself gave his face image to St. Veronica as she wiped his face on the way to Golgotha. These are all stories, but carefully made icon is god given gift, and so icons are called '*achairo poetos*' or not made by hand.

P. Solomon Raj